# FREE WOMEN OF SPAIN

To mary —
Yes, it actually is a book!
                    Best,
                        Martha

# FREE WOMEN OF SPAIN

## Anarchism and the Struggle for the Emancipation of Women

MARTHA A. ACKELSBERG

INDIANA UNIVERSITY PRESS

*Bloomington and Indianapolis*

Portions of this book appeared in somewhat different form in *Women Living Change*, edited by Susan C. Bourque and Donna Robinson Divine, © 1985 by Temple University, reprinted by permission of Temple University Press; and in *Feminist Studies* 11, no. 1 (Spring 1985), reprinted by permission of the publisher, *Feminist Studies*, Inc., c/o Women's Studies Program, University of Maryland, College Park, MD 20742; and in *Communal Societies*, vol. 5 (Fall 1985), reprinted by permission of the publisher, National Historic Communal Societies Association.

The paper used in this publication meets the minimum requirements of American National Standard for Information Sciences—Permanence of Paper for Printed Library Materials, ANSI Z39.48-1984.

♾ ™

Manufactured in the United States of America

Library of Congress Cataloging-in-Publication Data

Ackelsberg, Martha A.
   Free Women of Spain : anarchism and the struggle for the emancipation of women / Martha A. Ackelsberg.
       p.     cm.
   Includes bibliographical references and index.
   ISBN 0-253-30120-3 (alk. paper). — ISBN 0-253-20634-0 (pbk. : alk. paper)
   1. Mujeres Libres (Organization : Spain)   2. Women anarchists—Spain—History—20th century.   3. Anarchism—Spain—History—20th century.   4. Feminism—Spain—History—20th century.   5. Spain—History—Civil War, 1936–1939—Women.   I. Title.
HX925.A27  1991
335'.83'082—dc20                                              90-42665

1   2   3   4   5   95   94   93   92   91

*A las compañeras de Mujeres Libres, en solidaridad*
*La lucha continúa*

Puño en alto mujeres de Iberia
hacia horizontes preñados de luz
por rutas ardientes,
los pies en la tierra
la frente en lo azul.

Afirmando promesas de vida
desafiamos la tradición
modelemos la arcilla caliente
de un mundo que nace del dolor.

¡Que el pasado se hunda en la nada!
¡Qué nos importa del ayer!
Queremos escribir de nuevo
la palabra MUJER.

Puño en alto mujeres del mundo
hacia horizontes preñados de luz,
por rutas ardientes
adelante, adelante
de cara a la luz.

Fists upraised, women of Iberia
toward horizons pregnant with light
on paths afire
feet on the ground
face to the blue sky.

Affirming the promise of life
we defy tradition
we mold the warm clay
of a new world born of pain.

Let the past vanish into nothingness!
What do we care for yesterday!
We want to write anew
the word WOMAN.

Fists upraised, women of the world
toward horizons pregnant with light
on paths afire
onward, onward
toward the light.

Mujeres Libres' Anthem
Lucia Sanchez Saornil
Valencia 1937

# CONTENTS

*Illustrations follow page 107*

# ACKNOWLEDGMENTS

Many individuals and groups contributed to the creation of this book. Chief among them, of course, are the men and women of the Spanish anarchist and anarcho-syndicalist movements and especially the women of Mujeres Libres, who gave generously of their time and energy, told me their stories, and otherwise took me into their lives. It is impossible to find words to thank them; if the courage and integrity they shared with me finds even a faint echo in this volume, I hope it begins in some measure to repay my debt. Jacinto Borrás, Felix Carrasquer, Josep Costa Font, Gaston Leval, Arturo Parera, José Peirats, and Eduardo Pons Prades shared their personal knowledge of anarchist collectives and helped me make some of my initial contacts with members of Mujeres Libres. Matilde Escuder, Lola Iturbe, Igualdad Ocaña, Concha Pérez, and Cristina Piera in Barcelona, Federica Montseny in Toulouse, and Amada de Nó and Teresina Torrelles in Béziers, each spent hours discussing with me their experiences in the years preceding, during, and following the civil war and social revolution. Finally, Pura Pérez Arcos, Azucena Fernandez Barba, Pepita Carpena, Mercedes Comaposada, Anna Delso, Soledad Estorach, Sara Berenguer Guillén, Suceso Portales, Dolores Prat, and Enriqueta Fernandez Rovira opened their homes to me—often not at terribly convenient moments—and inspired me with their stories and their courage.

Others in Spain also provided crucial support and resources. Mary Nash shared her extensive knowledge of women in Spanish working-class movements. Mary's work on Mujeres Libres opened the field of women's history in Spain; she has been an important and generous colleague and friend. Through her, I met Ana Cases and Bernard Catlla, who took me into their home in Lérida and made possible my exploration of the Lérida collective, Adelante. Verena Stolcke, Juan Martínez-Alier, and their daughters, Nuria and Isabel, welcomed me into their family, provided a place for me to stay during the many months I conducted my research in Barcelona, and have become valued friends and colleagues. Rafael Pujol, Albert Pérez-Baró, Nazario González, Enric Fusteri Bonet, Ramón Sol, and Mercedes Vilanova shared their research and provided important introductions and resources at one stage or another of this research.

My debts are also great to those on this side of the Atlantic. José Nieto, Clara Lida, Temma Kaplan, Edward Malefakis, and Suzanne Berger were particularly helpful at the initial stages. It was an early article of Temma's that first alerted me to the existence of Mujeres Libres; I am grateful for her comments and criticisms over the years on various aspects of this manuscript. I feel particularly fortunate to have had the opportunity to know the late Ahrne Thorne. His own commitments and energy were matched only by his extensive network of friends and associates, into which he welcomed me. Through him, I came to know Anna Delso, Pura and Federico Arcos, and Paul Avrich. Federico maintains an extraordinary private collection of material related to the Spanish anarchist and anarcho-syndicalist movements. He and Pura both willingly and enthusiastically opened their collection and their home to me, and they have taken a personal interest in the completion of this project. Their careful reading of the manuscript, their comments, and Pura's efforts at "translation"—both of my words into Castilian and of Mujeres Libers' activities and commitments into contemporary terms—have been invaluable. Lisa Berger and Carol Mazer helped me to contact Dolores Prat and Concha Perez.

I am also deeply indebted to archivists in libraries and archival collections on both sides of the Atlantic who made the process of digging up materials on Mujeres Libres and on Spanish anarchism a very pleasurable one. I would like to acknowledge, in particular, the assistance of those in the Reference and Interlibrary Loan departments of the Smith College Library, the Industrial Relations section of Firestone Library, Princeton University, the Rare Books and Manuscripts division of the New York Public Library, the Labadie Collection at the University of Michigan, the Hoover Institution Library at Stanford University, the Bibliothèque de Documentation Internationale Contemporaine, Université de Paris, Nanterre, the Institut d'Études Politiques, Paris, the Casa del Arcediano, Instituto de Historia de la Ciudad (Barcelona), Fundación Figueras (Barcelona), Biblioteca Arús (Barcelona), Biblioteca de Catalunya (Barcelona), Ateneu Enciclopedic Popular/Centro de Documentación Histórico Social (Barcelona), Ministerio de Hacienda (Lérida), Hemeroteca Municipal (Madrid), the Archivo Histórico Nacional/Sección Guerra Civil-Salamanca, and International Institute for Social History (Amsterdam). During most of the time I was doing my research, the archives in Salamanca, which are a mine of information on the period of the Civil War, were under the control of the Spanish military. The change of government in Spain in recent years has improved working conditions—and the condition of the archives—dramatically. But I remain indebted to Paco and Miguel of the "old regime," who, despite our obvious differences, were unflagging in their willingness to search for files, pamphlets, and newspapers and to arrange for photocopying. Conditions of work at the International Institute were far superior. I spent a number of months there very early in my research on Spanish anarchism, and I returned years later when the

CNT and FAI archives were opened to the public. I am particularly grateful to Rudolf de Jong, formerly director of the Spanish section, for his continued advice and support, and to Thea Duijker, Mieke Ijzermans, and Mr. G. M. Langedijk for facilitating my research.

A number of groups and organizations have offered moral or financial support at various stages of this undertaking. I began this research as a member of the Project on Women and Social Change at Smith College, an interdisciplinary faculty research group funded by the Andrew W. Mellon Foundation. Project funds and a fellowship from the American Association of University Women enabled me to spend a semester in Spain at the initial stages and, together with faculty development funds from Smith College, to make additional trips to Spain, France, and Canada. Ongoing discussions and seminars with Project colleagues—especially Susan C. Bourque, Donna Robinson Divine, Sue J. M. Freeman, Miriam Slater, and Penny Gill—were crucial in my thinking through the direction of the research, particularly at the early stages. Student research assistants Anne Balazs, Robin Stolk, Barat Ellman, and Susan Jessop helped to organize the material I had collected and to review existing literature on women and social revolutionary movements. The assistance of Reyes Lázaro, in transcribing tapes, translating some of my papers, and in facilitating access to people in Spain, has been invaluable.

I began writing this book while a fellow at the Bunting Institute of Radcliffe College, one of the most supportive and exciting intellectual environments I have ever experienced. Seminars, colloquia, and informal discussions with fellows provided incentive and inspiration. I am particularly indebted to members of the "mother-daughter group," especially Ann Bookman, Caroline Bynum, Hope Davis, Bettina Friedl, Gillian Hart, Deborah McDowell, Janice Randall, Blair Tate, and Gretchen Wheelock. Friendships with Katie Canon and Karen Brown, which also began that year, have been another essential part of the writing process.

During the 1987–1988 academic year, while on sabbatical from Smith College, I was a fellow at the Institute for Research on Women and Gender at Columbia University and a member of the Women's Studies Theory Group at Hunter College. Each of those affiliations provided opportunities to develop and discuss my research in progress. In addition, colleagues at the Center for European Studies, Harvard University have invited me to participate in colloquia and seminars over the years and have provided opportunities for valuable exchange of ideas.

Finally, no academic work—especially one this long in the making—arises fully developed from the head of one person. Members of the Government Department at Smith College bore with me through the many years of this project's gestation. I am deeply grateful for their support. Students in my feminist theory and urban politics courses and seminars at Smith contributed to the development of my ideas about community and provided important challenges to the thinking that has gone into this book. Members of the Smith Women's Studies Program Committee and of the Five College Women's Studies Committee—especially Jean Grossholtz, Marilyn Schuster, Vicky Spelman, and Susan Van Dyne—have been both colleagues and friends and have helped me to keep my study of Mujeres Libres in its larger context. Marina Kaplan reviewed some of my translations. Kathy Addelson, Paul Avrich, Susan Bourque, Irene Diamond, Donna Divine, George Esenwein, Kathy Ferguson, Philip Green, Barbara Johnson, Juan Martínez-Alier, Vicky Spelman, Verena Stolcke, Will Watson, Iris Young, and Nira Yuval-Davis all have read parts of this manuscript and offered helpful comments. Myrna Breitbart, Pura and Federico Arcos, Jane Slaughter, and Judith Plaskow read the entire manuscript. Their comments and criticisms have been invaluable. Finally, Judith Plaskow helped me to maintain both a sense of humor and a sense of proportion.

Alex Goldenberg gave up a corner of his living room and took me into his life during the years I was writing this book; I am grateful for both gifts.

# ABBREVIATIONS

AIT  Asociación Internacional de Trabajodores (International Workingmen's Association), Anarchist International

AJA  Asociación de Jóvenes Antifascistas (Antifascist Youth Association), sponsored by the Communist Party

AMA  Asociación de Mujeres Antifascistas (Antifascist Women's Association)

BOC  Bloc Obrer i Camperol (Workers' and Peasants' Bloc)

CENU  Consell de l'Escola Nova Unificada (New Unified Educational Council)

CNT  Confederación Nacional del Trabajo (National Confederation of Labor), anarcho-syndicalist trade union federation

FAI  Federación Anarquista Ibérica (Iberian Anarchist Federation)

FIJL  Federación Ibérica de Juventudes Libertarias (Iberian Federation of Libertarian Youth), anarchist youth organization

JJLL  Juventudes Libertarias (Libertarian Youth), another name for FIJL

PCE  Partido Comunista de España (Spanish Communist Party)

POUM  Partido Obrero de Unificación Marxista (Workers' Party of Marxist Unity), Trotskyist

PSOE  Partido Socialista Obrero Español (Spanish Socialist Workers' Party)

PSUC  Partido Socialista Unificado de Cataluña (Catalan Unified Socialist Party)

SIA  Solidaridad Internacional Antifascista (International Antifascist Solidarity), anarchist-affiliated international relief organization

UGT  Unión General de Trabajadores (General Workers' Union), Socialist-affiliated trade union federation

AHN/SGC-S  Archivo Histórico Nacional, Sección Guerra Civil, Salamanca

AMB  Archivo Muncipal, Barcelona

AMHL  Archivo, Ministerio de Hacienda, Lérida

IISG/CNT  Internationaal Instituut voor Sociale Geschiedenis, Amsterdam, Archivo CNT

IISG/EG    Internationaal Instituut voor Sociale Geschiedenis, Amsterdam, Emma Goldman Archive
IISG/FAI   Internationaal Instituut voor Sociale Geschiedenis, Amsterdam, Archivo FAI-CP
NYPL-EG    New York Public Library, Rare Books and Manuscripts Division, Emma Goldman Papers
NYPL-RP    New York Public Library, Rare Books and Manuscripts Division, Rose Pesotta Papers

# FREE WOMEN
## OF SPAIN

# INTRODUCTION

In 1936, groups of women in Madrid and Barcelona founded Mujeres Libres, an organization dedicated to the liberation of women from their "triple enslavement to ignorance, as women, and as producers." Although it lasted for less than three years (its activities in Spain were brought to an abrupt halt by the victory of Franco's forces in February 1939), Mujeres Libres mobilized over 20,000 women and developed an extensive network of activities designed to empower individual women while building a sense of community. Like the Spanish anarcho-syndicalist movement in which these women were rooted, Mujeres Libres insisted that the full development of women's individuality was dependent upon the development of a strong sense of connection with others. In this respect, as in a number of others, Mujeres Libres represents an alternative to the individualistic perspectives characterizing mainstream feminist movements of that time and of our own.

The story of my discovery of these women and their activities spans many years and many miles, explorations in archives as well as conversations with former activists. But my coming to understand the significance of their visions and achievements is inseparably intertwined with our mutual and ongoing struggles to communicate across differences of culture, age, class, and political context. As many of these women took me into their homes and shared their stories, I tried to hear them on their own terms and to attend to both the similarities and the differences between us. As I have wrestled with the issues of identity, difference, community, and empowerment that have alternately energized and demoralized the civil rights, peace, and feminist movements in this country, I have come to appreciate ever more deeply the perspective Mujeres Libres has to offer contemporary feminists and social activists. This volume derives, in part, from my desire to make its history more generally available.

In the first part of this chapter I introduce some of the women who will be the subjects of the larger story to follow. In the second section, I lay out the themes and concerns that frame the volume theoretically.

The first woman I met from Mujeres Libres was Suceso Portales, who was spending the summer of 1979 in the small village of Móstoles, outside of Madrid. My route to her was to be typical in its circuitousness. While engaging in research on the processes of rural and urban collectivization in Spain during the Civil War, I met a number of

1

young anarchists in Madrid and Barcelona. Among these were young women in newly constituted groups taking the name Mujeres Libres. In both Madrid and Barcelona, the young women with whom I spoke told me that they had made several attempts to meet with the *viejas* (the older ones) who had been involved with the original Mujeres Libres. Apparently, those meetings which did take place had often been characterized by arguments and misunderstandings. When I finally found someone who could give me the name and address of a vieja, Suceso Portales, the information was accompanied by a warning: "You won't like her," my informant confided, "she is a reactionary and has very strange ideas."

Despite this warning, Suceso, like virtually everyone from Mujeres Libres I met, captivated me immediately. She was a very animated, active woman in her mid-sixties with gray-black hair. Her granddaughter, then aged eleven, was in and out of the small room in which we met, occasionally listening to our conversation and asking questions of her own—questions which Suceso always took the time to answer with patience, respect, and care. We talked for hours about her experiences in the CNT and FIJL,[1] her sense of the need for an independent and autonomous women's organization working within the ideological and political framework of the libertarian movement,[2] her evaluation of Mujeres Libres' accomplishments and disappointments, and contemporary feminism.

Suceso had affiliated with Mujeres Libres in central Spain in 1936, and served as national vice-secretary of the organization. She discussed Mujeres Libres' orientation to working-class women, the emphasis on education and empowerment, and the organization's relations with the larger anarcho-syndicalist movement. But I was most fascinated, intrigued, and perplexed by her attitudes toward feminists and feminism—attitudes which were, in many ways, the mirror image of those which the *jóvenes* (the young ones) had of Mujeres Libres: "We are not— and we were not then—feminists," she insisted. "We were not fighting against men. We did not want to substitute a feminist hierarchy for a masculine one. It's necessary to work, to struggle, *together* because if we don't, we'll never have a social revolution. But we needed our own organization to struggle for ourselves."

I was surprised by her assumption that "feminism" meant opposition to men or the desire to replace male hierarchy with female hierarchy. A product of the early feminist movement in the United States, I had always assumed that feminism meant opposition to hierarchies of any sort. Nevertheless, I was beginning to see the source of some of the tensions and misunderstandings between the young women in Madrid who *did* define themselves as feminists and this vieja, for whom feminism was anathema. As I was to discover, these differences in perceptions of what feminism means were hardly unique to Suceso. Through the three years of Mujeres Libres' formal existence, and to this day, its members committed themselves to the emancipation of women without defining themselves as "feminists."

Much of my fascination with Mujeres Libres arose from my desire to understand this distinction and its significance. What did it mean that these women were unwilling to identify themselves as feminists? I soon came to suspect that, although the political contexts of Spain in the 1930s and the United States in the 1980s differ markedly, there might be some similarity between Mujeres Libres' refusal to identify as feminist and the hesitation of many working-class women and women of color in this country to adopt the feminist label. Might there be a lesson here for contemporary feminists, struggling against the claim that feminism is a white, middle-class movement?

But there was more to my fascination. Suceso bemoaned the narrowness of vision of contemporary feminists, the lack of a larger organizational and ideological framework of orientation: "They are lacking in a *formación libertaria* [a phrase often used in anarchist/libertarian circles to refer to background or ideological context]. We had a much broader vision." In her view, the jóvenes did not understand what direct action or any of the other basic principles of libertarian organization meant. They appeared fearful of organizing anything, lest it create new hierarchies, "but that way, you can't accomplish anything."[3] Further, they focused too much attention on abortion, birth control, and sexuality: it's true that a woman's sexuality should be her own, but why is it necessary to make a political issue of it? Finally, she wondered, "How can they call themselves feminists when they go around wearing crosses?"[4]

For some questions I have no answers. I was then, and still remain, puzzled by Suceso's (and others') evident discomfort with making "political" the "personal" issues of love and sexuality, for example. Feminism had convinced me that "the personal is political," but did not anarchism make similar claims? The answers to other questions proved simpler, though often surprising. What she described as "feminists who wear crosses," for example, were young women who wore women's symbols (♀) to signify their feminism![5]

The next woman I met, Lola Iturbe, had been a strong supporter of Mujeres Libres, though not an activist. Together with her *compañero*, Juanel (Juan Manuel Molina, a former secretary-general of the FAI), she edited the anarchist newspaper *Tierra y Libertad* in Barcelona. Lola spoke of her experiences growing up poor, as the daughter of a single mother, in turn-of-the-century Barcelona. She was born in 1902 and, at age nine, began working long hours at incredibly low pay (she received 50 *céntimos* a week) as an apprentice to a seamstress. Her mother ran a *pensión* frequented by "men of the organization." Through these visitors, Lola learned of the CNT and found the acceptance she had been denied in the larger society. By the time she was fourteen or fifteen, she too had joined the organization.[6] It was Lola who told me, during the course of one of these conversations, that Mercedes Comaposada, one of the three women who had founded Mujeres Libres, was still alive and living in Paris.

But another accident intervened before I met Mercedes. I was interviewing Eduardo Pons Prades (then a journalist with *Diario de Barcelona*) about his experiences as a young man with the collectivized wood industry in Catalonia. He sent me to Perpignan, just over the border in France, to meet Jacinto Borrás, former CNT activist and editor of a journal devoted to rural collectives in Catalonia. During our conversations, I told Borrás I was interested in meeting women who had participated in the revolution. At first, his response was enthusiastic. But when I asked for names and/or addresses, he was unable to think of anyone who was healthy enough or "capable" enough to talk with me—a response that had already become all too familiar: few of the male activists with whom I spoke seemed to take many of their women comrades very seriously.

Nevertheless, I pressed him to come up with the name of even one woman who might be willing to talk with me. He hesitated, then called his daughter, Eglantina. She picked up the phone, and from the moment the voice answered on the other end, I knew that Azucena Fernandez Barba was someone I definitely wanted to meet. Eglantina's face and voice were alight as she spoke, and after grabbing some flowers from their garden (Azucena loved flowers, she informed me), Eglantina had me in her car within minutes, en route across town to Azucena's flat.

Azucena was born in Cuba in 1916 of Spanish exile parents, and came to Spain when her parents returned from exile in 1920. When I first met her, I found her seated in her small dining room, surrounded by flowering plants. She spoke animatedly about her experiences during the years before the war and about the history of her family. Azucena and her six sisters and brother were "raised on anarchism . . . with our mother's milk." Her grandfather, Abelardo Saavedra, was one of the early anarchist teacher-preachers who had been jailed repeatedly and later exiled for having committed the crime of teaching migrant workers in Andalusia how to read. As a result, Azucena and a number of her siblings were born in Cuba.

I spent many hours with her, discussing what it had been like to grow up in an anarchist family, her introduction to and participation in anarchist activities and organizations, and her sense of the complicated place of women in the Spanish anarcho-syndicalist movement.[7] But she insisted that the person I should really speak to was her sister, Enriqueta. She was the real *militante* (activist) and a member of Mujeres Libres.

It was not until six months later that I had the opportunity to meet Enriqueta Fernandez Rovira herself. I had already discovered that the mere mention of her name inspired the same reaction in just about everyone with whom I spoke: "Oh, Enriqueta," they would say, making their voices deep, hunching their shoulders and tightening both fists to make themselves look (as much as relatively frail older women can) like prizefighters flexing their muscles. Yet, despite this buildup, I was not fully prepared for the quiet power of her presence.

I met Enriqueta under far-from-ideal circumstances. It was Christmas vacation time in France, and her small house was filled with the activity of four of her grandchildren. We found time to talk either after they had gone to sleep or amid the bustle of midmorning requests for snacks or permission to engage in this or that game. And all her frustrations with the "poor manners" of these energetic young people provided a bittersweet counterpoint to her own stories of being considered "outrageous" even by her anarchist parents when she and her young friends went off on mixed-sex bicycle trips to the countryside or to the beach in the early 1930s.

Enriqueta was also born in Cuba, in 1915, and moved to Spain with the rest of the family in 1920. Anarchist activists were constantly in and out of their house, and the "ideas" were a normal part of the conversation. In many ways, her parents represented two of the different strands of anarchism prevalent in the movement in those years. As she put it,

> My father was a man of ideas, an anarchist, but much more than my mother, he was a pacifist. He would get upset if he saw a single drop of blood. He was a revolutionary, but a pacifist. He believed the revolution should come through culture and education. He hated guns. Never wanted to see them . . . that was not his style. He was more quiet. . . . Not my mother. She was more of an activist.[8]

The children learned early on that to be a member of a community is to be available to take care of others and to be willing to dedicate one's person and one's life to the common cause. The ideas they shared with others—particularly within anarchist-inspired youth groups in which Enriqueta and Azucena were both very active—unified them as a group, while separating them from others:

> In those days, we were . . . the whores, . . . the crazies, because we were the ones who pushed ahead. . . . I remember when my father died—it was very sad. . . . My mother said, "Papa didn't want roses, but I would like some. Go and get a dozen roses for your father." . . . So I went to the florist . . . [who] said to me, "What? You're here, and your father is dead? And I said, "what has one thing got to do with another? Do you think I feel no sorrow because I've come here? Do you think I don't feel the pain of my

father's death? I've come to get some roses for him." "But it's not your place, child, your place is in the house. Joaquín should come get the flowers. And you're not wearing black?" And I said, "No, my pain I carry inside. I don't wear it outside."

The commitment to anarchist values existed for Enriqueta and her family for as long as she could remember. The children's participation in groups and activities sponsored by movement organizations deepened that commitment and turned it into an important focus of their lives. The community gave them the strength to face the ridicule of their neighbors, as well as the scepticism even of their anarchist parents, about the appropriateness of young girls going out in mixed groups. It enabled them to find their own voices, dream their own dreams, and carry out the visions they may have learned from their parents but soon transformed into their own. Because of her long involvement in the movement, Enriqueta was chosen by the CNT for a highly sensitive job as one of the central telephone operators in Barcelona during the war. She continued to be active in the anarchist movement and in the CNT, and she eventually joined Mujeres Libres.

It was also with the help of Eglantina that I first met Sara Berenguer Guillén, who had been Secretary of Propaganda of Mujeres Libres in Catalonia. Eglantina picked me up one December morning from Azucena's house in Perpignan, and drove me to the lovely house in the small village of Montady (near Béziers), where Sara and her compañero, Jesús Guillén, have made their home. Sara is a small woman who, despite the numbers of family and friends who were visiting a few days after Christmas, readily made time to talk with me about her experiences. When I returned for a second visit some years later, Sara was as welcoming as she had been earlier. We spent an exhausting few days together, talking almost nonstop about Mujeres Libres, and interviewing many other women in the area who had been involved either in Mujeres Libres or in other organizations of the libertarian movement. These women included Teresina Torrellas Graells, Conchita Guillén, and Amada de Nó.

Sara had not been involved with movement organizations before the war, although her father was a CNT militant. She began to work with the CNT only at the outbreak of the war, when her father went off to the front and she wanted to do something "to help the revolution." She joined Mujeres Libres late in 1937, although initially she opposed the idea of a separate organization for women:

> I did not agree with the idea of Mujeres Libres. I thought, the struggle affects both men and women. We are all fighting together for a better society. Why should there be a separate organization? One day, when I was with a group from the Juventudes, we went to a meeting Mujeres Libres had organized at the Juventudes headquarters, where they also

had an office. The boys started making fun of the speakers, which annoyed me from the outset. When the woman who was speaking finished, the boys began asking questions and saying it didn't make sense for women to organize separately, since they wouldn't do anything anyway. The debate was impassioned. The tone of their comments disgusted me even more, and I came to the defense of Mujeres Libres. . . . In the end, they named me delegate from our neighborhood to the meeting of the Federación Local of Mujeres Libres of Barcelona.[9]

In addition to her activism in Mujeres Libres, Sara served during the war on the revolutionary committee of her *barrio* (neighborhood), Las Corts, and as secretary to the Catalan Regional Committee of the Building, Wood, and Decoration Industry (CNT). She also worked for SIA (Solidaridad Internacional Antifascista), an international anarchist relief organization. She fled to France when Barcelona was invaded in January 1939, remaining there as an exile and, over the years, participating in the Spanish exile underground. Early in the 1960s, together with Suceso Portales, she participated in publishing a newsletter, *Mujeres Libres*, in exile. She has written a number of volumes of poetry, and has recently published her memoirs of the war years.[10]

Not everyone who was involved in the movement, however, came from anarchist family backgrounds. Pepita Carpena, for example, was born in Barcelona at the end of 1919, and grew up as the child of working-class parents who evinced little or no interest in working-class organizations. She was introduced to "the ideas" for the first time in 1933 by anarchist union organizers who attended gatherings of young people in hopes of rounding up potential union members.[11] As she described it,

They would go to dances, activities, and the like where we young people would hang out, look for the boys, tell them about a meeting at a union hall at a particular time, and they would go. Well, as I tended to hang out more with boys than with girls, when they would invite the boys to the meetings at the union, I would go, too. That's how I got involved.

The metalworker's union, which took her in almost as a young mascot, became her home away from home. When her parents objected to her going out to meetings at night, she urged her father to go with her. After seeing who the people were and the way they treated her, he never complained again. Instead, he boasted to his friends about his daughter who was freeing the proletariat!

Through her associations with the metalworkers, Pepita soon learned much about unions and about anarcho-syndicalism. They encouraged her to organize the young women workers where she was employed as a seamstress, which she did. And when her boss fired her on some pretext (because of her union organizing), her compañeros from the metalworkers' union came to her aid and had her reinstated. She continued her militancy in the CNT and in the Juventudes Libertarias (the Libertarian Youth) through the early 1930s and into the first year of the war. When her compañero was killed early in the war, the metalworkers' union paid his salary to her as a stipend so she could continue to organize women workers for the war effort. She describes herself as someone who had assumed the equality of women for as long as she could remember, and she was, at best, initially indifferent to the creation of a specifically women's organization. But as a result of her experience in the Juventudes, in particular, she soon came to recognize that need, and she became an active member of the Catalan regional committee of Mujeres Libres during 1937–1938.[12]

More than any of the other viejas, Pepita has managed to communicate with the jóvenes across barriers of time, class, and geography. She is aware of contemporary feminist debates, even if she often takes issue with the terms in which they are posed. In her post as archivist and curator of the Marseilles branch of the Geneva-based CIRA (Centre Internationale de Recherches sur l'Anarchisme), Pepita travels frequently throughout Spain and Europe, speaking about the revolution and about her activities in Mujeres Libres. Her openness and her willingness to discuss issues that were controversial within Mujeres Libres have made her an invaluable informant and a very special friend.

I first met Mercedes Comaposada in Paris in January 1982 in the one-room apartment filled with books where she had been living for forty-three years. Her compañero, the artist and sculptor Lobo, had the room next door. Everyone had described her to me as a woman who was very handsome, yet delicate and frail. She is, in fact, a very small woman, but lively and absolutely in possession of her faculties. On those occasions when we walked outside, I was astounded at the speed with which she seemed almost to run through the streets. Even in her late eighties, she retained that "distinguished" presence which so characterized her in the eyes of the young women she was to educate in classes sponsored by Mujeres Libres.

Mercedes was born in Barcelona in 1900 to a strongly committed socialist father. Late in her teens, she left home to study in Madrid, and there she discovered the CNT. When invited by compañeros in the CNT to give a series of classes at the local union hall, she was appalled at the ways in which they treated the women who attended, and shortly thereafter, together with Lucía Sánchez Saornil, who had had similar experiences, she committed herself to educating and enculturating women, encouraging them to develop the full range of their potential. Within a few years, their dream had taken shape as Mujeres Libres.

Mercedes insisted that "we never called ourselves 'founders,' only initiators." Although her use of the term *initiator*, rather than *founder*, implies a rejection of personal power or authority, Mercedes clearly sees herself as the sole legitimate spokesperson for Mujeres Libres. She has been working for some years to organize and edit the organization's papers, and she is wary of those who attempt to publish or speak about them before she has completed her work. Although she has refused all invitations to speak about Mujeres Libres at anarchist and/or feminist gatherings (apparently out of concern that her remarks would be misunderstood or taken out of context), she has also been critical of others who have agreed to do so, on the grounds that they were too young then or came into the organization too late to really understand what it was about. Her position is obviously a complicated one, and our relationship has been somewhat problematic as a consequence.

Through Mercedes, however, I also met Soledad Estorach, one of the originators of the Barcelona group that was to become part of Mujeres Libres in the fall of 1936. When I first met her in Paris in January 1982, she looked much younger than her sixty-six years. We spent many hours in her small flat, talking about her youth, her involvement in the CNT and in Mujeres Libres, and her views on the situation of women in society. She had been described to me as a dynamo, the one who really *was* Mujeres Libres in Barcelona. Everything I saw and heard of her certainly confirmed that impression.

Soledad grew up in a small village about two hundred kilometers from Barcelona, although, as she explained, she did "not live the traditional life of a *campesina*." Her father, who had spent many years living outside of Spain and who taught classes for adults, also taught Soledad to read and write—skills virtually unknown to young girls of her class. The knowledge she gained from him was political as well: "He had very advanced ideas that affected me deeply—especially notions of justice." Her mother's family was very different: "They were landholders and very religious."

Her father died when she was eleven, and Soledad had to begin working. A teacher in a neighboring village who had been a friend of her father's continued her lessons for a few hours each week. The family managed to remain in the village until she was about fifteen. By then, however, she was under increasing pressure from her mother and her mother's family to marry, to find a man to support her and her family. But, as she put it, "I was faithful to my father, his world, and his ideas. I wanted to travel as he had, to learn. . . . I didn't want to live my life within the four walls of a house. I wanted to travel, to conquer the world. I persuaded my mother to let me go to Barcelona, where I could work in an uncle's shop, make money to support the family, and also get an education."[13]

She went first and was soon joined by her mother and younger sister. Initially she worked in her uncle's shop, but economic crisis forced him to close his business, and Soledad had to find other work. She went into domestic service, but her hours were long (from 5 A.M. until 1 A.M.!), and the pay was insignificant. So, after a short while, she began working in a factory, hoping both to earn more money and to have more time for her "education." Late in 1930 she also began attending night school and meeting compañeros from the CNT, which was still operating clandestinely.

In 1931, after the fall of the monarchy, she found her way to an *ateneo* (a storefront school and cultural center), where she met Abelardo Saavedra (the grandfather of Enriqueta and Azucena), who impressed her deeply with the power of his beliefs. "He was," she recalled, "for young people like a book that never closed." She joined the youth group at the ateneo and became a *militante*. Soon she was spending virtually all of her time in meetings or preparing for meetings, elated by the community and the excitement of collective action. By 1934 she was discussing with other women activists the difficulties that women often experienced within the CNT, and they established a sort of mutual support network, the Grupo cultural femenino, CNT (female cultural group, CNT). When, after the establishment of Mujeres Libres in Madrid in 1936, Mercedes came to Barcelona, the Catalan group quickly agreed to associate themselves.

I should mention one more vieja, Pura Perez Arcos, who lives with her compañero, Federico Arcos, in Windsor, Ontario. Pura was born in Valencia in 1919, and moved with her family to the village of Játiva three years later. Both her father and grandfather were transport workers and members of the CNT, and Pura had grown up hearing "much talk about injustice." At her insistence her parents sent her to elementary school with an older cousin who was living with them, and she stayed in the school, eagerly soaking up the knowledge, even beyond the expected school-leaving age of eleven or twelve. She felt particularly fortunate when the Republic was proclaimed in 1931, because the new government established more schools—including secondary schools—and she was able to continue her education. When her father was transferred to Barcelona in 1933, however, the high cost of living there meant that Pura had to leave school and go to work. A few months later the family settled in the barrio of El Clot, where Pura was able to continue her education at night in the Escuela Natura, a rationalist school. There she met young anarchists, joined an ateneo, and became involved in the libertarian movement. During the war and revolution, she returned to Valencia and spent time on a collective. She was also active in Mujeres Libres, and worked with Soledad Estorach in Barcelona and with Suceso Portales in Valencia.

After the war and several years spent in the underground anti-Franco movement, Federico made his way to Canada, got a job in an automobile plant, and settled in Windsor. Pura remained in Spain for some years, suffering through the horrors of the early Franco era. She joined Federico in 1959 and worked in Windsor as a nurse until her recent retirement. Now she spends her time reading, taking courses at the local universities, and producing pressed-flower pictures. Over the years she has maintained active contact with Sara Berenguer Guillén in southern France and with Mercedes and Soledad in Paris, and she is helping to organize and edit the papers of Mujeres Libres. Her insight and help—particularly in translating the activities and visions of Mujeres Libres into contemporary language—have been invaluable.

As I have studied the literature of Mujeres Libres and of the Spanish anarchist movement, spoken and corresponded with the women I have met, and attempted to understand their lives and activities, three themes have arisen to provide a focus for this book: community, empowerment, and diversity. Mujeres Libres, like the Spanish libertarian movement, was collectivist and communalist in orientation, which meant that it was committed to a vision of society in which the self-development of each is connected to the development of all.[14] Freedom and equality, individual identity and community, were understood to be mutually interdependent, each the precondition for the other. The women of Mujeres Libres therefore understood consciousness-change and empowerment to be both individual and collective processes. They believed that empowerment could take place only in the context of communities and/or organizations that acknowledged and valued the diversity of their constituents.

With respect to their understanding of the relationship between individuals and communities, Mujeres Libres and Spanish libertarians would have taken sharp issue with the classical liberal formulations of this relationship so common in contemporary U.S. culture. They shared with socialists the sense that individual identity and community, rather than being at odds with one another, are inextricably linked. Marxists, anarchists, feminists, and other social constructionists have insisted that human needs and consciousness are products of our social relationships, and, thus, to speak of individuals outside of a social context makes little or no sense. They further insist that what we understand as "freedom" is itself a social product.[15]

But much recent feminist social-historical research and theorizing have gone beyond even this formulation, emphasizing the importance of communal/collective networks in constituting people and providing the contexts for consciousness and empowerment.[16] This emphasis on networks and social context is giving rise to new conceptualizations of politics, as rooted not in *individuals* and their needs and concerns, but in what we might term "social subcollectivities," with a consequent focus on their constitution, their boundaries, and power relations

within them.[17] For contemporary feminist researchers, this approach
has led to explorations of the place of networks, community, and connection in the lives of women, both in earlier times and in the present.[18]

Spanish anarchists and the women of Mujeres Libres clearly recognized the importance of such connections and of the social constitution
of personhood, and like their earlier "sisters" in the British utopian
socialist movement (though, apparently, without any direct knowledge
of that group's existence or activities), they attempted to develop organizational forms and activities that would enable people to experience
them. As I will show in chapter 2, this perspective led them to address
people in a variety of contexts, including in rural communities and
urban barrios, as well as in workplaces. For the women of Mujeres
Libres, this perspective also meant an emphasis on the significance of
gender, both in constituting communities and in creating the conditions
for consciousness-change and liberation.

The second, related theme that emerged from my engagement with
this material concerns issues of power, domination, and empowerment.
Spanish anarchists and anarcho-syndicalists developed, and attempted
to act upon, an understanding of the nature of power and hierarchy in
society—and of strategies to overcome it—which differed significantly
from both Marxist and liberal strategies and which speaks directly to
the concerns of much contemporary feminist theorizing about the interaction of hierarchies of gender, race, and class. Although the range of
feminist scholarship on this topic is enormous and growing, theoretical
frameworks have tended to fall into three well-known categories—
liberal feminists, socialist feminists, and radical feminists. These categories are differentiated according to their understanding of the nature
and sources of the subordination of women in societies and of the
relationship between gender inequality and inequalities based on class,
ethnic-cultural, religious, or other differences.

Anarchists agree with socialists, socialist feminists, and radical feminists that the factors involved in understanding social inequality—and
sexual inequality, in particular—go beyond mere discrimination. Yet
Spanish anarchists echoed many of the concerns of earlier utopian
socialists, differing from Marxists (and from contemporary socialist-
feminists and radical feminists) in important ways. Instead of treating
either class relations or sexual divisions as the most basic form of
subordination on which all others depend, anarchists saw hierarchy,
formalized authority, as an equally crucial problem. They recognized
various types of subordination (e.g., political and sexual, as well as
economic) as more or less independent relationships, each of which
would need to be addressed by a truly revolutionary movement.

In her study of British Owenites, Barbara Taylor argues that those
early utopian socialists developed an analysis of society and domination that treated people as being rooted in collectivity. Further, they

recognized a need to address both gender and class as manifestations of domination. Nevertheless, as she points out, this multifaceted analysis of oppression was relatively short-lived. Within a few years, there was no place for "feminism" in socialist notions of solidarity. "Sex-equality radicalism," which had been an important aspect of utopian socialism, was lost when scientific socialism developed, emphasizing class as the central category of analysis. In the consequent "splitting" that occurred, feminism lost its class analysis and socialism lost its feminist dimension.[19]

Although the power of Marxist analysis derives precisely from its insistence that economic relationships are at the root of all relations of domination and subordination in society, many feminist critics insisted early on that this monolithic approach to oppression was also Marxism's limitation. Marxist socialist analysis had no room for an independent understanding of the subordination of women, which exists in socialist as well as in capitalist societies, irrespective of the "mode of production." But to "add women and stir" to a Marxist analytical model yields only confusion, since it destroys the power that derives specifically from the claim of that analysis to root *all* hierarchies in economic relations.

In its insistence that hierarchy needs to be addressed and uprooted, independent of economic relations, anarchism seems, by contrast, to offer an analytical model that could accommodate multiple relationships of domination and subordination without necessarily insisting that one is more fundamental than the others. Precisely because it acknowledged this multidimensional character of subordination, the experience of Mujeres Libres can be a very fruitful source for contemporary feminists struggling to develop an understanding of women's subordination and empowerment that can attend to differences of ethnicity, race, and class.

In locating individual identity in community and recognizing hierarchical power structures (whether based on gender, religion, or class) as limits to the development both of communities and of the individuals who constitute them, Mujeres Libres attempted to develop strategies for empowerment *(capacitación)* that would enable previously subordinated women and men to realize their own capacities. Feminists and democratic activists in the United States are, of course, struggling with related questions: What does *empowerment* mean? How can we empower ourselves (or others) without creating new relationships of "power over" others? Starhawk's recent analysis of power as "power over," "power within," and "power with" represents one example of these contemporary feminist—and, specifically, ecofeminist—explorations.[20] The experience of Mujeres Libres can contribute much to this discussion.

Finally, related to these issues is the question of diversity. Although

Spanish anarchists insisted on the importance of community and on the mutual interdependence of community and individuality, they also argued that shared visions need not be based on sameness and that communities can not only incorporate, but be strengthened by, diversity.

That vision, of course, is easier to point to than to live out. The story of Mujeres Libres is, in many ways, one of an attempt to build a movement that would incorporate at least one set of differences—those based on gender. The women of Mujeres Libres, working within the context of the Spanish anarchist movement, pressed their comrades, both male and female, to rethink what their community was, who belonged to it, whom it served, and how it operated. In the process, they pushed both anarchist theory and anarchist practice in exciting new directions.

This dimension of their activity poses important challenges and opens possibilities for us today. It is not coincidental that, as we increasingly acknowledge the power of communal connections in our own lives, contemporary U.S. feminists and democratic theorists are exploring just what we mean by *community*. Within the larger feminist movement, it has been women of color who first and most consistently raised the question of the place of community in personal identity and insisted that any truly feminist vision—and community—must be one that not only tolerates but also nourishes diversity.[21]

More recently, white feminists have begun seriously discussing the meaning and significance of diversity among women.[22] Increasing numbers of white women are coming to realize that there may be no such thing as "woman" and that our identities as individual women are crucially connected to the particular ethnic, religious, and cultural groups that also contribute to our identity. Of course, many women of color, working-class women, Jewish women, and members of other oppressed groups have been all too aware of the significance of such differences, insufficiently reflected in the larger "women's movement."[23] What, then, does this mean for feminist organizing or feminist theorizing? In recognizing class or ethnic differences among women, must we abandon any notion of commonality?

Mujeres Libres focused on gender differences between women and men within the larger libertarian movement, rather than on class or ethnic differences among women. Nevertheless, the struggles they underwent to recognize and validate difference while insisting on equality are certainly instructive. In addition, I believe that some of their wariness about feminism may have stemmed from their understanding of themselves as *working-class* women and of the differences between the needs and experiences of working-class and middle-class women. Thus, although the issues they addressed were framed rather differently from our own—they focused primarily on gender differences within a working-class movement, rather than on class or ethnic differences within a women's movement—the struggles they confronted, the strategies they devised, their successes, and their failures may yet prove valuable to us.

In the early years of this century and through the period of the Spanish Civil War (1936–1939), anarchists and anarcho-syndicalists in Spain developed not only a theoretical perspective, but also a network of economic, political, and cultural organizations and activities that provided a context in which to test their perspectives on community and diversity, domination and empowerment. Spanish libertarians strived to create communities that respected the individuality of their members, while at the same time they insisted that individuality could be developed and experienced only in community. The women who founded Mujeres Libres were all firmly committed to the goals of the movement and deeply involved in its organizations. Each had been nurtured by it. Many described themselves as having come to a full sense of who they were only in and through the activities of the groups they joined, whether unions, storefront schools and cultural centers, hiking clubs, or the like. The libertarian community became essential to their newly developing sense of self.

Yet, at the same time, they felt that something was missing for women. The realization was a painful one: the community they experienced through the anarcho-syndicalist movement was so important to them that they feared anything that might undermine its unity and integrity. Still, each came to insist that, both for the sake of her own and other women's development and for the sake of the movement itself, a separate organization devoted to women's emancipation was essential. That decision was not an easy one for any of them, and it often met with stiff opposition from their comrades, both male and female.

My purpose here is to chronicle the struggles of these women and, in the process, to illuminate our own: to review the theoretical and activist traditions in Spain that gave birth to the libertarian movement, to attempt to understand how and why these women came to believe that an autonomous women's organization was necessary, to examine how they came to understand the relationship between their project—and their autonomy—and the long-term goals of the libertarian community, and to explore how they were received by the mainstream organizations of that movement. While contemporary feminist and democratic struggles for a more egalitarian society differ significantly from theirs, we, too, strive to create relationships that can nurture without stifling and communities that can provide meaningful contexts for commitment. By linking our stories to theirs, I hope we can not only learn from, but be empowered by, our history.

# *I*

# ANARCHIST REVOLUTION AND THE LIBERATION OF WOMEN

When the Republic came, many people went to storm the prisons to free the prisoners, and I went, too. There was some guy there shouting, "Abajo la política! [Down with politics!] Abajo la Guardia Civil! [Down with the Civil Guard!] . . . all sorts of abajos." And then he yelled, "Viva la anarquía!" [Long live anarchy]. And I thought, "Aha, here is an anarchist." This was my first encounter with an anarchist—and he did not look like he was a terrible person. He had a good face.

—Soledad Estorach

People would say to us, "Were you children baptized?" and we would say to them, "We weren't baptized." "How terrible, what girls! Such beautiful children"—because we were six handsome sisters ( I mean from the standpoint of health) and one brother—"being brought up without God, you are like dogs!" And we would say, "No, you are the ones who are like dogs, that you need a master."

—Enriqueta Rovira

Domination in all its forms—whether exercised by governments, religious institutions, or through economic relations—is for anarchists the source of all social evil. While anarchism shares with many socialist traditions a radical critique of economic domination and an insistence on the need for a fundamental economic restructuring of society on a more egalitarian basis, it goes beyond Marxist socialism in developing an independent critique of the state, of hierarchy, and of authority relations in general. Where socialists have traced the roots of *all* domination to the division of labor in the economy, anarchists have insisted that power has its own logic and will not be abolished through attention to economic relations alone.

Anarchism aims to abolish hierarchy and structured relations of domination and subordination in society. It also aims to create a society based on equality, mutuality, and reciprocity in which each person is valued and respected as an individual. This social vision is combined with a theory of social change that insists that means must be consistent with ends, that people cannot be directed into a future society but must create it themselves, thereby recognizing their own abilities and capacities. In both its vision of the ideal society and its theory of how that society must be achieved, anarchism has much to offer contemporary feminists. The anarchist analysis of relations of domination provides a fruitful model for understanding the situation of women in society and for relating women's condition to that of other oppressed groups. A theory of social change that insists on the unity of means and ends and on the strengths of the oppressed provides a striking contrast to many existing theories—and most existing practice—of social revolutionary movements.

Furthermore, some nineteenth-century anarchist writers and activists, both in Spain and elsewhere in Europe and the United States, specifically addressed themselves to the subordination of women in their societies and insisted that full human emancipation required not just the abolition of capitalism and of authoritarian political institutions but also the overcoming of women's cultural and economic subordination, both inside and outside the home. As early as 1872, for example, an anarchist congress in Spain declared that women ought to be fully the equals of men in the home and in the workplace.

Yet neither the theory of anarchism as it developed in Spain and elsewhere in Europe during the nineteenth and early twentieth centuries nor the practice of anarcho-syndicalism in Spain was egalitarian in the full sense of the word.[1] Although many writers seemed to acknowledge the importance of women's emancipation to the anarchist project and the importance of women to the movement, few gave those concerns top priority. As was the case with socialist movements throughout Europe, many anarchists treated the issue of women's subordination as, at best, secondary to the emancipation of workers, a problem that would be resolved "on the morrow of the revolution."

The founding of Mujeres Libres represented an effort by women within the Spanish anarcho-syndicalist movement both to challenge the movement to fulfill its promise to women and to empower women to claim their places within that movement and within the larger society. At the same time that the founders were frustrated by the failure of the movement to adequately incorporate women and issues of concern to women, they nevertheless remained convinced that the movement provided the only context for achieving a true liberation of women.

My aim in this book is to make clear just what Mujeres Libres' vision was and to explore its relevance for contemporary feminists and social change activists. But in order to do so, we must first locate it—as did the women of Mujeres Libres themselves—in the context of anarcho-syndicalist theory and practice. In this chapter, I examine the works of Spanish anarchist writers and others in the "communalist anarchist" tradition who provided the theoretical grounding of the Spanish anarcho-syndicalist movement. My aim is to highlight their approaches to the understanding of women's subordination, their critiques of hierarchy and domination, and their understanding of the process of fully integrating a concern with the subordination of women into a theory of radical social transformation. But I also wish to explore the ambiguities evident in these analyses, the ways that—despite the apparent awareness at the core of anarchist theory that relations of domination were manifold and complex—attention to the subordination of women was repeatedly given lower priority than the oppression of male workers. This contextualization of Mujeres Libres' program and activities should lay the basis for a demonstration of the ways Mujeres Libres' programs effectively addressed the weaknesses of anarcho-syndicalism at the time and constituted both a critique and extension of Spanish anarcho-syndicalist theory and practice.

I focus here on Spanish anarcho-syndicalist analyses of domination and subordination, on the vision of an egalitarian society, and on the process of empowerment, specifically as related to the situation of women. Exploration of these concerns on a theoretical level can then serve as backdrop and counterpoint to the more historical analysis of the roots of Mujeres Libres in the anarcho-syndicalist movement, which I undertake in chapter 2. In fact, for anarchists, theory and practice were hardly distinguishable in this sense. The theoretical positions we will be discussing in this chapter were developed in the context of historical struggles, at the same time that they contributed to the development of those struggles. I separate them here only for analytical purposes.

## Domination and Subordination

Anarchist visions are politically, socially, and economically egalitarian. Politically and socially, an anarchist society is a society without government, without institutionalized hierarchical relationships or patterns of authority. Anarchists claim that people can organize and associate themselves on the basis of need, that individuals or small groups can initiate social action, and that centralized political coordination is not only harmful but also unnecessary. The right or authority to direct or command a situation should not inhere in roles or offices to which some people have privileged access or from which others are systematically excluded. Finally, anarchists are committed to nondominating relationships with the environment, as well as with people. Anarchists have focused not on conquering nature, but on developing new ways to live (as much as possible) in harmony with it.[2]

Virtually all major social thinkers in the West have assumed that social order requires leadership, hierarchy, and, in particular, political authority. Many argue that social life, especially in a complex society, could not exist without structures of power and authority. "Society means that norms regulate human conduct," and norms require authorities with power to enforce them.[3] In a slightly different vein, social contract theorists have argued that political authority is necessary to create a stable social order, the precondition for moral choice. Theorists of social movements argue that it takes a strong person (or persons) to unite disparate individuals into a coherent unit and give them direction. Organization, in turn, *requires* that some people be in positions to give orders and that the rest—whether as "good citizens" or as "good revolutionaries"—be prepared to take and follow them.[4]

Anarchists argue in response that formal hierarchies are not only harmful but unnecessary and that there are alternative, more egalitarian ways in which to organize social life. Most important, along with socialists and, more recently, feminists, anarchists have insisted that human nature is a social construct; the way people behave is more a product of the institutions in which they/we are raised than of any inherent nature. Formal hierarchical structures of authority may well create the conditions they are presumably designed to combat: rather than preventing disorder, governments are among its primary causes.[5] Hierarchical institutions foster alienated and exploitative relationships among those who participate in them, disempowering people and distancing them from their own reality. Hierarchies make some people dependent on others, blame the dependent for their dependency, and then use that dependency as a justification for the further exercise of authority.[6]

Many Spanish anarchists used the existing subordination of women in society as an example to demonstrate the power of social institutions to create dependent persons. While there were many views among Spanish anarchists about the nature of women and about the appropriate role for women in a future society, most anarchist writers seemed to agree that women were severely disadvantaged in Spanish society and that existing inequalities between men and women were largely the product of social conditioning and male power. As early as 1903, for example, José Prat argued that "women's 'backwardness' is a consequence of the way she has been, and still is, treated. 'Nature' has nothing to do with this. . . . If woman is backward, it is because in all times man has kept her inferior, depriving her of all those rights which he was gradually winning for himself."[7] Gregorio Marañon and Mariano Gallardo, while acknowledging that there were significant sexual differences between women and men, argued that societal gender inequalities were the result of denying opportunities to women: "Woman's . . . presumed inferiority is purely artificial, the inevitable consequence of a civilization which, by educating men and women separately and distinctly, makes of the woman a slave and of her compañero a ferocious tyrant."[8]

Spanish anarchists, like contemporary feminists, argued that the exercise of power in any institutionalized form—whether economic, political, religious, or sexual—brutalizes both the wielder of power and the one over whom it is exercised. On the one hand, those who hold power tend only to develop an ever-increasing desire to maintain it. Governments, for example, may claim to represent a "common interest" or "general will." But this claim is false and masks the state's role in preserving and maintaining the economic and political power of the few over the many.[9]

On the other hand, the exercise of power by some disempowers others.[10] Those in positions of relative dominance tend to define the very characters of those subordinate to them. Through a combination of physical intimidation, economic domination and dependency, and psychological limitations, social institutions and practices affect the way everyone sees the world and her or his place in it.[11] Anarchists argue that to be always in a position of being acted upon and never to be allowed to act is to be doomed to a state of dependence and resignation. Those who are constantly ordered about and prevented from thinking for themselves soon come to doubt their own capacities. Along with contemporary feminists,[12] anarchists insist that those who are defined by others have great difficulty defining, or naming, themselves and their experience and even more difficulty acting on that sense of self in opposition to societal norms, standards, and expectations.[13]

Anarchists, therefore, oppose *permanent* structures of authority in which particular people seem to find their "calling," arguing that authority relations in society ought to be more fluid: "People are free. They work freely, change freely, contract freely."[14]

## Community and Equality

Many theorists, of course, have argued that, despite the negative effects of hierarchical structures, domination and subordination (whether in the political, economic, or sexual realm) are necessary for social life. In response, anarchists describe alternative ways to organize society that embody both freedom and equality in the broadest sense. Such visions locate individuals firmly in a communal context and require attention to economic relationships, to mechanisms for coordination, to sexuality and male-female relations, and to those ongoing systems of education and socialization that make it possible for a society to perpetuate itself over time.

In place of inequality as a basis of organization, anarchists offer mutualism, reciprocity, and federalism. In place of hierarchy and domination, they propose to empower everyone to achieve his or her full potential, thus obviating the need for social, political, or sexual inequality. I will highlight those aspects of the anarchist theory of revolution that were to be of particular significance for Mujeres Libres and through which we will see most clearly Mujeres Libres' contribution to the development of the theory and practice of nonauthoritarian social change: the social nature of freedom, the vision of an egalitarian society, and the process of consciousness-change and empowerment.

Freedom, or individual liberty, was a basic premise of the Spanish anarchist tradition. "Individual sovereignty" is a prime tenet of most anarchist writing; the free development of one's individual potential is one of the basic "rights" to which all humans are born.[15] Yet Spanish anarchists were firmly rooted in the *communalist*-anarchist tradition. For them, freedom was fundamentally a social product: the fullest expression of individuality and of creativity can be achieved only *in and through community*. As Pilar Grangel (a teacher who was also active in Mujeres Libres) wrote, describing the relationship of individuality and community: "I and my truth; I and my faith. . . . And I for you, but without ever ceasing to be me, so that you can always be you. Because I don't exist without your existence, but my existence is also indispensable to yours."[16] They made frequent appeals to Kropotkin's claim that social life was regulated not by an antagonistic struggle for survival, but by "mutual aid": "Without association, no life is possible."[17] Only in a fully egalitarian society, devoid of hierarchies of economic class, political, or sexual privilege, would everyone be free to develop to the fullest and would individual initiative be able to flourish.[18]

The focus on individuality and individual initiative, and the communal context that nourishes it, provided a potential context for Spanish anarchists to address male-female differences. This perspective generated an awareness—at least on a theoretical level—of human diversity, of the variety of ways people can contribute to the social whole, and of the benefits to the society of the incorporation of different groups. But the working out of this vision, whether in theory or in practice, as related to sexual differences was much more limited. As contemporary feminists and minority activists have made us well aware, it is not always obvious how to ensure respect and equality in nonhomogeneous communities. Many supposedly egalitarian social forms have ignored differences between men and women, for example, or assumed they were irrelevant to politics, thus effectively reproducing the subordination of women.[19]

The limits of the Spanish anarchist vision become clear as we examine their understandings of the basic constituents of social organization. Most Spanish anarchist writers located economic relationships at the center of their vision, insisting that the basic principle of social organization must be economic, rather than political. Economic relationships must be as nonhierarchical as possible, with respect both to the remuneration that people receive and to the structure of work. They differed among themselves as to what ought properly to constitute equality of reward, varying between collectivism (to each according to contribution) and communism (to each according to need). Nevertheless, all agreed that relative equality of reward was essential to the functioning of a just society. This was so both because economic inequalities are easily converted into social or political power and, more basically, because most human labor is collaborative and it is virtually impossible to assign value to an individual's contribution to a collective task.[20]

To say that economic equality must be at the root of a society based in reciprocity and mutuality, however, is insufficient to define what the overall structure and organization of that society might look like. For communalist anarchists, society was best conceived as a series of voluntary associations that, while recognizing individual autonomy, could still provide for the overall coordination essential to freedom and justice. Social order was to be achieved through the voluntary cooperation of locally based, decentralized units rather than through formal political structures. They pointed to railways, international postal services, and other forms of communication as models of networks, set up by voluntary agreement, that functioned efficiently to provide services to people without the intervention of some higher authority.[21]

This central focus on economic structures, however, particularly in a society characterized by a sharp sexual division of labor, raised serious questions for women. How would women be involved? Would a new society challenge and overcome the sexual division of labor? Or would it leave that division in place and strive to achieve a kind of "separate but equal" status for women? An emphasis on economic structures as the root of social organization effectively belied the anarchist insistence that domination and subordination had many facets and that economic issues were not the only ones that needed to be addressed. In fact, as we will see in chapter 2, debates about the core institutions and structures of the new society were to be quite divisive during the pre–Civil War period, although they rarely focused on the implications of these decisions for women's position or participation.

Most of the debate instead focused on what sorts of organizations would form the basis of the new society. Those who were to become known as anarcho-syndicalists (and who, by 1910, represented the majority position within the CNT) envisioned a society with unions at its base.[22] Unions would be coordinated both locally and industrially through federations to which each union (or group of unions) would send a delegate. This vision, however, provided little opportunity to nonworkers (including children, the unemployed, old people, the disabled, and nonworking mothers) to participate in social decision making.

Others, identified as "anarchists" rather than as anarcho-syndicalists, insisted that unions represented too narrow a base for coordinating a libertarian communist society. Soledad Gustavo, Federico Urales, and Federica Montseny, for example, argued that unions are products of capitalism and that it does not make sense to assume that they would be the basis for organization and coordination in a transformed economy: "There are workers because there are bosses. Workerism will disappear with capitalism, and syndicalism with wages."[23] Both Gustavo and Federica Montseny pointed to another tradition with a long history in Spain, the *municipio libre* (free commune): "Especially in agricultural villages, where the syndicalist solution is not appropriate even in a transitional sense, I reserve the right to pursue the revolution from the moment that we proclaim free communes throughout Spain, on the basis of the socialization of the land and of all the means of production, placed in the hands of producers."[24] Interestingly, these two women who argued for a more community-focused organizational base were also two of the more outspoken supporters of women's emancipation—although, to my knowledge, neither explicitly connected her concern for women's emancipation with this organizational focus on community as opposed to workplace. As we will see in chapter 2, community-based organizing strategies were often more successful than workplace-based ones in addressing issues of concern to women and in galvanizing women's participation.

Eventually, most theorists and CNT activists attempted to combine the municipio libre with the union, although the terms of the combination still tended to favor the syndical solution. Isaac Puente, for example, argued that the municipio libre in cities should actually be the local federation of unions. In rural areas, the town would hold everything within its boundaries as common property; the communal decision-making body would be composed of "everyone who works." The only ones exempted from this requirement would be the young, the sick, and the aged.[25] This resolution, of course, based social and political rights on *economic* productivity, even in the "free commune."

As we will see in the next chapter, to the extent that there was any resolution of questions of organizational structure and vision, it was achieved through the practice of the anarcho-syndicalist movement, rather than through theoretical debates in the press. It is important to note here that the Spanish movement differed from most other European working-class movements of the late nineteenth and early twentieth centuries in the place it accorded to activities and organizations that were not strictly union-based. The differences between the Spanish and other movements took on particular significance in the context of discussions about "woman's place."[26]

Significantly, neither Montseny's nor Puente's discussion of the free commune mentioned women—or, for that matter, unemployed men. As for the latter, we might well be meant to assume that, in a properly ordered society, there would be no unemployment—except of those who refuse to work—and that refusal to participate in the common business would justify deprivation of political rights. Nevertheless, the position of women was much less clear, since these writers did not state whether both men and women would work (they make no mention of arrangements for child-care or child-rearing); whether they would count women's domestic work as work (but, then, would there be a "union" to certify that women are working properly in their homes?); or whether they simply did not expect to recognize women with small children as full citizens. While Puente seemed to assume that all women would be workers, Mella addressed women as wives and daughters, rather than as workers: "Workers: your obligation is to throw yourselves into the struggle. Your wives will go with you, as they are no less slaves of the brutality of the bourgeoisie."[27] Marañón argued that motherhood was incompatible with work (since motherhood was, or at least should be, a full-time occupation if done properly). Nevertheless, he argued that work was important for nonmothers, whom he seemed to treat as a special, even possibly abnormal, class of women.[28]

## Sexuality and the Subordination of Women

In fact, the lack of agreement on these issues is evidence of a divergence among anarchist writers not only about the place of women within working-class organizations, but also about the nature of women's subordination and of what would be necessary to overcome it. Mary Nash has suggested that two differing streams of thought about the nature of male-female relationships developed among Spanish anarchists during

the course of the nineteenth and early twentieth centuries.[29] One, draw-
ing on the writings of Proudhon (and exemplified in Spain by Ricardo
Mella), treated women essentially as reproducers who make their contribution to society in and through their role in the home. According to
this view, what was necessary for women's emancipation was the re-
valuation of women's work in the home; her work outside the home
must always be secondary to that of men. The second stream (similar to
a Marxist perspective), which found theoretical roots in the writings of
Bakunin (and was exemplified, at least in its productivist aspects, in the
works of Isaac Puente), insisted that women were the equals of men and
that the key to women's emancipation was their full incorporation into
the paid labor force on equal terms with men. In this view, if women
were to overcome their subordination, they would have to join the labor
forces as workers and struggle in unions to improve the position of all
workers.[30] The official position of the CNT followed the latter view,
though it should be noted that the acceptance of a *theoretical* commitment to women's equality in the workplace was no guarantee that the
majority of CNT members would act in accordance with that commitment. As we will see in chapter 2, the practice of the movement rarely
lived up to its stated beliefs in this regard.

Nevertheless, there were also those within the libertarian movement
who insisted that organizing women into unions—even if it were possible to do so—would not, in itself, be sufficient. In their view, the
sources of women's subordination were broader and deeper than economic exploitation at the workplace. They argued that women's subordination was as much a cultural phenomenon as an economic one and
reflected a devaluation of women and their activities mediated through
institutions such as family and church. Thus, in an article revealing her
understanding of the process of revolutionary change as it affected
male-female relations, "Javierre" commented on reports from *Pravda*
on the numbers of "new Soviet men" who had abandoned pregnant
women: "Politics, alone, cannot make men morally ready for a common
life. . . . [These men] no more learned to be a man by Marxist baptism
than they did by Christian baptism."[31] Furthermore, at least some
Spanish anarchist writers located woman's subordination in her reproductive role and in the double standard of sexual morality. These,
too, would have to change—through the adoption of a new sexual
morality and the widespread use of birth control—if women were to be
fully equal partners in a revolutionary society.

Even this broader understanding was not without ambiguity.
Kyralina (Lola Iturbe, the journalist who was to become an active
supporter of Mujeres Libres) insisted on the need for an analysis and
practice that took into account broader cultural phenomena. Yet her
article "Anarchist Communism Will Liberate Women" reveals a belief,
common to anarchist cultural critics early in the twentieth century,

that the abolition of private property will lead to free love and the emancipation of women: "Only the reign of libertarian communism can provide a humane solution to the problem of women's emancipation. With the destruction of private property, this hypocritical morality will fall by the wayside, and we will be free. . . . We will experience love with the complete freedom of our appetites, respecting all the various forms of amorous and sexual life."[32]

For many anarchist writers and activists, a reorganization of sexual and family life and a reconstitution of women's roles were essential components of the revolutionary vision. In this attention to the "private" relations of family and sexuality, Spanish anarchists shared much both with nineteenth-century utopian socialists and with contemporary feminists.[33] But there was more than one way to apply an anti-authoritarian analysis to sexual and familial relations. What was to be the structure and nature of families and family relations in a new anarchist society? And how was woman's social participation to relate to her familial or reproductive roles? Was the unquestioned authority of the husband/father in the family to be preserved, as Proudhon and his followers advocated, or was that authority, too, to be abolished and replaced with voluntary egalitarian relationships? Some Spanish anarchists apparently agreed with Proudhon; others advocated asceticism, opposed the use of alcohol and tobacco, and advocated monogamy or sexual chastity. The majority of writers who addressed this topic in the early years of the twentieth century, however, advocated gender equality and free love. This last group insisted that true freedom meant the full expression and development of all human capacities, including the sexual. To them, prevailing social ideals of chastity, monogamy, and fidelity reflected a legacy of Christian repression and would be replaced in an ideal anarchist society by free love and egalitarian family structures.

This latter position gained strength and legitimacy during the 1920s and 1930s, particularly as the works of Sigmund Freud, Havelock Ellis, and other sexologists began to be known. By the 1930s, Spanish anarchists—writing in such journals of cultural criticism as *La Revista Blanca* and *Estudios*[34]—were combining Freudian psychology, neo-malthusian rhetoric, and doctrines of free love to develop a broad picture of the importance of sexuality and sexual emancipation to human development and, ultimately, to social revolution.

A plethora of contributors to *Estudios* during the 1930s argued for a new sexual ethics, one based on the positive value of sexuality and opposition to the double standard of sexual morality for men and women. These writers ridiculed anarchists who advocated chastity and the repressing of sexual urges. They insisted, to the contrary, that enforced abstinence led not only to the classic double standard (resulting in prostitution and the oppression of women) but also to stunted lives and, at worst, criminal behavior. They argued, following Freud, that sexuality was a basic life force and an important component of both psychic and social health. Rather than repress sexual feelings or divert them into prostitution, the writers concluded, people should learn more about sexuality—and practice birth control.[35]

Dr. Felix Martí-Ibáñez, the "dean" of anarchist writers on psychosexual health matters, outlined a new perspective on the place of sexuality in human life.[36] First, he insisted on the importance of genital sexuality—for both men and women—as a component of human growth and development and of successful marriages. His articles rejected the church's view that marriage existed only for the perpetuation of the species, and he insisted, instead, that marriage must be understood as a way of life, voluntarily chosen by two people. Whether in a marital or a nonmarital context, sex involved not just procreation, but recreation. Successful sexual relationships (whether marital or not) required a valuing and respecting of sexuality for both partners and a recognition that sexual union and satisfaction could be an end in itself, not just a means to produce children. Consequently, successful marriage would involve knowledge and use of birth control. His articles were intended both to articulate this new view of the place of sexuality in human life and to make information about birth control available to the proletariat.[37]

Martí-Ibáñez further argued that a new understanding of sexuality was necessary. For too long, he said, sexuality had been confused with genitality. He criticized the practice of enforced chastity, arguing that it denied important human needs. At the same time, he insisted that sexual energy could be channeled in a number of different directions and need not necessarily be expressed through genital contact: "Let us recognize that *the genital*—erotic impulses, the sexual act—is but one small part of *the sexual*, and that apart from this aspect, sexuality has many others (work, ideals, social or artistic creation, etc.). . . . Sexuality can express itself either erotically or through work in its various forms.[38] Nevertheless, he asserted, if efforts to redirect sexual energy were not successful, neither young women nor young men should hesitate to have sexual experiences—as long as they did not assume that sex must be linked with love or that it required a woman to give up her sense of self or her sense of self-respect![39]

Despite their calls for new and freer attitudes toward sexuality, however, virtually all these writers identified "normal sexuality" with heterosexuality. This identification was usually implicit rather than explicit—their discussions of sexuality assumed and asserted the "normal" or "natural" attraction between people of the opposite sex. In his series on "Eugenics and Sexual Morality," Martí-Ibáñez did address himself explicitly to the question of homosexuality. In an article focused primarily on the history of attitudes toward homosexuality, he at-

tempted to distinguish between "sexual inversion" ("congenital homosexuality") and "sexual perversion" (that practiced "voluntarily, out of
snobbery or curiosity, or for utilitarian ends"). Despite his efforts to
delineate the two types, the article acknowledged that it is often difficult to determine which cause is primary. Finally, he asserted that there
was nothing immoral about homosexuality and, therefore, that homo-
sexual behavior should not be punished (any more than we would find it
appropriate to punish a kleptomaniac who cannot help stealing!). At the
same time, however, he made clear his belief that homosexuality was
deviant and that homosexuals were "victims" of "sexual inversion."[40]

Many writers recognized the potentially liberating impact of new
attitudes toward sexuality for women. Abandonment of traditional attitudes toward chastity (which had always bound women much more
strongly than men—apparently even in anarchist circles) would free
women to explore and express their own sexuality. More specifically,
many writers—both men and women—had viewed women's reproductive activity as the key to their subordination. As long as married
women were subject to their husband's sexual desires (an aspect of
marital relations that was apparently only rarely questioned at that
time) and as long as there was no way to regulate fertility, women
would be subject to the emotional, physical, and psychic drain of repeated childbirths and the managing of a large household. The disabilities fell most dramatically on women of the working class. The
control of fertility, then, could be particularly liberating for women.
María Lacerda de Moura, a frequent contributor to *Estudios* on issues of
women and sexuality, criticized anarchist men who opposed the dis-
semination of birth control information among the working classes:
"For them, a woman is just a fertile and inexhaustible womb, destined
to produce bourgeois soldiers or, more accurately, red soldiers for the
social revolution." On the contrary, she insisted, birth control could
become a fundamental arm of the struggle for the liberation of
women.[41]

As had feminists and birth control advocates in the United States and
in a variety of European contexts, Lacerda, Marañón, and other Spanish
anarchists argued that both working-class families and individual
working-class women suffered from the production of more children
than a family could properly maintain and that the emancipation of
women must also involve the choice of whether, when, and how often to
become a mother. But they also insisted on the benefits of birth control
for individual women: it could relieve women, both married and unmarried, of the fear of pregnancy and thus allow them to enjoy sexual
relations more fully.[42]

Some analysts took these arguments further, linking malthusianism,
birth control, and class analysis to articulate an anarchist neomalthusianism. Dr. Juan Lazarte argued that the meaning and consequences of

pregnancy and birth varied with social class. Frequent pregnancies could be disastrous to a woman's health and also to the health and stability of a family already strapped for resources. And the more children a family had, the higher the rates of infant mortality. In short, as Malthus had argued, the poor were particularly hurt by unlimited reproduction. But with the availability of birth control, working people could replace "restraint" (of which Malthus did not believe the poor were capable) with birth control, which a conscious working class could use as a component of a strategy toward its liberation. With smaller families, workers' wages could sustain higher levels of health and strength. Limiting births could also lead to a smaller wage force, reduced unemployment, more power for workers, and even an end to wars.[43]

Finally, in addition to making possible the separation of procreation and pleasure in the expression of sexuality, these new attitudes toward sexuality had important implications for anarchist understandings of love and marriage. Many anarchists had claimed that permanent monogamous marriage constituted a form of despotism, which required a virtual renunciation of self on the part of women, and that free love (by which they meant the right of both men and women freely to choose a sexual relationship without benefit of clergy or state and freely to end it when it was no longer mutually satisfying) was the only appropriate manifestation of the natural tendencies of both men and women. Some of these writers assumed that, even in an ideal society, existing differences between men and women with respect to sexuality would continue to exist or that new ones would emerge; others insisted that existing differences were largely the product of social conditioning. But all assumed that, whatever the source of those differences, both men and women would be able to experience their sexuality more fully and more satisfyingly in a society that accorded full equality to women.[44]

Critiques of both chastity and monogamous marriage were common during the 1920s and 1930s, and numerous articles appeared advocating either free love or "plural love" in its place. Beyond arguing for free love, many anarchist writers insisted that monogamy itself was a product of the desire for possessiveness, rooted in private property and in the subordination of women, and that it would disappear in a future anarchist society.[45] Amparo Poch y Gascón, who was to become one of the founders of Mujeres Libres, wrote in *Estudios* in 1934 that traditional notions of monogamy made a woman, "whether she was still in love or not, a permanent possession of the man to whom the church or the judge gave her." But, she argued, properly understood, monogamy "does not mean 'forever,' but as long as . . . the will and feelings of the lovers lasts." Furthermore, if women as well as men held such attitudes, all would be freer and more satisfied.[46]

María Lacerda de Moura departed even further from accepted notions of monogamous love and marriage. "Love," she insisted, "has always been in open struggle with monogamy." In a truly egalitarian society, in which men and women were respected equally, monogamy would be replaced by plural love, the only form of sexual expression that would allow all people (in particular, women, who had been denied any sexual autonomy) the full growth, expression, and meeting of their sexual needs. By allowing both women and men to have more than one lover at a time, she insisted, plural love would eliminate most problems of jealousy, allow women to be truly free to choose their mate (or mates), and end prostitution and the sexual exploitation of women (since unmarried, sexually active women would no longer be stigmatized and vulnerable).[47]

Nevertheless, many writers were not as sanguine as she was. At the very least, they recognized that doctrines of either free love or plural love would be much more complicated to apply in practice than in theory. Many writers, especially women, were quick to point out that few anarchists actually practiced what they preached when it came to equality for women. Soledad Gustavo noted, for example, that "a man may like the idea of the emancipation of women, but he is not so fond of her actually practicing it. . . . In the end, he may desire the other's woman, but he will lock up his own."[48]

In response to criticisms raised of Clara, the sexually emancipated female heroine of her novel *La Victoria*, Federica Montseny argued that the notion of a weak, adoring woman protected by a strong man, though appealing to some male anarchists, was hardly a libertarian vision. Very few women may have been ready to live according to, or even to conceive of, a free and unlimited mutual freedom. But "there [were] even fewer men capable of accepting her."[49]

In Montseny's view, the fact that few Spanish women were morally ready for their emancipation, enslaved as they were by traditional attitudes and beliefs, presented a more serious problem than did male resistance to sexual and economic equality. Emma Goldman had argued that women needed internal emancipation to know their own value, respect themselves, and refuse to become psychic or economic slaves to their male lovers. But, Montseny lamented, Goldman gave no real guidance about how to achieve that liberation.[50]

In the case of familial and sexual relations, as in the economic realm, the ideal was equality with difference. Both women and men should be free to develop and express their sexuality, inside or outside what we might now term a "committed sexual relationship." Both should be free to enter—and to leave—sexual relationships without bringing down on themselves social condemnation or ostracism. Families, too, should be egalitarian institutions—the unquestioned authority of the father ought to be replaced by reciprocity and mutual respect.

These, then, are the major components of the anarchist social vision—a society in which all people are respected equally and mutually, in the sexual as well as the economic and political realms, a society organized around people's contributions to the ongoing life of the community, in which there are no relations of domination and subordination and in which decisions must be made by all and acceptable to all. But how is that society to be achieved? How are the "new anarchist man and woman" to be created?

### Revolutionary Transformation: Consistency of Means and Ends

Recognizing the social construction of relations of domination and subordination is, of course, not the same as changing them. The complexities of the anarchist perspective on revolutionary change become clear when we examine the attempts of Spanish anarchists to deal with overcoming subordination in general and the subordination of women in particular. How would it come about that self-interested, disempowered people—and anarchists were quick to admit that people living in capitalist societies were hardly immune to the self-interest that those social and economic arrangements reinforce—would come both to recognize their own capacities and to direct their attentions to the needs of others? How were people to achieve the inner emancipation that would enable them to recognize their own worth and demand recognition from the larger society? How would they develop a sense of justice appropriate to living in an egalitarian society? And how would such a society generate continued commitment to its values? More specifically, if women's subordination is a product of social institutions, and if social institutions disempower those who would attempt to overthrow them, how are those institutions to be changed?

One of the defining characteristics of the communalist-anarchist tradition is the insistence that means must be consistent with ends. If the goal of revolutionary struggle is a nonhierarchical egalitarian society, then it must be created through the activities of a nonhierarchical movement. Otherwise, participants will never be empowered to act independently, and those who lead the movement will direct the postrevolutionary society. In the words of one participant in the civil war experience, "a la libertad sólo se llega por caminos libertarios" [one only achieves freedom through libertarian means].[51] As Kropotkin had written about the dilemmas of parliamentary socialists, "You thought you would conquer the State, but the State will end up conquering you."[52]

But where existing practices disempower people, how are they to become empowered? The anarchist commitment to an egalitarian, nonhierarchical revolutionary process seems to require that people recognize their own abilities in order to participate. Successful anarchist revolution apparently depends on the prior achievement of what is perhaps the most complex aim of the revolutionary movement itself: popular empowerment.

The solution to this paradox is to be found in anarchist understandings of the revolutionary process. People are expected to prepare themselves for revolution (and for living in a communitarian society) by participating in activities and practices that are themselves egalitarian, empowering, and therefore transformative. There can be no hierarchy structured into the process of social change. The way to create a new society is to *create* new reality.

### Direct action

We can best understand the Spanish anarchist perspective on empowerment and the process of consciousness-change by examining their commitment to decentralism and "direct action." Decentralism referred to an insistence that revolution must be, at its core, a local phenomenon, growing out of the concrete realities of people's day-to-day lives. A revolutionary movement develops from people's struggles to overcome their own subordination, and it must speak to the particularities of their situation. Thus, as we will see, one important new institution that Spanish anarchists created was the ateneo libertario (storefront cultural center), which served as a school, a recreational group, and gathering place for working-class young people in the years preceding the war. As Enriqueta Rovira explained, describing one such group,

> We were in a group called Sol y Vida [sun and life] with both boys and girls. . . . We did theater pieces, gymnastics, went on trips to the mountains, to the sea. . . . It was both a cultural and a recreational group. . . . There was always a little [educational] talk of some sort. And in that way, ideas got stirred up, they created a sense of being compañeros and compañeras. True, people went to union meetings and the like, but relations within our group were more intimate, the explanations more extensive. That's where we were formed, most deeply, ideologically.[53]

Direct action meant that the goal of any and all of these activities was to provide ways for people to get in touch with their own powers and capacities, to take back the power of naming themselves and their lives. It was to be distinguished from more conventional political activity even in a democratic system.[54] Instead of attempting to make change by forming interest groups to pressure politicians, anarchists insisted that we learn to think and act for ourselves by joining together in organizations in which our experience, our perception, and our activity can guide and make the change.[55] Knowledge does not precede experience, it flows from it: "We begin by deciding to work, and through working, we learn. . . . We will learn how to live in libertarian communism by living in it."[56] People learn how to be free only by exercising freedom: "We are not going to find ourselves . . . with people ready-made for the future. . . . Without the continued exercise of their faculties, there will be no free people. . . . The external revolution and the internal revolution presuppose one another, and they must be simultaneous in order to be successful.[57]

Direct action activities that arose from day-to-day needs and experiences represented ways in which people could take control of their lives. As feminists have learned, whether through consciousness-raising groups or in community organizing, participation in such activities would have both internal and external effects, allowing people to develop a sense of competence and self-confidence while they acted to change their situation. Engagement of this sort empowered people and fortified them to act together again. Soledad described the effects of active participation in the movement on her life and on her friends: "It was an incredible life, the life of a young militant. A life dedicated to struggle, to knowledge, to remaking society. It was characterized by a kind of effervescence. . . . It was a very beautiful youth, of camaraderie. . . . I was always involved in strikes and actions, anywhere. We lived on very little. . . . The men and boys earned somewhat more than we did—but we didn't really resent it. . . . Sometimes, it seemed we lived on air alone."[58] The sense of empowerment was also clear in Enriqueta's recollections: "For the love of those compañeros, and that vision so strong, we would have battled with the Virgin Mary herself!"

Further, direct action not only empowered those who participated in it, it also had effects on others through what anarchists termed "propaganda by the deed." Often, that term meant bomb-throwing, assassination attempts, and the like. It had another meaning, however, referring to a kind of exemplary action that attracted adherents by the power of the positive example it set. Contemporary examples of propaganda by the deed include food or day-care coops, collectively run businesses, sweat equity housing programs, women's self-help health collectives, urban squats, or women's peace camps. While such activities empower those who engage in them, they also demonstrate to others that non-hierarchical forms of organization can and do exist—and that they can function effectively.

Obviously, if such actions are to have the desired empowerment effects, they must be largely self-generated, rather than being devised and directed from above. Hence, the anarchist commitment to a strategy of "spontaneous organization," noncoercive federations of local groups. The aim was to achieve order without coercion by means of what we might call "federative networking," which brought together representatives of local groups (unions, neighborhood associations, consumer coops, or the like). The crucial point was that neither the individual groups nor the larger coordinating body could claim to speak or act for others. Ideally, they would be more forums for discussion than directive organizations. Spontaneous organization would demonstrate in practice that those who had experienced oppression were still capable of rational thought and action, able to come to know what their needs were and to develop ways to meet them.[59]

## Preparation

Finally, and most important, direct action could take place only within a context of "preparation." In the words of Federica Montseny, "Una revolución no se improvisa" (one doesn't improvise a revolution).[60] Although all people had within them a sense of equality and justice based in their participation in social relationships, that almost instinctive sense was insufficient to lead to revolutionary action. Preparation was necessary both to point out to people the communal nature and context of their plight and to enable them to recognize the possibilities of their collective action. Without such preparation, "revolution" would lead only to the reinstitution of authority in new forms. In fact, many anarchists, writing in the years just after the Russian Revolution, pointed to the USSR as a negative example of how hierarchy was easily reimposed in the absence of sufficient preparation.[61]

However paradoxical it may seem, people must be prepared to act spontaneously on their own behalf. Along with Marx, anarchists believed that the best preparation, the best technique for what we call consciouness-raising, was action. "Capitalism is mortally wounded, but its agony will be prolonged until we are ready to substitute for it successfully. And we will not achieve that by pretty-sounding phrases, but by demonstrating our constructive and organizing capacity."[62] People would develop a critical, revolutionary consciousness through reflection on the concrete realities of their lives—a reflection often sparked by their own and others' activities.[63]

Attention to the particular needs and situation of women, and to the activities of Mujeres Libres, can help to explicate the multidimensional nature of this understanding of the process of consciousness-change and to highlight its relevance to many contemporary debates. I noted above that Spanish anarchists argued that one important context for preparation was participation in working-class organizations, particularly unions. Yet, following Bakunin and breaking with Marx, they had also insisted that urban industrial workers were not the only people capable of coming to a revolutionary consciousness. Rural peasants and members of the urban petit bourgeoisie, as well as industrial workers, could develop a consciousness of their own oppression and join in a revolutionary movement.[64] Many women, in particular, criticized the emphasis of the movement on the male urban industrial proletariat. Emma Goldman, for example, who was to be quite active in support both of the Spanish revolution and of Mujeres Libres, had earlier argued that "anarchists agree that the main evil today is an economic one," but as she pointed out, "they maintain that the solution of the evil can be brought about only through the consideration of *every phase* of life, the individual, as well as the collective; the internal, as well as the external phases."[65] It was most obviously true for women, but also true for men, that the workplace is not the only context for relationships of domination, nor is it therefore the only potential context for consciousness-change and empowerment. A fully articulated movement must transform all hierarchical institutions, including government, religious institutions, and—perhaps most dramatically for women—sexuality and family life.

Preparation, then, could and must take place in a variety of social contexts, in addition to the economic. Both Enriqueta and Azucena spoke of imbibing anarchist perspectives more or less unconsciously "with our mother's milk":

> My mother taught us anarchism, . . . almost like a religious person teaches religion to her children—but without imposing it on us, as the religious one does . . . whether by her actions, by her way of expressing herself, and by always saying that they hoped for, longed for, anarchism. . . . It's almost as if she didn't *teach* them, we *lived* them, were born with them. We learned them as you would learn to sew or to eat.[66]

For those who became part of the movement later in life, the learning process was obviously a different one. Pepita Carpena, for example, was introduced to the ideas by union organizers who frequented young people's social gatherings in hopes of attracting young adherents to the cause. Soledad Estorach, who was to be very active both in the CNT and in Mujeres Libres in Barcelona, gained much of her initial information about "anarchist communists" by reading newspapers and magazines.

Anarchists had long recognized the interdependence of educational practices, narrowly defined, and participation in ongoing institutions, where social approval and disapproval provided continuing mechanisms of social control.[67] Proudhon's notion of "imminent justice"—the claim that we develop a conception of justice through our relationships with other people—was taken up directly by a number of Spanish anarchist writers. Mella argued that the only proper regulator of society is the sense of justice, which people learn through their participation in institutions that recognize and validate their own worth and the equal worth of others. The collective feeling that develops out of such participation would translate into a sense of justice more powerful and

permanent than any imposed on people by church or state.[68] "To practice justice," Proudhon had insisted, "is to obey the social instinct." It is
through our patterns of interaction with one another that we learn and
experience both who we and others are and what justice is. The best and
most effective educational system therefore is society itself.[69]

Another major factor operative in the development of a sense of
justice is public opinion, what Mella referred to as "moral coercion"
[coacción moral]. Our moral sense develops out of the "exchange of
reciprocal influences," which, although it may come initially from outside ourselves, eventually is taken in as a sense of justice and becomes
the basis for our own self-regulation. A well-ordered egalitarian society,
left to itself, will generate people with the proper sense of justice;
anyone who seems lacking in such a sense will be held in check by the
opinions of others. Over time, those opinions will have an educative
effect; public opinion will be internalized as conscience.[70]

The goal of anarchists, then, was to eliminate those institutions—for
example, church, state, judges and courts—whch impeded the development of such a moral sense by taking over the responsibility of looking
after others and oneself. Once such authorities were eliminated, reciprocity would become a norm of action; simply living in the community—participating in its activities, in the context of an open
educational system, and in communal ownership and disposition of
property—would be sufficient to foster and safeguard the development
of the individual's sense of justice, in turn necessary to sustain the
community.

The complexities of this position are revealed quite clearly when we
look specifically at efforts to address women's subordination and empowerment. Both those who emphasized a union-based strategy and
those who insisted on the broader cultural components of women's
subordination recognized that women were devalued and disempowered, culturally and economically. Both accepted the perspective
that means and ends are intimately connected. But how were those
principles and perspectives to be realized in practice? How were
women in early twentieth-century Spain, who thought of themselves
(and were viewed by others) as dependent on men, to begin behaving in
ways that developed their own sense of competence and capacity?

These questions are, of course, crucial ones for any would-be revolutionary movement, since a sense of one's own capacities and powers is
precisely what oppressors attempt to deny to the oppressed. But even
agreement on the importance of the perspective did not guarantee
unanimity on its implications for practice. In fact, the question of how
best to address and challenge the subordination of working-class
women within Spanish society was never effectively resolved within the
anarcho-syndicalist movement. Mujeres Libres was created precisely

because of a disagreement among movement activists about how to achieve that empowerment.

The issues were played out quite dramatically during the course of interviews I was conducting in 1981. A group of former activists were meeting and reminiscing about their years in the CNT and FIJL. After some discussion of the role of the FIJL and ateneos in opening the minds of young people to new ideas in the twenties and thirties, the conversation turned to the liberation of women. Two different but strongly held positions were put forward. One was articulated by a man who identified himself as a strong supporter of women's emancipation, who was quite articulate about the ways in which even anarchist men tended to take for granted their compañeras' subordination to them. He argued that, precisely because of women's cultural subordination, anarchist men had a responsibility to take the lead in changing these patterns. Women's taking paid jobs would not be sufficient: "There are too many men whose wives work and who still do all the housework." After so many years of socialization, women were all too ready to accept traditional roles. Men, who have the understanding and the sense of their own capacities, he insisted, must take the initiative and encourage their compañeras towards greater self-direction and autonomy.

Another position was articulated by a woman who had been an activist in the Juventudes during the thirties and whose life had been fundamentally changed through her participation in it. She, too, was committed to the liberation of women. But she strongly opposed her compañero's insistence that it was up to men to take the initiative. She argued that his focus on what contemporary feminists call "the politics of housework"[71] was misplaced. The basic problem, she insisted, was not who washes the dishes or cleans the house, but that a woman be able to go where she pleases and say what she pleases. The root of women's subordination was ignorance. In her words, "toda mujer que se cultura un poco desarrolla armas" [every woman who gains some culture (educates herself) develops weapons]. "What matters to me is that a woman be able to open her mouth. It is not a question of cleaning plates." While her interlocutor insisted that a woman's responsibility for all the housework and for the family would prevent her from participating fully in communal activities, this woman insisted that "going to meetings is not the issue. Going to meetings is a kind of sport. What is important is work and reading."

It soon became clear that the fundamental issue between them was not the primacy of work, reading, or housework. It was initiative. While he insisted that, given the weight of cultural subordination that women had to bear, the initiative would have to come from men, she insisted that "a compañero never ought to say to a woman, 'liberate yourself, and I'll help you.' A woman has to liberate herself. It's all right for men to help, but the *initiative* must come from the woman. It must be her issue."

That the debate sounds so contemporary should not be surprising. It was taking place among people who, while they did not grow up with the contemporary feminist movement, had obviously been influenced by it. Nevertheless, the issues they raised and the particular ways in which they discussed them echoed the written debates of the early part of this century. In 1903, José Prat had urged women to take responsibility for their own emancipation. Some years later, Federica Montseny had insisted that one way for women to work toward the abolition of the sexual double standard was for them to take themselves seriously, to stand up and punish the men who had seduced and abandoned them, rather than to cower in shame. And Soledad Gustavo, echoing Emma Goldman's claims about internal emancipation, insisted that if there were to be a new order of sexual equality, women would have to "demonstrate by their deeds that they think, are capable of conceiving ideas, of grasping principles, of striving for ends."[72]

The question they were all addressing was precisely that of empowerment and the overcoming of subordination: how best to accomplish them consistent with a commitment to recognize both the impact of cultural conditioning and the potential for autonomy of each person. Nevertheless, the question of the *significance* of women's subordination and of its place within the anarchist project was far from resolved, whether in the theoretical writings of Spanish anarchists or, as we shall see, in the activities of the movement. Debates continued within the movement throughout the 1930s and led ultimately to the founding of Mujeres Libres.

# II

## COMMUNITY MOBILIZATION AND UNION ORGANIZATION
### WOMEN AND THE SPANISH
### ANARCHIST MOVEMENT

The years from 1868 to 1936 served as preparation for the social revolution that broke out in response to the generals' rebellion against the Spanish Republic in July 1936. The struggles that took place during those years changed the face of Spanish society and politics, as well as the consciousness and self-perception of the thousands of people who participated in them. As Spanish anarchists themselves have been quick to point out, revolutions do not spring up out of nowhere; they require a strong and broad base. Organizationally, that base was set during the seventy years beginning in 1868, the year in which anarchism was officially introduced into Spain.

A number of studies of anarchism and anarcho-syndicalism in Spain have argued that the successful uniting of "collectivist" and "communist" ("reformist" and "revolutionary") tendencies into anarcho-syndicalism during the period 1910–1919 marks the great creative achievement of the movement and its single most important contribution to the history of social-revolutionary anarchism.[1] Yet, while the resolution of tensions between these two seemingly contradictory perspectives was surely one important achievement of that movement, I wish to focus here on the recognition that effective revolutionary organizing must involve more than workers organized into unions at their workplaces. In a country with an economy and society as diverse as that of late nineteenth- and early twentieth-century Spain, a movement for social change had to bridge the differences between industrial and rural laborers, the organized and the unorganized, men and women, and reach into many areas of people's daily experiences. It is that recognition—even more than the strategic compromises it was able to forge—which marked the success of the Spanish libertarian movement. Its exploration helps us to comprehend both the role of women within the movement and the founding of Mujeres Libres as a separate organization.

By the time of the Civil War, anarchist activists had created a vast and complex network of programs and organizations uniquely structured to meet the particular needs of widely differing groups within the Spanish working class. In February 1936, the CNT boasted a membership of approximately 850,000 members, organized in non-hierarchically structured unions, federated both by industry and by region. [See Appendix A.] Its unique combination of revolutionary goals and somewhat "reformist" tactics enabled it to sustain a vast membership while retaining a strong revolutionary character. On the other hand, the movement as a whole did not limit itself to union organizing in the narrow sense. During this same period, it was supporting and developing educational programs for both adults and young people, which included a network of storefront schools and cultural centers, a broad-based national youth organization, and journals and newspapers that made anarchist critical perspectives on culture, politics, and social issues available to large numbers of people throughout the country.

The variety of those programs and organizations allowed the movement to speak to and from the experiences of vastly differing groups of people: from urban industrial wage laborers to rural day-laborers, the unemployed, housewives, domestic workers, and even children. While I cannot possibly provide a detailed history of the movement during this period, I wish to trace the broad outlines of the development of the various sources of activism. My aim is to explore, in particular, how the Spanish anarchist movement established roots in what we would now term community, as well as in workplace organizing, and to examine the implications for women and marginal workers of this broad-based organizing strategy.

### Precursors: Regionalism, Collectivism, and Protest

In her study of the development of the anarchist movement in rural Andalusia, Temma Kaplan argues that the effectiveness of the movement depended on its success in engaging entire communities of people (including women), rather than just male wage-laborers, in protest actions. The communal strategy allowed the movement to engage those whose lives were not defined primarily by the context of paid work: "Unions could improve the conditions of their own members, but did not appreciably alter the lives of the people outside."[2] In a recent study of the development of anarchist ideology in Spain, George Esenwein takes issue with this claim that anarcho-collectivists (those who advocated a union-based vision of anarchism) were necessarily unresponsive to the needs and concerns of nonproducers. He asserts, to the contrary, that collectivists did make provisions for nonworkers in various proposals for sharing the wealth. Although I tend to agree with Kaplan that a communal perspective offered a broader basis for popular mobilization than a union-based one, my concern here is to emphasize the significance of organizational strategies that extended beyond the workplace, narrowly construed. Esenwein effectively seems to grant this point, both in his discussion of "anarchist associational life" and in his analysis of the move to overcome these divisions through what was referred to as "anarchism without adjectives."[3]

Of course, the patterns of work, community, and protest varied with local conditions, particularly as between rural Andalusia and the more urban industrial cities and towns of Catalonia, where anarcho-syndicalism also was to establish strong roots. Nevertheless, in urban areas as well, the movement encompassed nonunion as well as union-based elements. To understand the success of communalist anarchism in Spain, it is important to examine the traditions of localism and of collective/communal action that provided a context for the movement.

Attachment to village and to region had been a feature of Spanish politics for generations. Regionalism was given further impetus with the introduction of utopian socialism during the 1830s and 1840s, and the federalist-republican agitation of the 1860s and 1870s. Local and regional sentiments were supported by (if not rooted in) significant economic differences. Patterns of land tenure differed substantially from one region to another and contributed to the sense of disconnection among the parts.[4] In the southern regions of Andalusia and Extremadura, for example, the dominant form of landholding was the *latifundio*, a farm of thousands of acres, worked by *braceros*, day laborers who constituted the Spanish rural proletariat. By contrast, the average landholding in Galicia, in the northwest corner, was tiny— often of one hectare or less. Only in Catalonia and in the Basque provinces of Alava and Navarra did middle-sized holdings (of ten to one hundred hectares) predominate and make a significant contribution to agricultural income.[5]

By the end of the eighteenth century, much of rural Spain was dominated by large entailed holdings, ecclesiastical and civil, creating a rural population sharply divided into two classes, "an oligarchy of large property-owners . . . and a great mass of impoverished peasants."[6] Both the concentration of agrarian wealth and the devastations of rural poverty were marked in Andalusia. In Sevilla, for example, noble holdings constituted 72 percent of the wealth in the "kingdom of Seville." Six old seigneurial families owned land representing approximately 90 percent of all rural holdings in the province. In Andalusia as a whole, two seigneurial houses had holdings worth 48.85 percent of the total of all latifundial wealth in the region. Feudal property relations were such that there was no incentive for owners (many of whom were absentee landlords) to increase the amount of land under cultivation or to improve production techniques.[7]

The Napoleonic Wars and the loss of colonial markets in the Americas proved disastrous to this system, however, and a small commercial and industrial bourgeoisie came increasingly to press for reforms to allow for agricultural development. When liberals came to power in 1835, they instituted a series of agrarian reforms meant to raise money for the government and to increase the economic productivity of the country by selling land to those who would be more active in its management. Legislation in 1837 disentailed the holdings of the church and village councils, putting them up for sale on the open market. It also abolished *mayorazgo* (primogeniture), opening the property of the nobility to the market.

In Andalusia and Extremadura, the results of the reform efforts were mixed, at best. The ecclesiastical disentailment earned the regime the lasting enmity of the church, while actually worsening the situation for many peasants and small landholders.[8] Furthermore, the disentailments came nowhere near transforming the countryside in the sense hoped for by the reformers. The largely landless rural laborers had no money to buy these parcels. Instead, they were purchased either by those who had previously held them under seigneurial rights or by a group of "new nobles," men who had made their money in commerce and who were rewarded with titles by the new regime. In effect, the reforms transformed seigneurs into capitalists, increased property concentration, and led to the expulsion of peasants from lands they had traditionally cultivated as well as the consequent proletarianization of the displaced population. Although the formal structures of land tenure changed, the actual patterns of landholding changed little, if at all. The liberal revolution in agriculture succeeded only in establishing new class inequalities.[9]

The effects of the reforms were similar elsewhere. In Aragón, Susan Harding has argued, the reforms established the control of *caciques* (local bosses) over local politics, "stalling the development of capital-intensive agriculture in the countryside," and limiting the ability of the national government to support the modernization of agriculture.[10] On the other hand, Susan Tax Freeman found different effects in the village she studied in Castile. Although initially the reforms concentrated property in the hands of a single man, the release of the peasant farmers from the burdens of tithing and first fruits allowed them to accumulate some surplus and, ultimately, to buy land themselves. Nevertheless, the relative equality that characterized that village was unusual in the broader Spanish context.[11]

Uneven economic development compounded the tensions over land redistribution. The Spanish economy remained largely agrarian until well after the Civil War, though there were pockets of industrialization.[12] By the turn of the century, Catalonia could claim large numbers of textile workers, almost 40 percent of whom were women.[13] The other major industrializing region was Asturias, the center of coal mining. Finance was centered in Madrid and Vizcaya, and in the large cities and towns of many of the central and northern provinces there was a small middle class, composed of tradesmen, teachers, lawyers, doctors, and bureaucrats.

Class differences were extreme. They were perhaps most dramatic in the South. In lower Andalusia, for example, many laborers lived in urban agglomerations of roughly fifteen to twenty thousand inhabitants. An overwhelming majority had no land of their own: men did day or weekly labor (when work was available) at meager wages in the surrounding fields and many women worked as domestic servants. Diets were barely adequate, with the majority of calories supplied by oil and bread. The average worker was severely undernourished.[14] Many kept themselves from starving by poaching, gathering wood, or burning charcoal to sell on the market. The situation was worsened by the midcentury reforms, which denied peasants the use of common lands at a time when many church-related charitable institutions had ceased to exist.[15]

Living and working conditions in industrial areas were only marginally better. At midcentury, for example, approximately half of the average Barcelona industrial worker's wages were spent on food and half of that went to bread. Meat was virtually absent from the diet. In the Catalan textile industry, according to an 1892 report, the average worker labored twelve to fifteen hours per day in a poorly ventilated, poorly lit, overly hot room. Approximately 40 to 45 percent of the workers were men, an equal number were women, and the remaining 10 to 20 percent were children, many of whom had begun working at age six or seven. The average life expectancy for a worker was half that for a man of the "wealthy class."[16] With the shift to more modern industrial techniques, class tensions were increasingly unmediated by local paternalist traditions.[17]

There were also sharp gender divisions. In all but the most advanced industrial areas (and, to a considerable degree, even there), men and women lived almost entirely separate lives. Most women were economically dependent on men (whether their fathers or their husbands), their lives circumscribed within the larger domestic arena—though it should be noted that their identification with the domestic arena did not mean that they did not engage in labor. Rural women had responsibility for the *huerta* (the family agricultural plot, which produced vegetables for home consumption), even though their labors were usually not acknowledged as work. In industrial areas, increasing numbers of single working-class women worked for pay either as domestics or in textiles (some in factories, most as outworkers in their own homes). Again, they worked for extremely low wages.[18] Most women's social circles consisted of other women: family members, neighbors, fellow workers, or those they met at the market place. Men, conversely, tended to operate in a largely male world, whether in the factory, at union meetings, or in local bars.

Illiteracy compounded both class and gender divisions. In rural areas, in particular, very few schools were available. Oligarchical authorities feared the potential radicalizing effects of education, treating "any effort at spreading culture as something demonic." In 1860, for example, 84 percent of the population in the province of Sevilla, 79 percent in Cadiz, and 83 percent in Huelva were illiterate.[19] Even when schools were available, few poor families could afford to send their children, and if a child did attend, it was usually a boy. In 1878, only 9.6 percent of all Spanish women could read, and as late as 1900, women's illiteracy stood at 71 percent.[20] Illiteracy added to the difficulties that women of all classes experienced in controlling conception or caring for children.[21]

Clearly, successful organizing would have to respond to this economic, cultural, and political diversity. Anarchist perspectives—the commitment to direct action and spontaneous organization, and the recognition that organization ought to flow from, and speak to, people's felt needs—were especially well suited to this task. But anarchist organizers were also able to draw on collectivist traditions, which had long flourished in Spain.

Agrarian collectivism is characterized by a belief that (in the words of Joaquín Costa, its preeminent scholar) "individual property cannot legitimately apply except to those goods which are the product of individual effort; since land is the work of Nature, it cannot legitimately be appropriated."[22] Evidence of such beliefs and of intellectual and religious traditions supporting them can be found in Spain as early as the sixteenth century. For the next three centuries, the Spanish countryside was the scene of periodic uprisings of varying intensities and degrees of organization, demanding relief from poverty and land redistribution. By the mid-nineteenth century, in the aftermath of the dislocations resulting from the disentailments, both social banditry and popular revolts increased, while taking on a more explicitly political tone.[23] Although some commentators have dismissed these revolts as "spontaneous," "millenarian," and "prepolitical,"[24] Bernal argues that they represented peasant resistance to the changes resulting from the midcentury reforms and that this resistance—which initially took the form merely of disputing what they perceived as the "usurpation" of common lands—eventually turned into direct action to occupy the lands they felt should rightfully be theirs. In his estimation, 1857 marked the important beginnings of a working-class consciousness.[25]

The agricultural crisis of the 1850s and 1860s shook the countryside with hunger and unemployment through the winter and spring of 1868. This, in turn, provided a backdrop to a bourgeois revolution against the monarchy of Isabel II. Peasants and day laborers joined in the republican enthusiasm, attempting to turn the process into a social as well as political revolution and demanding redistribution of the land. Municipal revolutionary councils refused to back these demands, however, and the social revolution was suppressed. When Bakunin's emissary, Giuseppi Fanelli, arrived in Spain in 1868 carrying the anarchist message, he found fertile soil for his ideas among the craftspeople and day-laborers of Andalusia.

### Anarchism, Anarcho-Syndicalism, and Popular Mobilization

Formal anarchist organizing in Spain began with Fanelli's arrival in October 1868. During the last quarter of the nineteenth and the first quarter of the twentieth centuries, Spanish anarchism grew into a mass-based popular movement, virtually the only one of its kind in the world.

Fanelli's visit coincided with the excitement generated by the September 1868 revolution and the disappointment of landless southern workers over the failure of the Constituent Cortes to redistribute land in 1869. The tale of Fanelli's arrival and initial tour through Spain makes a fascinating story, one that quickly became part of the folklore of the movement.[26] Fanelli went to Spain as a representative of a Bakuninist faction within the International Workingman's Association; thus, the "socialism" he introduced into Spain in 1868 was what came to be known as collectivist anarchism. Marxist socialism was not introduced into Spain until two years later, and it never caught on as strongly, at least not with workers in Barcelona or Andalucia.[27]

In Andalusia, the ideas Fanelli brought provided language and images for the transformation of the braceros' yearning for land into a more complete political vision. In Barcelona and Madrid, he met with members of working-class and artisan clubs, which represented incipient working-class organizations. The failure of the 1868 revolution spurred these groups to become independent of republicanism and to adopt a more explicitly antipolitical stance.[28] In June 1870, the Spanish Regional Federation of the International Workingman's Association was formed, marking the formal beginning of the anarchist movement in Spain.

The goal of the association was simply stated by Rafael Farga Pellicer: "We desire that the power of capital, the state, and the church be ended, so that we can construct, on the ruins, anarchy, the free federation of free workers' associations."[29] The congress committed itself to a strategy of syndicate-based resistance (i.e., using the strike as a weapon against employers), solidarity across union lines, federalism, and rejection of political action. It adopted the policy that came to be known as "anarcho-collectivism," a faith in organized workers to overthrow government by force of arms.[30]

But the diversity of Spanish society was reflected in a lack of unity within the organization itself: the new policies were interpreted variously by different groups and in different regions of the country. Catalan workers, for example, were the largest regional group by far and the only organized group of industrial workers. While they gave explicit allegiance to revolutionary goals, most tended to be reformist in practice (i.e., focusing on the day-to-day concerns of workers), and concentrated their efforts on organizing in and within unions. In rural Andalusia, skilled workers tended to be anarcho-collectivists because, as Kaplan suggests, the collectivist program "promised economies gained from collective labor, but individual union ownership of whatever was produced." Among the unskilled and unemployed, the preference was for "anarcho-communism," which differed from anarcho-collectivism in its more communal orientation. "Not only would there be collective ownership of all productive resources, but also common ownership of everything produced. Each person, whether worker or housewife, healthy or infirm, young or old, should have whatever he or she needed from the common storehouse."[31]

These differing perspectives gave rise to important differences in strategy. Anarcho-collectivists understood the movement to be based in unions, which, because of the structure of the Spanish economy, were overwhelmingly male and urban. On the other hand, anarcho-communists, who drew on the tradition of "free communes," emphasized direct action tactics and viewed their "potential constituency [as] the entire community of the poor, including self-employed craftsmen, peasant tenants and small landholders, rural and urban proletarians, housewives, children, and the jobless."[32]

By 1888, the Spanish movement formally committed itself to anarcho-communism. The consequences of this tactical decision were mixed. On the one hand, Temma Kaplan argues that it enabled the movement to unite union-based organizing with community-based support and provided the groundwork for what was later to be known as the unique Spanish creation, "anarcho-syndicalism":

> By placing increased stress on workers' centers, coops, mutual aid associations, and women's sections, collectivism and communism were able to overcome the localism of the former and the willful dissociation of the latter. . . . The general strike, really a mass mobilization of the community, could take advantage of the weight of numbers . . . enabling militant unions and equally militant community people to march together against an oppressive system.[33]

On the other hand, George Esenwein argues, the direct action strategy of "propaganda by the deed"—a central tenet of the communist anarchists—often proved disruptive to a more ordered associational life.[34]

Both the philosophical differences and their strategic implications continued to be discussed and debated over the ensuing decades. Meanwhile, many of the ideas were spread through the rural countryside by a combination of "propaganda by the deed" and by the work of dedicated anarchist militants, known as *obreros conscientes*. Among those traveling teachers was Abelardo Saavedra, grandfather of Enriqueta and Azucena. Born in Cadiz, around 1864, of staunchly conservative parents, he "picked up the ideas" while at the university. Azucena spoke proudly of the work her grandfather did in the countryside:

> He devoted himself to spreading the ideas. He thought to bring about the revolution: not with a gun, but with culture. He wanted to bring culture and education to the *jornaleros* [day-laborers]. It was what we would call today a literacy campaign, like what Fidel de Castro [*sic*] is doing in Cuba. . . . But without a Christ to fund him. . . . He went to the *cortijos*—always with the police right behind him, mind you!—and taught people to read. He was always in and out of jail. Once he was jailed for three days for gathering workers together to read.

Times were hard and any anarchist was an easy target for punishment on the slightest pretext:

> "The year Alfonso XIII married [1906], my grandfather was exiled and my father was put in jail. . . . Someone had thrown a bomb during the wedding, and that became the justification for a severe repression. After a year in jail, my father, too, was exiled, and the whole family went to America [Cuba]."[35]

The activities of these traveling teachers, together with activism and strikes, helped to generate an air of expectancy and excitement in the Andalusian countryside. Government repression forced the strikers and, ultimately, the movement underground until the First World War. But anarchists had succeeded in demonstrating the effectiveness of a strategy that built on people's *communal* and neighborhood connections—developing workers' centers, storefront schools, and the like—and insisted on the linkages between work and community, workers and the poor, women and men.[36]

Compared to working-class movements in other western European countries, industrial union activity in Spain was late, weak, and slow to develop.[37] The union activity that did exist in Catalonia was largely reformist in character, seeking to improve wages and limit hours. Nevertheless, as the syndicalist tactic of the revolutionary general strike made its way into Spain from France at the end of the century, reformist unionism coexisted with the tactic of the general strike. In a pattern similar to that in Andalusia, Catalan general strikes incorporated many people besides unionized factory workers, including significant numbers of women. But in Catalonia and to some extent in Madrid and Valencia, there were also increasing numbers of female workers with reputations for militancy, particularly in cigar making and in textiles.[38] In textiles, for example, a rapidly growing industry in Catalonia at the turn of the century, women constituted between 80 and 90 percent of the labor force in many Catalan communities. Because of the rapid growth of the industry, the importance of female labor within it, and the small but growing unionization of those women workers, two types of activism—union-based and community-based—developed more or less simultaneously.[39]

Recent scholarship challenges the belief that Spanish women were less open than men to unionization. While Spain had a very low percentage of women in the labor force compared to other major European countries, and although both men and women in Spain affiliated with unions and participated in strikes at rates considerably below those of their western European brothers and sisters, factory-based Spanish female textile workers readily affiliated with unions and participated in strikes at rates almost equal to those of men. Occasionally, managers were able to bring in (nonunionized) female workers as scabs at times of labor unrest, but there is little evidence that this was a common practice.[40]

Working conditions for industrial workers in Spain at the turn of the century were poor, especially for women in the textile trades. A 1914 report by a corps of labor inspectors found that virtually all factories employing women and children were operating illegally: the factories were "dirty, lacking ventilation and sun, located in the most unhealthy areas of buildings, and with no regulation other than the arbitrary whim of the owner."[41] A 1902 law had reduced the maximum workday for women in textiles to ten hours, but the report acknowledged that many women were still forced to work for sixteen or more hours at a time. And all received wages that could only be characterized as "wages of hunger," often less than half of what male textile workers received for the same, or more difficult, work.[42]

Despite the growing numbers of women workers, however, and the generally acknowledged deplorable state in which they found themselves, neither anarchists nor socialists were consistent in addressing the concerns of women workers or in supporting equality for women within unions. Paralleling the debates about the role and status of women within the anarchist movement, mid-nineteenth century Spanish utopian socialists had exhibited ambiguous attitudes towards women's equality and participation. Some argued that woman's place was in the home, educating children and maintaining domestic tranquility. Others rejected the domination of men over women even in the household, and argued that equality for women would have to be won both at the workplace and in the home. Over time, concern for women workers was relegated to a secondary, if not tertiary, status within Spanish socialist theory and practice. Socialists even went so far as to argue at a party congress in 1881–1882 that women's work ought to be prohibited.[43] Nevertheless, beginning in 1886, Spanish Socialist Party (PSOE) pronouncements advocated a commitment to equality for women—at least in the abstract—arguing that both the emancipation of women and the emancipation of the working class required the incorporation of women in the labor force on equal terms with men and the participation by women in socialist unions.

Independent activity by Spanish socialist women was relatively unsuccessful. As early as 1903, some denounced male dominance and challenged the sexual division of labor, both in the household and in the paid workplace. A number of socialist women's groups were formed in Madrid and Bilbao between 1902 and 1906. But those advocating the organization of women along sex-specific lines were never more than a tiny minority within the movement. A socialist women's group, founded in March 1906 in Madrid, was incorporated as part of the PSOE in 1908 with 75 members, and grew to 183 by 1910. Nevertheless, these women constituted a very small percentage of the total membership of socialist unions or the PSOE (75 out of 25,000 members of the Casa del Pueblo in Madrid in 1908, and 36 of 2,900 members of the PSOE in Madrid in 1910).[44]

Even the relatively moderate position of Virginia González—that women's primary role was as "helpmeet" to men and socializer of the new generation of socialist children—rarely received a respectful hearing within socialist circles. Most socialists, even those concerned with the oppression of women workers, saw the solution solely in syndical terms. In general, socialists were slow to address women's issues and relatively unsuccessful in attracting women militants, whether to unions or to the party.[45]

Margarita Nelken, another Spanish socialist who was to become a deputy to the Cortes (the Spanish parliament), took a somewhat more militant position, arguing that exploitation of women workers hurt male workers as well as women. "Equal pay for equal work," she asserted, "as much as it is a feminist maxim, is also a principle of defense for male workers." She urged the party to undertake massive programs of education, as well as improvements in wages and working conditions for women, and to organize women into unions so that, together with men, they could work for the social transformation that all desired.[46] She lectured widely, within and outside the PSOE, developing, in effect, her own version of a socialist feminism. But while the socialists eventually supported woman's suffrage, they never directed the attention she felt was necessary to overcome other aspects of women's subordination. They did not adopt equal pay, maternity leave, or improved working conditions for women as central goals of the movement, and they never devoted serious attention to organizing women workers. In the end, neither Nelken nor the socialists succeeded in making "the greater participation of women a necessary part of the leftist struggle to survive."[47]

Anarchists were somewhat more attentive to the particular needs of women workers, a phenomenon probably not unrelated to the fact that women workers were most common in those areas where anarchist unions were strongest. In its 1881 congress, for example, the Spanish Regional Federation of the AIT declared that women "can exercise the same rights and meet the same responsibilities as men."[48] Anarchist congresses repeatedly called for the unionization of women workers and for equal pay for equal work. Nevertheless, as we have seen, there were also anarchists who viewed women more as revolutionary "helpmeets" than as active revolutionaries. And although women actively joined unions in the late nineteenth century and may even have constituted a majority of members in some textile locals, they were rarely represented in the leadership. Teresa Claramunt, one of the most famous anarchist orators and organizers of the period, complained in an article published in 1891 that men insisted on running predominantly female unions.[49] One result of her call for women to take charge of their own unions was the formation in 1891 of the Agrupación de Trabajadoras de Barcelona (Barcelona women workers' group). Apparently, however, the group had little success in remedying the situation, since men were still representing women at the time of the La Constancia strike in 1913.

While the organizing of women in unions was proceeding on the syndical front, neighborhood/community activism was given a boost with the introduction into Catalonia (in 1899–1900) of the revolutionary general strike. In May and December of 1901, workers and community people effectively closed down Barcelona for brief periods. The first real test of the general strike in industrial Spain, however, came in February 1902, when a general strike in support of metallurgical workers mobilized thousands of workers and brought virtually all production in Barcelona to a halt for a week. Significantly, the strike also engaged many women, both as striking workers and in neighborhood-based demonstrations. This established a pattern of multifaceted women's activism that was to be repeated during the next fifteen years of worker agitation in Barcelona, Madrid, Valencia, and elsewhere. Teresa Claramunt was instrumental in the 1902 strike, both as propagandist and as leader of women demonstrators.[50]

Over the next few years, the anarchist movement in Catalonia developed the strategy that provided a means to resolve the dilemma of syndicalism vs. communalism, reformism vs. revolution: anarcho-syn-dicalism. It combined revolutionary (anarchist) perspectives with re-spect to long-term goals with somewhat more reformist (syndicalist) strategies in the short term. A new synthesis began to be articulated as early as 1907 with the founding of the Federación Barcelona de Soli-daridad Obrera (Barcelona Federation of Labor Solidarity), followed in 1908 by the Catalan Federation of Solidaridad Obrera. In these organi-zations, workers joined forces behind a "revolutionary leadership, on the condition that it remain reformist in its practice,"—i.e., that it not ignore the day-to-day job-related concerns of workers. Finally, in Oc-tober 1910, the CNT was created. Its organizational structure, as well as its ideology, combined revolutionary syndicalism with anarchist com-munism, establishing a strong revolutionary base for the movement over the course of the next thirty years.[51]

At the same time, the new synthesis largely neglected the more com-munalist, direct-action, and woman-involving strain of popular ac-tivism, which had been manifest throughout this period, most dramatically during the "Tragic Week" in Barcelona, July 26 to August 1, 1909. Cristina Piera was twelve years old at the time of the events and was working as an apprentice in a textile factory. She described the strike as follows:

> We were in Badalona, ready to go to work, and they said, "Hey, today is a holiday." I was pleased, as you can imagine. . . . Anyway, then they began to shoot. . . . That revolution was because they were sending lots of soldiers to Melilla, where there was a war. . . . And then, well, the people revolted, and they began to take the bridge—the bridge in Badalona, which is called "Butifarreta" [little sausage], and they took it, and they blocked the rails, so that the train couldn't pass, so that the soldiers couldn't go. And then began the week-long battle, which is what they call the "Tragic Week."[52]

Lola Iturbe noted the importance of women during the Tragic Week: "In 1909, the great 'Tragic Week,' . . . there was a lot of activity on the part of women, in the matter of the streetcars, of burnings, of . . . demonstrations, of women who threw themselves on the train tracks to prevent the troops from going to Morocco."[53] Joan Connelly Ullman's detailed study of the events of the Tragic Week is punctuated throughout with references to particular women who took leadership roles and to women (and children) who spurred activism at the neigh-borhood level.[54]

What is particularly interesting here is the focus on neighborhood-based community antiwar activity. One impetus for the general strike was syndical in nature: the closing of a textile factory had resulted in massive worker layoffs. The strike, in turn, provided the context for considerable anticlerical violence. But in the memory of many men and women who participated in the marches and street demonstrations, what was primary was the effort to stop the call-up of reservists.

It is precisely the mix of these motives in memory and action that constituted the particular power of the demonstrations: there were aspects that appealed, in specific ways, to a variety of people, each of whom could find his or her place in response to the conditions of his or her life—a prime example of direct action. Yet the lesson here—the uniting of wage-laborers, unemployed workers, and women who saw themselves rooted primarily in the domestic arena—was not immediately reflected in the policy of the growing anarcho-syndicalist movement.

The CNT was founded in Barcelona just one year after these events. Its program combined attention to classical "syndical" concerns—minimum wages, maximum hours (they aimed for an eight-hour day), elimination of piece work, and unionization—with more "revolutionary-communal" ones, such as abolishing child labor (for children under fourteen of both sexes), struggling for cheaper rents and the elimination of rental deposits, setting up "rationalist schools" for workers (both night schools for those who worked and day schools for young children), overcoming the subordination of women, creating a base of revolutionary workers, and strategizing for a general strike. Significantly, these demands were made not just on behalf of urban-industrial workers, but on behalf of rural-agricultural workers as well.[55]

With this program, the CNT demonstrated the beginnings of an understanding that successful revolutionary organizing must reach beyond the bounds of the workplace. In its commitment to setting up and funding schools for workers, in its support for controlling rents (even to the point of considering a general strike in support of tenant demands), and in its attention to the subordination of women in the household as well as at work, it seemed to recognize that workers' concerns were far broader than their "work." It provided a framework within which rural, agrarian-based groups could federate with urban, industrial ones. And it stated clearly that "syndicalism" was a means to an end, not the end in itself.

Yet, the projects that flowed from the congress focused on more traditional working-class organization and did not take fully into account the implications of the community mobilization, which had been so striking the previous year. Thus, for example, the congress declared that "we consider that the key to women's moral redemption—subordinated as she is today to the protection of her husband—is work, which will raise women's condition to that of men. That is the only way of affirming her independence." In a rare statement that articulated the relationship between the exploitation of women and the exploitation of workers in general, the congress went on to assert:

The decrease in hours of work for many of us is an indirect consequence of the difficult work women are doing in factories; meanwhile, many of us allow our compañeras to get up before five o'clock in the morning, while we sleep later. And when the woman finishes shedding her blood for twelve hours, to support the vices of her exploiter, she returns to her house and, instead of rest, she encounters another bourgeois: her compañero who . . . expects her to take care of all the domestic tasks.

The congress's program for action, however, neglected entirely the issue of the subordination of women to their husbands within the household.[56]

The founding conference of the CNT thus represented a compromise between communist-anarchists and syndicalists in some aspects of strategy, but it did not yet reflect a recognition that working-class solidarity and action could be strengthened by the activities of those who were not defined, or understood, as workers. While the fullest expression of that perspective did not come until the era of the Civil War, women's activities in the intervening years and then in the subsistence strikes of 1918–1919 were to be further examples of the power of women's collective action and, consequently, of the limits of the strictly syndical strategy.

Women continued to be active in protest during the years of repression following the Tragic Week. Many female textile workers joined unions during those years and participated actively in strikes. In fact, the years 1910 to 1920 marked the real "take-off" both of the unionization of female textile workers in Catalonia and of their participation in strikes.[57] From 1905 to 1909, official records list 7,370 male and 1,051 female strikers in Barcelona (with women representing 28 percent of the workforce, but only 12.4 percent of the strikers); those same records list 61,918 female and 72,954 male strikers for the period 1909 to 1914. In 1913, women surpassed men in numbers of strikers (56,788 to 23,286). Women's participation and leadership was crucial to the general textile workers' strike in Sabadell in 1910, that of Reus in the summer of 1915, and the Barcelona textile workers' strike of August 1916.[58]

The general strike of textile workers of 1913 (known as "La Constancia"), in which the participation of anarchist women was critical, was typical in many ways. Reports of the events referred to female workers who "served as ringleaders well known to the crowd." While strike meetings were presided over by men, "often women spoke as leaders of more or less formal groups." Eventually, the male leadership of the union recommended a return to work on the promise of a ten-hour day; but the women refused, insisting on waiting for official publication of the new law. As one woman said at the meeting to discuss strategy, "If the men wish, let them go back to work, and the women will continue the strike!"[59]

Women's participation carried the strike considerably beyond the bounds of the workplace. Street demonstrations wound through working-class neighborhoods into some of the central plazas of Barcelona, keeping the issues and events of the strike constantly in the public eye. Thousands of women joined in these demonstrations, including large numbers of those who were not themselves union members. Temma Kaplan has argued that this strike was an example of the power of women's networks to erode the supposed boundaries between workplace and community and to draw on women's multiple roles as sources of strength for the community. Women were involved in similar sorts of activities in Madrid, Valencia, and Vizcaya as well.[60]

Active participation in unions and even in strikes, however, did not necessarily lead to formal recognition for women. Some small numbers served as officers of unions, but most were formally involved with union activity (if at all) only at the level of the shop floor. Through the early 1920s, the overwhelming number of even predominantly female textile unions were led and officially represented at congresses by men.[61]

The vast majority of women were not unionized, of course, since most were not working for wages in factories, and neither anarchists nor socialists devoted much effort to organizing those who worked at home as outworkers or as domestic workers in the homes of others. The working conditions of these female homeworkers were even more deplorable than those for factory workers. Home-based piecework escaped all forms of protective labor legislation on the grounds that the home was sacred and that a law regulating homework would be impossible to enforce in any case. Those working at home often put in twelve, fourteen, or sixteen hours a day, receiving an average take-home pay (discounting what they had to pay for needles, thread, and transportation to and from the place where they picked up and delivered their work) of 1.80 pesetas a day.[62]

Juan Paulís' Las obreras de la aguja (female needleworkers), published in 1913, called for the creation of a nationwide union of needleworkers that would include both factory and homeworkers, struggling together for the regulation of hours, wages, and working conditions. Although the book was cited as one of the most influential of the era by a number of the women I interviewed (all of whom had been needleworkers), it seems to have had relatively little effect on the practices of existing union organizations. Homeworkers were largely ignored by both the CNT and the UGT, on the grounds that they were too difficult to organize, although Catholic syndicates were apparently quite successful in appealing to homeworking women in the needle trades. Their vision of harmony between classes, however, and their goal of awakening "a love on the part of [women] workers for their task, for one another, and for their employers . . . and of their employers for them," was hardly compatible with either anarchist or socialist trade unionism.[63]

The links between factory-based women and community women solidified during the so-called women's war in Barcelona in 1918. By contrast with the general strikes discussed above, which had begun at workplaces and spread from there into working-class communities, the 1918 women's war was begun and carried out by neighborhood women for community ends. In reaction against increases in the cost of living induced by the First World War, women took to the streets of Barcelona in early January 1918, attacking coal trucks and demanding controls on the price of coal. Over the course of the next few weeks, the demonstrators moved through textile areas, calling on women workers to join them in striking. They requisitioned supplies from foodstores and communal slaughterhouses, demonstrated in market areas, and moved, as they had in 1913, into public plazas to confront political authorities and demand justice. Strikes that had begun over quality-of-life issues eventually broadened their goals to include improving conditions of women's work, reducing rents, rehiring of railroad workers, increasing job alternatives and education for women, calling for an end to war and a return to peacetime concerns, as well as for an end to hierarchy in unions and the family and an end to the church's sponsoring of piecework shops that contributed (in the view of the women) to the exploitation of women workers. In all, demonstrations lasted for more than six weeks, and employers and government officials alike were in awe of the women's strength and tenacity and the radicalism of their demands.[64]

The CNT viewed the women's actions with ambivalence. Although it had declared a one-day general strike in November 1916 to protest the rising cost of living, the CNT rarely made connections between workplace-based issues and those relating to women's subordinate status in either the workplace or the community. The CNT had been severely weakened by a protracted and ultimately unsuccessful general strike in Barcelona in August 1917 and by the repression that followed it. Thus, it was largely unorganized women who initiated and maintained the subsistence strikes of January 1918.

A few men in the CNT recognized and applauded the roles of these women. Others were threatened by the independent action of women: "The hour for justice has sounded with the heroic greatness of the women. Either we take advantage of it or we should give our balls to the dogs to eat."[65] Those who appreciated its significance, however, were clearly in the minority. When the Catalan Regional Federation of the CNT held its congress at the end of June 1918, not a single female delegate was present. Few of the predominantly female industries or workplaces were unionized, and those that were (e.g., La Constancia) were represented by men.[66] Only one of the major speakers at that congress addressed the role of women in the January 1918 strikes. Enric Rueda, a delegate representing the lampmakers of Barcelona, declared: "The woman . . . has clearly demonstrated her capacity to participate in social struggles. . . . After August, when we were persecuted, surrounded by the brutality of the bourgeois regime . . . our compañeras knew to take to the streets to demand what, for the most part, no one wanted to give them: their rightful bread. . . . Today, they incite us to defend freedom, inspire us to continue with our struggles."[67]

Although the organization did pass resolutions advocating the unionization of women, these focused almost entirely on incorporating women into already existing unions, ignoring large numbers of women who worked in nonunionized textile shops, those who toiled as outworkers in their own homes, and (despite a later organizing drive) those who worked as domestic servants.

Strike activity continued, of course, in the succeeding years. In 1919, for example, textile workers in Ripoll (another textile town in Catalonia) mounted a strike for the eight-hour day that lasted for nine weeks. Since the town was almost completely dependent on the mills, suffering was widespread. Dolores Prat, who was about fourteen years old at the time, remembers the poverty, the hunger, and the public soup kitchens. She developed a great anger at scabs. In fact, she dates her own militancy from this period. When, in the months after the strike, her father suggested that it was time for her to start earning her living, she rejected both the prospect of becoming a teacher ("I had had enough of nuns at school") and his offer to set her up with a small fruit and vegetable stand ("I would end up giving away all the food to the hungry workers, so what would be the point?"). She decided, instead, that she would become a worker, "so that I could go to the factory to protest!"[68] She soon joined the CNT and became a member of her factory committee. During the war, she served as Secretary of the Sección Fabril of the textile workers' union in Ripoll.

CNT efforts to unionize women and other disadvantaged workers continued through the 1920s, hindered, as were all organizing efforts, by the repression of worker activity under the dictatorship of Primo de Rivera (1923–1929). When the Republic was declared in 1931, women could be counted, along with men, as members of and activists in the CNT. But, for all the reasons I have noted (particularly the continued focus of the CNT on unionizing factory workers, and the relative inattention to women's specific situation) participation in union activity, or even in mass community mobilizations, was only a part of women's "preparation." It remains for us to explore the networks of schools, ateneos, and cultural institutions that also developed during the first third of the twentieth century and that were of particular importance to women.

## Education as Preparation

While they considered participation in resistance movements to be important learning experiences for workers, Spanish anarchists also recognized the need for more "formal" education. The commitment to self-direction meant a focus on education. Given the high levels of illiteracy in Spain at the turn of the century, it was clear that a movement committed to working-class empowerment through direct action and self-organization would have to devote at least some of its energies and resources to adult and child literacy. It was one of the great strengths of the anarchist movement—and one of the achievements of which members were proudest—that it developed a network of schools, journals, and cultural centers to address these issues.

To teach people to read and write was to empower them socially and culturally; it became, truly, a revolutionary act. It was for this reason, of course, that traveling teachers like Abelardo Saavedra had been persecuted and jailed in Andalusia and Extremadura at the end of the nineteenth century. And it was with this perception of the importance of education that Spanish anarchists (and later Mujeres Libres) embarked on a massive program of "enculturating" working people, both rural and urban. Although many of these programs were undertaken by unions and initially directed toward union members, they served a population considerably larger.

Anarchist-supported educational institutions took a variety of forms during this period, but common perspectives animated all. Basically, they aimed to increase literacy and broaden the cultural base of working people. Specifically, that meant that schools, cultural centers, and journals attempted to communicate to their students or readers a sense of excitement about the world, a message that the world was theirs to explore and not simply the context of their daily oppression. People were encouraged to question, to value their experiences and perceptions, and to learn from one another, as well as from their teachers. These programs also aimed to communicate a different set of moral values, to replace the resignation and acceptance of subordination taught in church-sponsored schools with a commitment to self-development in a context of mutualism and cooperation. Schools, cultural centers, journals, newspapers all encouraged people to "think for themselves, and to develop their sense of responsibility, commonality, and criticism."[69]

## Creating Institutions for Literacy and Culture

Levels of illiteracy varied markedly in Spain at the turn of the century. But everywhere, literacy rates for women lagged between ten and twenty percentage points (and sometimes as much as thirty points) behind those of men. By 1930, with greater access to education, rates of illiteracy fell for both men and women, but still ranged from highs of approximately 50 percent of men and over 60 percent of women in the southern provinces to lows of 25 to 30 percent of women and 20 to 25 percent of men in the Basque provinces.[70]

Official "state" education was of little help in meeting these deficits. Republicans, socialists, and anarchists had pressed for the establishment of lay schools as early as the mid-nineteenth century, but their efforts were largely unsuccessful until the educational reforms of the Republic in 1931. Church-run schools concentrated on discipline and rote memorization. In 1873 and 1874, during the 1880s, and again in the early 1890s, efforts had been made to change the relationship of church and state, so that the church no longer controlled the curriculum. The creation of nonconfessional lay schools was one of the major demands made by demonstrators during the Tragic Week in Barcelona, for example. But since the church provided most secondary education, even when schools were not officially run by the clergy, church-trained teachers tended to define their structure and function. As Azucena Barba summarized, "You went to the state schools with a rosary in one hand and a flag in the other."[71]

Clara Lida has argued that efforts to articulate and implement an alternative educational philosophy—of *enseñanza integral* (integral or holistic education)—can be traced back to republican and Fourierist schools in the 1840s and 1850s, and to anarchist and secularist schools in the 1870s and 1880s. Very few of these were financially accessible to the children of workers, however, and even if financial aid were available for the children, it was a rare family that could spare the income, however meager, that a working child could bring into the family. In addition, these lay schools fought a continual (and usually losing) battle with the state over their very right to exist.[72]

One response of anarchists to the effective inaccessibility of lay-controlled education was the founding of "rationalist schools." Although these have been associated most notably with the name of Francisco Ferrer y Guardia, they were the direct descendents of efforts at enseñanza integral. Born in Barcelona in 1859, Ferrer spent sixteen years in exile in Paris, where he came in contact with the educational ideas of Paul Robin, Tolstoy, Jean Grave, and others. He returned to Spain in 1901 to found the Escuela Moderna (modern school) in Barcelona. His goal was "to form a school of emancipation, which will be concerned with banning from the mind whatever divides men, the false concepts of property, country, and family, so as to attain the liberty and well-being which all desire and none completely realizes."[73]

Consistent with both anarchist principles and advanced educational theory at the time, Ferrer was committed to establishing a school that recognized education as a political act. If one hoped to enable children to live in a free society, the educational system itself had to encourage freedom to develop and explore. Science and reason were key concepts in the schools, and children were to be stimulated to direct their own education. Consistent, too, with his understanding of libertarian principles, Ferrer was firmly committed to coeducation (a practice virtually unheard of in Spain at the time) and to mixed-class education, which would provide a context for people to learn to live with diversity.[74] Given the rigidity of the existing system in Spain and anarchist suspicion of both church and state, it should not be surprising that Spanish libertarians attempted to establish "alternative schools"—institutions which, true to the anarchist belief in direct action and propaganda by the deed, would not only educate students but also serve as models for a very different educational philosophy and practice.

Ferrer's Escuela Moderna opened in Barcelona in September 1901, and it lasted, despite frequent closings because of state censorship, through 1906, when it was closed definitively. Cristina Piera, who attended the school for about a year at the age of nine, described the confusion: "The police would come to close the school, and then . . . we couldn't go. I went to the Escuela Moderna, and learned a fair amount there, but since they were always closing it, I ended up without much of an education."[75] The school was supported by parental contributions—according to what each family was able to pay. The classes were mixed by socioeconomic background and completely integrated by sex as well. All students, regardless of background or sex, studied a "scientific" curriculum that also included sex education, manual work, and the arts. Ferrer recognized the need for appropriate textbooks and began publishing them himself in 1902. The books were in great demand and came to be used in rationalist schools and ateneos throughout the country. In addition, the school building served as much more than a place for small children to go during the days. It was also a library and community center for adolescents and adults, offering classes, discussions, excursions, and the like for those of all ages who wished to learn.

While Ferrer's name has come to be the one most prominently associated with the rationalist school movement, rationalist schools certainly preexisted the Escuela Moderna, and hundreds were established throughout Spain in the early years of the twentieth century.[76] Igualdad Ocaña, together with her father and four brothers and sisters, started and taught in such a school in Barcelona in 1934–1935. Perhaps her description of what it meant to teach children in a free and open environment can provide some sense of the "modernity" of the "modern school movement":

> In our school, we tried to get a sense of each child's particular nature or character. We would tell them a story. And through this story, they would

reflect themselves. . . . They cried and they laughed. . . . We never had to yell at them. People talk about exercising 'authority.' But what authority can they have if they don't know how to control [children] with feeling, with love? . . .

You can help little creatures to become active, productive people, productive in ways that are true to themselves, because you have studied them, seen what they enjoy. . . . We taught mechanics, music, arts . . . We had mechanical toys, for example, to see whether, when he was playing with them, a particular child would awaken to a desire, a positive inclination to activity of that sort.[77]

Not surprisingly, given the type of attention they devoted to their students, teachers in rationalist schools were often revered, both by their students and by other members of the community. They functioned as powerful models, much as the obreros conscientes or traveling teacher/preachers (such as Abelardo Saavedra) had served for rural workers in nineteenth-century Andalusia. Sara Berenguer Guillén, who studied with Felix Carrasquer in the "Eliseo Reclus" school, Pura Pérez Arcos, who studied with the noted Juan Puig Elías in the "Escuela Natura," and others I interviewed all vividly recalled their experiences with teachers they respected. Igualdad Ocaña reported that students she meets now, forty years later, still talk of their experiences in the school her family ran. And Ana Cases discovered, during the course of research she was doing in 1981, that many of those who had studied with Josep Torres (known as Sol de la Vida) in Arbeca, a small village in Lerida, still had the notebooks and workbooks they had used in the 1920s.[78]

Many young people who eventually became militants in the anarcho-syndicalist movement attended one or another of these schools, but attendance was clearly not limited to anarchists or anarchist-sympathizers alone. Since they offered an alternative to the highly rigid structures and rote-learning methods of the dominant school system, the schools attracted considerable numbers of children from the progressive middle and upper classes as well.

Aside from the somewhat formally structured rationalist schools, the anarchist and anarcho-syndicalist movement created and supported a large number of ateneos. Many neighborhood educational/cultural centers were started by CNT locals; almost every working-class barrio of Barcelona had one during the early years of the Republic. For those who had never been to school, the hundreds of ateneos that sprang up around the country offered a chance to learn to read and write. Most had classes during the day for young children, and in the evening (usually from 7 to 9 P.M.) for older people, who would come after work. In the words of one participant, "The education in the school was a totally different kind of education. . . . Each person would talk about what he had read (which often varied a great deal, since sometimes we didn't understand what we were reading!), and then we would all talk about it, and think about what each had said. . . . As far as I am concerned, the school and the books were probably the greatest factors shaping my development."[79]

In addition to its importance as a place for learning basic skills and competences, the ateneo had important social functions. Ateneos were popular "hangouts" for young people, particularly during times when they could not afford even the ten céntimos to go to a movie![80] Because they were at least formally separate from the unions, many were able to remain open during periods of political repression, when unions were forced to close their doors and/or go underground. Consequently, they also served as important centers of communication.

Further, virtually all ateneos included theater, recreation, and—particularly for those in urban barrios—trips out of the city. In addition to offering opportunities for exercise and fresh air, these excursions were thought to provide moral and intellectual benefits: giving young people a chance to see firsthand the mountains, valleys, and rivers they might have learned about in classes; overcoming the narrowness of vision that comes from living in crowded urban environments; providing an occasion for them to experience "the influence of nature on the human spirit." Exposure to nature, one writer explained, will "allow young people to experience freedom, so that they will want to live it and defend it."[81]

As community-based organizations, ateneos offered opportunities for preparation that were particularly important for working-class women, who had relatively fewer contexts than did men to gain such experiences. Those women who became activists in the CNT and/or in Mujeres Libres reported virtually unanimously that their experiences in ateneos, schools, and cultural activities were crucial to that process. They learned to read and, equally important, developed meaningful peer relationships with boys of their own age—an experience that was otherwise closed to them in the highly sex-segregated Spanish society. Through the ateneos many young people experienced that *cambio de mentalidad* (consciousness-change) which was a crucial step in their becoming militants in the movement:

> The building belonged to the union (textiles). The Escuela Libre [Escuela Natura of El Clot] was upstairs, and the sindicato and our group, I think, were downstairs. . . . My sisters and I went to school at night. (We couldn't go during the day, because we had to work.) And—remember this detail, because it's important—in order to save money, the union had the women do the cleaning. . . . Afterwards, there would be meetings of Sol y Vida [the cultural group]. . . . True, people went to union meetings,

but relations within the group were more intimate, the explanations more extensive. That's where we were formed most deeply.[82]

In addition to the schools and cultural centers, the anarcho-syndicalist movement supported an enormous array of newspapers, magazines, and clubs that challenged conventional norms and provided channels for bringing alternative perspectives to a broader audience. The movement newspapers *Solidaridad Obera, CNT*, and *Tierra y Libertad* combined political commentary with extensive cultural criticism. Almost every issue had an article dealing with some aspect of education, and in the years before and during the war, many carried articles devoted specifically to women. *Tierra y Libertad*, for example, published a woman's page each week, in which many of the women who were to be active in Mujeres Libres tested out ideas about sexuality, work, or male-female relations and had an opportunity to communicate with the larger anarcho-syndicalist community. Magazines such as *La Revista Blanca* (Barcelona), *Natura* (Barcelona), *Estudios* (Valencia), and *Tiempos Nuevos* examined a range of issues from collectivist politics to birth control, nudism, and vegetarianism.

Particularly for people who lived in places relatively isolated from organized anarchist or anarcho-syndicalist activity, the press provided important sources of information and a "route in" to the anarchist community. Soledad Estorach, for example, who came to Barcelona at the age of fifteen, alone and isolated in her interest in what she termed "communism," read *La Revista Blanca* and, through it, made her way to the ateneo:

> I was reading newspapers and magazines and trying to find "communists.' . . . The first person I went to see, in fact, was Federica Montseny's mother, Soledad Gustavo, because she was a woman! I didn't know how to get in contact with these people. And I figured that those people who were writing about communism must somehow . . . live differently. I had been reading *La Revista Blanca*, and I saw that this woman Soledad Gustavo wrote for them, so I went to the address given in the magazine and asked to see her. I was shown right in. I guess they thought I was a compañera. She received me without any understanding. . . . I can't even remember just what I asked her. Probably "How do I find people?" And she said, "All you have to do is find an ateneo in your barrio" and she more or less threw me out. . . . Anyway, I went to the ateneo. The first man I met there was Saavedra, the grandfather of Enriqueta and the others. He was very old even then. But I fell in love with him immediately. . . . He showed me the library . . . I was entranced by all those books. I thought that all the world's knowledge was now within my reach.[83]

### Education as Empowerment

For all that the ateneos provided in the way of opportunities for young and old to learn to read and develop some "culture," probably their most important long-term effect was the creation of a community—a community of people who believed that they could effect change in the world. The network of friends and comrades established there provided participants important sources of both moral and material support through their years of struggle in the movement and during the Civil War. Men and women who had participated in these groups as boys and girls referred to their experience with words and expressions similar to those one might use to describe a lost love. Even those who had become most cynical and/or isolated from the larger movement in the intervening years spoke of those experiences with a near reverence. No doubt, their recollections have been romanticized over the years. But the experience of participating in these groups—groups in which people attempted to interact with one another as they hoped they would in the "anarchist paradise" they were struggling to create—had obviously marked them deeply.

For some of the girls, in particular, the experience of equality between men and women was especially energizing. It impelled considerable numbers of them to insist on their equality within the context of the larger movement. As Enriqueta noted, the ateneos provided both an incentive and a model for what was to be Mujeres Libres:

> I always felt strongly that women had to be emancipated. That our struggle was—and still is—more than just the struggle against capitalism. . . . We used to talk about that a lot [in the ateneo], insist that the struggle was not just in the factories, in the streets, or even in the ateneos. That it had to go into the house. The boys would sometimes laugh and make fun of us when we'd say those things. They said, it is the struggle of all of us, and we all should struggle together. But I would say, no, it's not just that. We need to express ourselves, to be who and what *we* are. We're not trying to take things away from you, but we need to develop ourselves, to demand our *own* rights.

Since the groups formed out of the ateneos were primarily for young people, they provided youth with opportunities to act at least somewhat independently of their parents—an almost unheard-of experience in Spain of that time. Even anarchist families had difficulty with the freedom their daughters asserted. "We had to ask permission every week when we were going to go on these excursions. Don't think that just because our parents were libertarios that we were free to do as we pleased! No, none of that! Every week we had to ask. And if the answer to "where are you going?" were something like "camping," then, whoa!

None of that. No, there were lots of controls, even of our activities in the ateneo." Azucena and Enriqueta developed ways around their parents' efforts at control. Often, they would put skirts on over their bermuda shorts, ride on their bikes to the edge of town, where they would no longer be seen by adults, and then remove the skirts and continue with the group to the mountains or the seashore![84]

The struggles continue. Ironically, while she was telling a related story, Enriqueta was engaged in a continuous, loving battle with her twelve-year-old granddaughter who was visiting for the Christmas holidays, a battle that recapitulated the tensions she had described in her own youth: "Sometimes," she mused, "I sit here and look at them and think 'what have I done?' But they don't really behave very well. I think there is too much permissiveness in the way they're raising children these days."[85]

Finally, their experiences in the ateneos were specifically important to the women of Mujeres Libres in a somewhat more complex way. As any number of women reported, even within those organizations, the same *machista*, masculinist atmosphere persisted, if not in thoughts or beliefs, at least in action. Mercedes Comaposada, for example, who was to become one of the founders of Mujeres Libres, reported the following about her own first experience of attempting to teach a class sponsored by one of the CNT unions in Madrid:

> In 1933, I went along with Orobón Fernandez to a meeting at one of the sindicatos. They were trying to help with the "preparation" of the workers, and asked me to come along. Lucía [Sanchez Saornil] was there, too. They wanted me to teach, since they had no women teachers. But it was impossible because of the attitudes of some compañeros. They didn't take women seriously. There is a saying: "Las mujeres—a la cocina y a coser los calcetines" [Women belong in the kitchen or darning socks]. No, it was impossible; women barely dared to speak in that context.[86]

Mercedes and Lucía responded to this experience by beginning the conversations that ultimately led to the founding of Mujeres Libres.

Conversely, others reported that it was often difficult to get girls to concentrate on learning to read, or to focus on the particular lecture at hand, at the ateneos. It would be necessary, they concluded, to develop classes and programs just for women and girls, where they could be approached independent of the boys, encouraged to develop their own potential, and enabled to recognize their own strengths beyond mothering.

In short, the movement's institutions for "preparation" provided important resources for the women who were to found Mujeres Libres—resources both positive and negative. On the positive side, participation in unions, in ateneos, schools, and in youth movement organizations offered opportunities for learning, for empowerment, and for making and cementing important networks of support. The cultural and educational institutions Mujeres Libres sponsored were clearly modeled on them. On the negative side, their experience with ateneos and schools demonstrated to many that groups oriented specifically to women would be necessary if women were to emerge as fully equal members of the libertarian community. As Mercedes summarized her own reflections,

> We had one million people against us. All the great revolutionaries—Alexandra Kollontai, Rosa Luxemburg, Clara Zetkin—tried to do something with women. But they all found out that, from within a party, within an existing [revolutionary] organization, it is always impossible. . . . I remember reading, for example, of a communication between Lenin and Clara Zetkin, in which he says to her, "Yes, all this you're talking about with respect to the emancipation of women is very good. A very fine goal, but for later." The interests of a party always come before those of women.[87]

# *III*

# CIVIL WAR AND
# SOCIAL REVOLUTION

## The Republic and the Popular Front

By the early 1930s, many of the deep cleavages dividing Spain along political, economic, social, religious, and gender lines had found political expression, whether in regionalist movements, labor unions, employer associations, or church-based organizations. At the time of the outbreak of the Civil War in July 1936, the CNT and UGT (the socialist trade union federation) each boasted a membership of between 850,000 and 1 million workers, committed to workplace-based and (in the case of the anarcho-syndicalists) community-based organizations to create a more egalitarian society. Given their size and the range of their activities, the very existence of these organizations was perceived as a threat to the traditional power of employer and landlord groups, the army, and the church.

After many years of authoritarian, "constitutional" monarchy, followed by the dictatorship of Primo de Rivera (1923–1929), Spain became a republic in 1931. This republic, however, had no solid social base, having been established virtually by default when King Alfonso XIII abdicated the throne after candidates favoring a republic scored a major victory in local elections. From 1931 to 1933, the country was led by a weak coalition of centrist and left-centrist republicans, desiring to break the power of the church, the army, and large landholders, but reluctant to take strong action against them for fear of alienating them entirely and provoking a military coup. They instituted a series of moderate reforms, including a program of land reform in Andalusia and Extremadura (which, however, did more in the way of investigation than of actual redistribution of land). They also supported secular education and limited the numbers of new military commissions. But the workers and agricultural laborers who were living in a state of near destitution became increasingly frustrated by the lack of change, while the traditional forces (military, church, and landholders) chafed against policies aimed at restricting their privileges. A center-right government took power from 1933 to 1935. It lifted many of the new restrictions on traditional powers and instituted more severe repression of leftist revolutionary activity, but it was unable to assure social peace.[1]

The elections of February 1936 sent into office a Popular Front government, pledged to free political prisoners and to move deliberately toward a more egalitarian society. But the coalition behind that Popular Front was tenuous at best. The slate presented in the elections reflected a hastily constructed coalition, with a platform that was less a compromise of all the differing views than "an acceptance of the Republican program by the workers' parties."[2] What united the groups was mostly negative—a desire to defeat the Center-Right coalition. But the Left's victory depended on the support of a considerably more revolutionary working-class electorate, united (to the extent it was) by the memory of joint struggle during worker uprisings in Asturias, in particular, in 1934.[3]

The election both revealed and masked the deep divisions in the country. Leftist parties, taken together, had won a narrow victory over those of the Right. Center parties experienced a notable drop in support. Spain was increasingly polarized between Left and Right. But the workings of the electoral system created a Cortes with a strong Center-Left majority.

The limits of these arrangements were made manifest in the months that followed. Although the Popular Front coalition won the election, neither socialists nor anarchists would accept formal roles in a government that, in their view, remained "bourgeois." The new Republican government attempted to put into action its program of liberal reforms, which included land reform and the reinstatement of the secular, regional, military, and education policies of the Republican-Socialist government of 1931–1933. Meanwhile, workers and peasants undertook their own efforts at more revolutionary change, expropriating latifundial land in many parts of Extremadura and Andalusia and engaging in industrial strikes and work stoppages in urban areas. Assassinations on both Right and Left contributed to an atmosphere of increasing social and political unrest.[4] Thus, when Generals Franco, Mola, Quiepo de Llano, and Goded led an attempted military coup on July 17–18, 1936, few people were surprised; the bonds holding the society together were already quite fragile.

## Rebellion and Revolution

Workers' organizations had long been expecting a coup attempt. Many of those with whom I spoke, both men and women, told of sleeping in union halls during the week before the uprising in order to be prepared for a call to arms. The government, however, was ill-prepared. Both the national and the Catalan governments had refused to accede to UGT and CNT demands to arm the workers, fearful that workers would use those arms against the Spanish Republic rather than defend it against a military coup. Nevertheless, when the four generals rose (on July 17 in Morocco, and July 18 on the mainland), the response of the populace was swift and strong, particularly in areas with large numbers of unionized workers, such as Catalonia, Madrid, and Asturias. Men and women, boys and girls stormed the armories to grab the guns and ammunition that the government refused to provide them. People took to the streets with whatever weapons they could find to confront the rebel army.

In the weeks and months that followed, anarchist and socialist activists drew on their experiences in labor unions, community groups, and informal cultural and educational centers to mobilize millions of people and take control over vast areas of the economy and society. Particularly in areas of anarchist strength such as Catalonia, workers took over factories and workplaces. In rural areas, workers' organizations expropriated large properties, small landholders pooled their lands and animals, and municipalities instituted new cooperative systems of cultivation. Soon millions of people were living or working in anarchist- or socialist-inspired collectives (both rural and urban-industrial), marketing through cooperatives, and restructuring their interpersonal relationships.

Reports by participants in these events can, perhaps, give some sense of the excitement in the air. For the first time, large numbers of working people felt in control of their world, participants in a process that was transforming it totally. As Pepita Carpena (who was fifteen at the time) described it:

> Great things were done in Spain. . . . You had to live it in order to understand it. I saw those compañeros who created the collectives, who organized the socialization . . . who took charge of things without any pay or compensation whatever, just so that the pueblo would have what it needed. . . . When I was fourteen and fifteen, I had experiences that would stay with me all my life . . . such a flowering of ideas-made-reality. . . . Even if I had died, I wouldn't have wanted not to have had that experience.[5]

Thousands of people took part in the events of the first days. Enrique Cassañes, together with his buddies from the FIJL, had entered the armory at San Andrés at dawn on July 19, joining with other anarchist militants to obtain arms to put down the rebellion. His mother, Cristina Piera, awoke that morning to hear the sirens blaring, and she followed the crowds to the armory. (Union organizations had sounded an alarm to signal that the rebellion had begun and to call out everyone in a general strike in opposition to it.) Her story was probably typical of that of many people who were not themselves militants in any movement, but who were caught up in the excitement of the moment: "I woke up in the morning and heard that people were in the armory. . . . So I went there. Everybody went. . . . I took a pistol and two ramrods [for rifles]. What I could carry. They had gunpowder there, too. . . . Even me, with the little I knew, and could do, I was there. People took arms and ammunition, and I took what I could."[6]

Soledad Estorach and four or five other members of a women's group in Barcelona had been meeting throughout the night of July 18 in a room lent to them by the builders' union, on the Calle de Mercaders, behind the Via Layetana (in the center of Barcelona). Marianet (Mariano Vázquez) and all the rest of the "high command" of the CNT had gone off to storm the military barracks at Atarazanas, at the foot of the Ramblas.

> They left us there alone at 5 A.M. when the sirens went off. There were people all over the Plaza de Macià, and the whole area, and everyone went off to get arms—because the Generalidad, at that point, still refused to arm the people. I joined that mass, too, for a while.

Still early in the morning, she went back to the union hall with the rest of the compañeras.

> There was shooting everywhere. . . . It was very frightening. We didn't know what was happening, or what we should do. We figured that, if the worst happened, and the compañeros couldn't prevail at Atarazanas, that we could make a refuge. So we went to the Casa Cambó, one of the most beautiful buildings in Barcelona, on the Via Layetana. We had a small pistol and a few sticks. . . .
> There was construction going on across the street, and there were lots of sacks of bricks around. We took them to make barricades, and brought some inside, too, to fortify the building. The doorman was very sweet. He let us in, but told us not to get the elevator dirty or he might lose his job!
> So we took all the stuff upstairs and made barricades and fortifications. And when the compañeros returned—victorious, of course—and saw how beautiful it was, they took it over as the Casa CNT-FAI.[7]

She went on to discuss the hours and days that followed, and the role of women in quelling the rebellion: "The most important thing women did—aside, of course, from the heroic things they did along with everyone else—was to go up to the roofs of the buildings, with paper loudspeakers, and call out to the soldiers to come to our side, to take off their uniforms and join the people."

Enriqueta Rovira, who was about twenty at the time, had been vacationing with friends at Blanes, on the Costa Brava. Compañeros from the Comité in Barcelona called the Comité in Blanes to let them know what was happening, and Enriqueta hopped the first train back to the city.

> Most of the action was in the center of Barcelona. I had a pistol—they had given me a pistol. Imagine me, who had never even had a toy pistol, because my mother was opposed to such things! But they had given me a pistol, and I was prepared to use it. But they soon said no. That this was no place for a woman. . . . I didn't know how to use it, and there were compañeros without arms. So they sent me—and all the women, all families—to build barricades. We also took care of provisions. Women in each barrio organized that, to make sure that there would be food for the men. . . . Everyone did something.[8]

## Popular Revolution and Collectivization

A massive popular revolution—in both rural and urban-industrial areas—followed these first heady days. Once the rebellion had been quashed in some of the major cities and opposing battle lines had been drawn, it was clear there would be civil war. The resulting political vacuum both required and made possible social experimentation on a massive scale. Somehow, social order would have to be reestablished and the economy kept going, even if under a new system of management (necessary because, at least in some areas, landholders and industrial managers had fled to the rebel-controlled zone).

Catalan industrial workers responded to the rebellion by taking over factories and running them under one or another variation of "workers' control." In many rural areas, laborers took over management of fields from absentee landlords, and small landholders pooled their land and farm animals to create agricultural cooperatives and collectives. Municipalities everywhere in Republican Spain set up new systems for public works, transport, food, and supplies. And, for a time, militias replaced the army, local "patrols" replaced the police, and popular tribunals replaced the criminal court system.[9]

Not all collectivization was voluntary. Nor did collectivization take place everywhere in Republican Spain; it was most prevalent in industrial Catalonia and Valencia, in rural areas of Aragon and Valencia, and to a lesser extent in rural Castile and Catalonia. Nor was it the case that all collectives were anarchist-inspired. Socialists collectivized in some areas, particularly in the central region, and in Catalonia many farms were collectivized by the Unió de Rabassaires. But the initiative tended to derive from the local level, even if strongly reinforced, for example, by pressure from anarchist militia columns nearby.

Years of participation in union struggles, and attention to the problem of coordination, alerted activists in the cities to the need for cooperation with their comrades in other industries and in the countryside.

One immediate need was for food. As José Peirats, the anarchist historian, who was a young man at the time of the outbreak of the war, explained:

> We realized that, since everything was closed down because of the strike, people might not have food to eat. And if they could not get food, they would not support the revolution. So we set up food distribution centers for the food we had available, and we loaded up wagons with finished products, manufactured goods, kitchen utensils, (which we got from the relevant unions) and took them to the surrounding countryside, where we exchanged them with farmers for food.[10]

Soledad Estorach, who also took part in these activities, revealed another side of the revolutionary fervor:

> We requisitioned the large movie houses and turned them into communal dining halls. Where did the food come from? From wherever we could get it! We'd go around to shops in the area and requisition it, and the poor shopkeepers would give up everything they had. They weren't very happy about it. Some of them said that we ruined them. But that couldn't be helped. Those were things of the first days of the revolution, and we had to get food to people. Later, of course, we took trucks and went to the big markets and got food from there.[11]

Signs of the social transformation were everywhere. Government and private buildings were expropriated and draped with UGT or CNT banners. Movie theaters were turned into public refectories. Taxis and trams were repainted with CNT and UGT insignia. George Orwell, who first visited Barcelona in December 1936, reported that "in outward appearance, it was a town in which the wealthy classes had practically ceased to exist.[12]

Creative energies found outlets both large and small. Activists were able to realize the ideas they had cherished for years. Soledad, for example, had long been fascinated by books. Although the meager wages she earned as a textile worker barely allowed her to support herself and her family, she had not lost sight of her goal of getting an education and "seeing the world." Soon she joined with compañeros from the Juventudes to begin to make that dream a reality: "We started the Universidad Popular [people's university]. We took over a beautiful French convent, and requisitioned books for a library from all over the city. I was ecstatic about the books. The compañeros were more educated than I, and were able to choose which ones were most appropriate. I would have taken them all!"[13]

The revolution transformed education on a broad scale. In Catalonia, CENU (Committee for the New Unified School) was created on July 27. Its goal was quite radical: the provision of free public education for all, from elementary through higher education, including the "workers' university" and the Autonomous University of Barcelona. Its aims were deeply influenced by anarchist educational theory, and anarchist educators were prominent in its organization and functioning. Juan Puig Elías, for example, president of the cultural section of the CNT and the director of the Escuela Natura, served as president of the CENU executive committee. The decree creating it gives a good sense of the nature of the enterprise: "It is the time for a new school, inspired by rationalist principles of work and of human fraternity . . . which will create a new school life, inspired by the universal sentiment of solidarity and in accord with all the concerns of human society, and on the basis of the total elimination of all forms of privilege."[14]

Emma Goldman, invited by the CNT to visit Spain and the revolution, was totally captivated by what she experienced, particularly in these early stages. Even before she went there for the first time, in September 1936, she had written to friends that it was the constructive aspect of the revolution which seemed to her the most important: "For the first time our comrades are not only fighting the common enemy. They are engaged in building. They are expressing concretely the thought of our great teacher, Michael Bakunin, that the spirit of destruction is at the same time the spirit of construction."[15] When she arrived in Barcelona, she was not disappointed. She wrote to Rudolf and Milly Rocker: "I have already visited all works in control of the CNT and operated by the workers themselves, the railroads, transport, oil and gas works, the aviation yards, and some of the clothing factories. And I was overwhelmed by the perfect condition and orderly running of everything. I was especially impressed with the peasants of a collectivized village. I have never thought such intelligence among peasants possible."[16]

The feelings of empowerment, or possibility, that accompanied participation in these activities stayed with participants for years afterward. As Enriqueta Rovira recalled: "The feelings we had then were very special. It was very beautiful. There was a feeling of—how shall I say it?—of power, not in the sense of domination, but in the sense of things being under our control, if under anyone's. Of possibility. A feeling that we could together really do something."[17]

### Industrial Collectivization

Preexisting structures of worker organization made possible a workers' takeover of much of the industrial economy, especially in Catalonia. At the same time, however, those structures defined and limited who would participate most actively in the takeover.

In Barcelona and surrounding areas, union organizations collectivized virtually all production, from barbershops to textile factories, electric power generation to bakeries, logging to furniture retailing. Factory committees formed to direct production and coordinate with other units within the same industry. Union organizations coordinated both the production and distribution of manufactured goods across industries and regions. In some of these industries—wood, hairdressing, and bread-baking, for example—reorganization meant not only changes in management but also closing down small, ill-equipped shops, building new and larger workplaces, and developing more efficient production techniques. The wood and building trades union, for example, coordinated all production and distribution from the forests to furniture stores, built a recreational center with a swimming pool at 10, Calle de Tapiolas near one of these new workplaces in Barcelona, and took over a nearby church for a day-care center and school for workers' children.[18] In Catalonia, a joint UGT-CNT committee took over operation of the entire energy industry, creating a Central Committee of Workers' Control of Gas and Electricity, which reorganized production relations and salaries, coordinated the distribution and exchange of resources with other parts of the country, and even attempted to arrange for the purchase of coal from German mines (while, of course, disguising the identities of the purchasers).[19]

In most collectivized industries, general assemblies of workers decided policy, while elected committees managed affairs on a day-to-day basis. In industrial collectives, much was done through *Comités de Fábrica* (factory committees). Workers' committees had existed in all unionized plants during the prewar period. Participation in them enabled significant numbers of workers to develop both knowledge of their enterprises and a sense of their own competence.[20] The committees readily adapted themselves to the revolutionary context, coordinating and organizing production and—in the words of Dolores Prat, who served on the factory committee where she worked in Ripoll—"seeing that all were working, and all were content." *Comités de empresa* (enterprise committees) constituted another layer of organization. These were composed of representatives from each of the unions, and they more or less managed the collectivized factory.[21]

In the immediate aftermath of the rebellion, for example, the coordinating council of the textile workers' union in Badalona (a small textile city outside of Barcelona) asked the factory committees to take control of the factories and keep careful records of income, production, output, etc. Within a week, another communique asked members to create a workers' control committee in each factory.[22] These committees, formed in a general assembly of the workers, with representatives from each section, became the basic units of "worker control." The committees kept records, assigned duties within the factory, and monitored coordination with other enterprises and within the industry as a whole.

Through them, the union coordinated production throughout the textile industry.[23] Similar structures and procedures existed in other industries. Yet Albert Pérez Baró, who served as overseer of collectivizations as an employee of the Generalitat, was critical of the actual workings of many of these committees. In his view, too many CNT militants confused *worker control* with *union control,* and they tended to deny or dismiss any conflicts of interest that might have arisen—for example, as to which factories were assigned what production goals, or regulation of competition and working conditions between factories.[24]

Overall, these structures proved extraordinarily effective, not only in maintaining production but also in instituting changes in both production and personnel policies. For example, textile workers who were manufacturing cloth and uniforms for militiamen developed new processes that allowed for the substitution of hemp for hard-to-get cotton as a basis for cloth. On the personnel side, one change made in the collectivized textile industry was the abolition of piecework for women and the incorporation of homeworkers into the factories. The CNT began seriously to unionize women and to bring them into factories to work for a daily wage. Furthermore, in some areas, at least, worker committees were able to put into practice long-held beliefs about a "right to work." Dolores Prat, for example, who was general secretary of the *sección fabril* of CNT textile workers in Ripoll, reported that when foreign orders fell after May 1937 and hours had to be cut back, they adopted a three-day workweek, dividing the available work among all those who had worked at the plant—thereby avoiding unemployment— and continued to pay everyone her or his basic salary.[25]

In many industries, especially metallurgical and industrial chemicals, women flooded into new factory jobs. Many unions cooperated with Mujeres Libres to institute training programs for these new workers. In Barcelona and Madrid, women ran much of the public transport system. Many CNT union journals devoted columns to women's issues, focusing especially on the integration of women into the work force and providing an appreciation of the contributions women were making to production in factories and to the work of the union.[26]

Nevertheless, it would not be accurate to say that women actually achieved equality with men in these industrial collectives. By whatever measure we might choose to define it—equal pay for equal work, equal participation in worker-management activities, or the extent of the sexual division of labor—the collectives fell far short of a goal of equality, whether along gender or other lines.

In the area of salaries, for example, the CNT clearly compromised with the theoretical goal of equality. Although the organization had long been committed to the *sueldo único,* a uniform salary for everyone working within the same factory or industry, industrial enterprises rarely achieved that goal. Factory committees in most industries maintained or reintroduced wage differentials between different "grades" of work in an effort to retain the cooperation of managers, supervisory workers, and technical personnel, although they attempted to equalize wages across different "ex-enterprises" within a collectivized industry.[27] One story frequently recounted to me concerned the workers in the Barcelona opera house. Apparently, a group of workers proposed that all workers (from ushers and stagehands to singers) should receive the same wage. The singers agreed—if the ushers and stagehands would take a turn at singing the lead roles! The proposal was quickly abandoned.

Differentials in wages paid to men and to women also continued. Pepita Carnicer reported that in the collectivized textile factory in which she worked in Igualada (in the province of Barcelona) during the war, where the overwhelming number of workers were women, there were three levels of wages. The highest were paid to the *hombres responsables*, who were all men: the director, the foremen, and the electricians. A second level of salary was paid to the regular employees ("mothers of families")—the *maestras* and *ordidoras*. And a third level applied to the apprentices.[28] Although women constituted a majority of workers in the textile industry, they continued to perform the lowest-paying jobs. Lower pay was justified on the grounds that women's work was not as heavy nor as difficult as men's. And the claim that "male" work was indeed "heavy" also excluded women from the higher-paying jobs.

The situation was somewhat different in areas where there had been organized activity by women in the pre–Civil War period. Teresina Graells reported that a women's group began meeting within the CNT textile workers' union in Terrassa in the early 1930s, and had succeeded in getting the union to adopt equal pay for equal work and maternity leaves as formal bargaining goals even before the war. That situation was unusual, however.[29]

Structures of participation and leadership also fell short of the egalitarian vision. The CNT envisioned an anarcho-syndicalist society structured largely by union organizations. Although participation and leadership in these organizations and in institutions of worker control were officially open to all, in practice male workers participated more regularly in plant committees and tended to monopolize leadership positions.[30]

There were some exceptions, particularly in heavily female industries. Pepita Carnicer reported that most of the members of the factory committee in the textile factory where she worked were women—her mother among them. Teresina Graells was an active member and leader of the women's organization in her textile union in Terrassa, and Dolores Prat was secretary-general of her union in Ripoll. But their experiences were apparently unusual. Especially where both men and women worked together in an enterprise, women remained relatively under-represented in leadership positions.

Furthermore, the syndicate-based vision of social organization neces-sarily excluded nonunionized people from active participation in soci-etal decision making. In theory, a "local union" (which included representatives from each industry or enterprise in a particular com-munity) addressed matters of broader community concern. But there was no specific representation in these meetings of nonunionized work-ers or (with a few exceptions) of nonunion anarchist organizations, such as the ateneos. Thus, both the definition of issues and decisions about them tended to be left to union members.

Given the relatively low levels of women's participation in union leadership, union dominance in social and economic decision making only perpetuated the effective exclusion from priority consideration of issues of particular importance to women. Male-dominated movement organizations continued to analyze women's situation in terms of what we would now call a public/private split. If they thought about women's emancipation at all, they understood it to take place within the work-place context. They were effectively blinded to the ways in which women's domestic roles might impinge on their "public" (i.e., union) participation.

In fact, the abolition of homework for women and their incorporation into the textile factories—regarded by the men who instituted it as one of the most significant achievements of collectivization, since it would allow for the incorporation of women into the work force as "equals" with men—demonstrates the problems with a public/private analysis that ignores the complexity of women's lives. Although the men who pressured for the change genuinely believed it would help women, the women who experienced it were not always in agreement. Homework had given women some opportunity to set their own hours and the pace of their work. Perhaps more important, it allowed them to care for children and family at the same time. Hours and wages improved significantly with the move into factories, but many women found it difficult to adjust to the new work discipline, which, in the absence of provisions for child care, may have made it harder for them to balance their multiple roles.[31]

"Double duty" continued for women who worked in the factories and then had to go home to prepare food, clean, care for children, or keep house for their families. While many people apparently recognized the burden this placed on women, few suggested that it could change.[32] At the same time, however, the lives of many women changed markedly as a result of extraordinary new opportunities for participation in a broad range of economic activities. The development of Mujeres Libres assured that there would be opportunities for women to expand their participation beyond the narrowly defined economic arena.

## Rural Collectives

There were even more pronounced changes in rural areas. In many small villages, particularly in Aragon, anarchists created municipal collectives of which all who worked the land could become members. In slightly larger villages, workers expropriated and collectivized the lands of large landholders, allowing those who had previously owned the land to continue working it, but assuring that all who had been sharecroppers or day laborers became full members of the collective. In other areas, the process of collectivization was more mixed: while some peasants and sharecroppers joined the collective as members, others remained outside as "individualists," perhaps joining in only as members of a producers' or consumers' cooperative.

Soledad Estorach traveled with representatives of the CNT, FAI, and FIJL through Aragon, Catalonia, and parts of Valencia in the first few months of the war. She described the role of these traveling activists in the process of collectivization:

> When we got to a village, we'd go to the provisional committee of the village and call a general assembly of the entire village. We'd explain our paradise with great enthusiasm. . . . And then there would be a debate— campesino style—questions, discussion, etc. By the next day, they'd begin expropriating land, setting up work groups, etc.
>
> We'd help them form a union or create work groups. Sometimes there would be no one in the village who could read or write, so some of these matters took a bit longer! We'd also make sure they named a delegate to send to the next *comarcal*, or regional, meeting. And we'd go out to the fields to work with them, to show them that we were "regular people," not just outsiders who didn't know anything about this. We were always welcomed with open arms. For those people . . . Barcelona was like God. People would ask us, "Is this the way they do it in Barcelona?" And if the answer was "yes," then that was enough![33]

On a collective in Lérida (about 175 kilometers west of Barcelona) called "Adelante!" expropriation of a few relatively large landholdings made collective members of those who had previously worked those lands as laborers or sharecroppers. Land was widely distributed in the Lérida area. Many people had some small plot of their own; few had extensive holdings. Although the properties expropriated to form the collective were not the largest holdings, they did represent properties of some significance.[34] Only a few of those who joined the collective, however, had been members of the CNT prior to the war. It was apparently their initiative which led to the establishment of the collective in October 1936.[35]

In Aragón, where patterns of landholding were different, the process of collectivization also differed. There, it was often the case that small landholders formed collectives by pooling land they had always worked. The collectives formed in this manner either left surrounding large land owners to themselves, "relieved" them of all their property beyond what was needed to support themselves and their families, or forced them to join the collective. In some areas of Aragón, most of those joining collectives had owned little property at all in the prewar period. A list of those entering collectives in the vicinity of Gelsa, for example, indicates that the majority of those who affiliated were sharecroppers who owned little or no property of their own.[36] Not surprisingly, the process and outcome of collectivization varied with the town and with the proximity of CNT-led militia units. While testimonies vary on the question of how much force was used in the creation of collectives, even many anarchist militants acknowledged that the march of CNT militias through an area helped create an "atmosphere" favorable to collectivization.[37] Susan Harding highlights the ambiguities:

> Anarchist collectivization in wartime was an intensely and inescapably contradictory experience. Most Aragonese villages contained a nucleus of supporters for the anarchist revolution, and many villagers joined collectives eagerly. . . . On the other hand, many villagers participated unwillingly in collectives and, for all, the climate of coercion created by the executions and threat of executions made real choice impossible.[38]

In Valencia, with the exception of a few communities with a long history of CNT militancy, the situation was similar to that in Catalonia. In the weeks after the threat of rebellion had dissipated (in Valencia, troops had remained in their barracks, loyal to the Republic), both the UGT and the CNT initiated efforts to collectivize latifundial land and land abandoned by owners disloyal to the Republic. But there were few latifundial estates, and relatively little of the cultivated land in the region was owned by "disloyalists." Nevertheless, through the initiative of the CNT, agricultural laborers in many villages took control of the land they worked and attempted to establish collectives. As it did in Aragón and in the central region, the CNT set up regional federations to assist the individual collectives with production and coordination. But even the federations had their limits. Aurora Bosch has argued, for example, that all too few CNT leaders and activists in the area had any idea what collectivization was about. Many collectives were little more than producers' and consumers' cooperatives.[39] Among the collectives that functioned effectively was one called "El Porvenir" [the future] in Tabernes de Valldigna, where Pura Pérez Arcos was to live during the last months of the war.

Regardless of the way in which the collectives began, work was usually done in groups on a cooperative basis. In smaller collectives, all workers gathered daily to discuss what work needed to be done and how to allocate tasks. In larger collectives, representatives of each work group would gather at regular intervals. General assemblies of the collective met on a weekly, biweekly, or monthly basis, and they took up issues ranging from hours and wages to the distribution of food and clothing.[40]

The achievements of these collectives were extensive. In many areas they maintained, if not increased, agricultural production, often introducing new patterns of cultivation and fertilization. In Valencia, the UGT and CNT together formed CLUEA (The Unified Levantine Council for Agricultural Exports), which collectivized the orange export industry, the country's largest source of foreign exchange. Although its operations were limited by the exigencies of war, lack of experience on the part of the workers who were running it, and the closing down of foreign markets, it did coordinate both production and export in a major agricultural industry. Elsewhere, collectivists built chicken coops, barns, and other facilities for the care and feeding of the community's animals. Federations of collectives coordinated the construction of roads, schools, bridges, canals, and dams. Some of these remain to this day as lasting contributions of the collectives to the infrastructure of rural Spain.[41] The collectivists also arranged for the transfer of surplus produce from wealthier collectives to those experiencing shortages, either directly from village to village or through mechanisms set up by regional committees. The redistribution thus effected was not total: transportation and communication were often lacking, and commitment to the process was far from unanimous. But, as Felix Carrasquer reported, consciousness-raising was a continuing process:

> There were, of course, those who didn't want to share and who said that each collective should take care of itself. But they were usually convinced in the assemblies. We would try to speak to them in terms they understood. We'd ask, "Did you think it was fair when the *cacique* [local boss] let people starve if there wasn't enough work?" And they said, "Of course not." They would eventually come around. Don't forget, there were three hundred thousand collectivists, but only ten thousand of us had been members of the CNT. We had a lot of educating to do.[42]

The problem was not a simple one. Except in those areas that had had some prior experience with *comunismo libertario*, collectivization represented a marked change from former ways of organizing life, and many laborers evidently had difficulty adjusting to the new system. *Solidaridad Obrera, Nuevo Aragón, Acracia, Castilla Libre,* and other CNT-operated newspapers ran articles discussing the functioning of collectives, appealing to the rural petit bourgeoisie not to be afraid of the revolution and to laborers not to hang on to old ways of doing things, no matter how familiar they might be.[43]

In general, and not surprisingly, rural collectives were somewhat more successful than industrial collectives in achieving the anarchist goal of equality, at least with respect to wages. There seem to have been two major pay schemes. One was to pay all collectivists a set amount per day. The other was the so-called family wage, which adjusted the amount of the wage to the size of the family in an approximation to the communist-anarchist goal of "to each according to his need."

Some collectives paid all workers the same wage, regardless of the type of work done. Those of Monzón and Miramel in Aragon, for example, paid men and women equally. But most collectives set fairly significant differentials between wages paid to women and those paid to men.[44] Even the family wage systems incorporated this unequal valuation of labor. "Adelante!" (in Lerida) and "El Porvenir" (in Valencia), for example, paid wages to the "family head" scaled according to the number, sex, and ages of people in the family. The head of family in "El Porvenir" received 4 pesetas per day for himself; 1.50 for his compañera; 0.75 for each child over ten; and 0.50 for each of those under ten.[45] Some collectives in Aragón operated with a combination of these two systems. In Fraga, for example, women who worked outside the home in the traditionally feminine task of tending and packing figs received the same daily wage for their work as did men. During those months when they "simply kept house, or kept up the family plot," they were not paid. The family wage paid to the husband or father was said to reflect their contribution indirectly.[46]

In addition, a traditional sexual division of labor seems to have prevailed in the distribution of work within the collective. The minutes of the Lérida collective, for example, suggest a widespread acceptance of the proposition that norms for women's work should be different from those for men's.[47] Evidence from other collectives reveals similar expectations. Everywhere, domestic chores fell automatically to women. And, except on small or very poor collectives, women worked outside the home only under unusual circumstances, such as the harvest, when all hands possible were needed.[48]

Finally, a traditional sexual division of labor also seems to have prevailed in the nature and extent of participation in leadership and decision making within the collectives. Both the minutes of "Adelante!" and interviews with male anarchists from other collectives suggest that women's involvement in communal decision making was rather limited. Given the devaluation of women's worth, such reports should not necessarily be taken as indicative of the levels of women's participation. Nevertheless, a number of women also reported that women were often silent in meetings—a silence they attributed to the fact that most women had had little experience in public speaking. As we will see, this was to be yet another concern that Mujeres Libres would address.

It is, of course, possible that, then as now, women did much and received little or no recognition for it. Soledad Estorach reported that there were some collectives in Aragón where the first delegates to the village committee were women. Why? Because men were often away from home for long periods, tending the flocks. Those who actually kept the villages going on a day-to-day basis were the women. From all reports, however, the leadership of women in these villages represented an exception to the general pattern, rather than the rule.

Still, the collectives had accomplished a great deal. Women participated actively in some rural collectives, and even took positions of responsibility in them. Degrees of personal freedom increased dramatically. In a significant number of areas, formal marrige ended, even if the nuclear family remained in the norm.[49] Working-class women began to act autonomously.

### Political Consolidation and Counter-Revolution

No account of the social revolution would be complete without a consideration of the political context in which it took place—both international and domestic—and the impact of changes in that context on the course of the revolution itself. I noted above that the rebellion marked the effective collapse of official governmental power. In the major republican strongholds, victorious workers' organizations quickly took responsibility for the establishment of public order. In most cities, formal institutions of government were replaced by Antifascist Militia Committees, consisting of representatives of the various parties and worker's organizations active in the community. What resulted was an attempt to reflect in *political* institutions the unity of purpose and of struggle that had been experienced in the streets.

Still, the political transformation was not total. While these committees took over the formal direction of communal life at the local level, preexisting institutions were not always totally destroyed. In Catalonia, for example, the Generalitat (the autonomous Catalan government) continued to function as the region's formal government, while popular forces organized the Central Committee of Antifascist Militias of Catalonia, with representatives from socialist, communist, and regionalist republican political parties, and the major working-class organizations, including the UGT and CNT, in numbers roughly proportional to their support in the population.[50] (The comparable institution in Aragon was the Consejo de Aragon, and in Valencia, Comité Ejecutivo Popular. In Aragón, however, unlike Catalonia or Valencia, there was no other formal governmental structure. The revolutionary committee ruled the region throughout the Civil War.) Nevertheless, this brief period of "dual power" ultimately allowed time for the reconsolidation of power in the hands of the government.[51]

These political shifts were heavily influenced by the international context of the Spanish Civil War. The war began in the summer of 1936, when Hitler had already established himself in power in Germany, and it ended in the spring of 1939, shortly before Germany's invasion of Poland marked the official outbreak of World War II. Those countries which could have been expected to be the natural allies of Republican Spain—England, France (which had its own Popular Front government), and the United States—adopted a policy of "neutrality," fearful of offending Hitler and Mussolini or of supporting the "Red" Spanish government. They refused not only to sell arms to the Republic, but refused even to allow trade in any materials that might be of strategic use. This policy was implemented with notable inconsistency: Franco's "nationalist" government somehow managed to purchase oil and gasoline from U.S. oil companies despite the embargo, for example. Meanwhile, although Hitler and Mussolini had also signed the "Nonintervention Treaty" in August 1936, they made it clear that they had no intention of abiding by its provisions. Over the years, they supplied arms, war materiél, troops, and massive air support to the rebel side (the most notable example of the latter being the Luftwaffe air raid on the Basque town of Guernica). The Republic was effectively isolated and abandoned. But for the support of the Soviet Union and Mexico, beginning in October 1936, it would probably have fallen to the rebels before the end of that year.[52]

Nevertheless, while Soviet aid may have been crucial in allowing the resistance to continue, it also affected the course of the social revolution and of the Civil War itself. Stalin actively supported the Popular Front strategy in an effort to build an alliance with the capitalist West against the fascists. Hence, it was in his interest to play down (if not to repress) the revolutionary aspect of the Spanish Civil War and to represent it to the West as a simple war of democracy against fascism.

As the war dragged on, and the support of the USSR became ever more central to the Republic, the influence of the Spanish Communist party (which had had a mere three thousand members at the outbreak of the war) over Republican policy grew. The *politics* of the Popular Front—defined as winning the war and defending the democratic republic—came increasingly to replace, and then to dominate, the worker-based revolutionary alliances. The PCE (Spanish Communist party) and PSUC (the Catalan Communist party) became the representatives of the petty bourgeoisie and small peasantry against the revolutionary workers' organizations. Very early, they adopted an explicitly counterrevolutionary policy, opposing popular militias and collectives and advocating the protection of private property.[53]

Libertarian movement organizations struggled to resist these policies, but the pressure was intense. As early as September 1936, the CNT was emphasizing the importance of antifascist unity. In a radio address in Madrid, for example, Federica Montseny declared, "Now we are neither socialists, nor anarchists, nor republicans, we are all antifascists, since we all know what fascism represents."[54] Toward the end of that month, three CNT members joined the Council of the Generalitat of Catalonia, which now had representatives of all the workers' organizations as well as political parties, and a few days later, the Central Committee of Antifascist Militias dissolved itself. Joining a political body, of course, was a clear deviation from traditional anarchist principles. *Solidaridad Obrera* justified the move in terms of the necessities of war: "In a war, there must be direction. A committee must be created that will be solely responsible for actions of a military character. And by the side of military technicians there must coexist a council that takes responsibility for assuring that all workers do their assigned tasks."[55]

Throughout October, *Solidaridad Obrera* issued repeated calls for the creation of a national defense council that would unite all the antifascist forces in a nongovernmental body. A politics of parties, they argued, would not be adequate for the task confronting them.[56] But the calls met with no positive response from Largo Caballero, the Socialist leader who was then prime minister. Finally, pressured to join the government or to lose access to arms and the coordination of the struggle, the CNT gave in.

Representatives of the CNT and FAI joined the government of Largo Caballero on November 2 (accepting four ministerial positions) in exchange for promises of arms to Catalonia and in hopes of preserving revolutionary gains. Emma Goldman shared the concerns of most non-Spanish anarchists about the implications of the move. She wrote to Rudolf Rocker, for example, that the move "far from having helped [has] injured our comrades and their work beyond belief."[57] In fact, as Goldman feared, the anarchists began to lose ground almost immediately, as the antirevolutionary forces gained ever more control over government policy, both locally and nationally. On October 24, 1936, the Generalitat issued a "Decree of Collectivizations and Worker Control," formally designed to "normalize" the collectivizations. Effectively, it limited the power of worker control committees. By November, representatives of the collectivized gas and electrical power industry were complaining that the Generalitat had forbidden the Central Committee of Workers' Control to withdraw any funds without the prior authorization of the Generalitat.[58] By December 1936, the popular militias were militarized; soon stringent controls were set on industrial and agricultural collectives, limiting the extent of worker control. As Emma Goldman noted, the anarchists were caught in the dilemma of either attempting to impose their will (as in a dictatorship) or participating in the government—both "reprehensible" options. Participation seemed the lesser evil.[59]

Within a few short months, political concerns overcame revolutionary aims, and the political alliance effectively defeated the revolutionary one. In Barcelona, Communist-led forces took the initiative against anarchists and the POUM in what became known as the "May events" of 1937, attacking the CNT-controlled central telephone building and arresting (and "disappearing") major POUM leaders. The CNT ministers took to the airwaves, urging their followers to lay down their arms so as not to give the Communists and the government a justification for further violence. But theirs was, at best, a temporary holding action; they did not have the power to reverse the direction of policy. Later that week, all four ministers resigned in protest.

The government then took on an increasingly counterrevolutionary role. It imposed constraints on many industrial collectives, limiting worker control in the name of war production. In August, Communist-dominated troops, led by Enrique Lister, marched through the Aragon countryside in an effort to reverse collectivization and restore lands to their "original" owners. Soon the government adopted an explicit policy of "war first, revolution afterwards."[60] Although many collectives continued in operation until they were overrun by Franco's troops at the conclusion of the war, the May events of 1937 marked the effective end of the expansive period of the social revolution. The sense that "the world was in our hands" had clearly come to an end.

Historians and former participants continue to debate the validity of the opposing anarchist and Communist positions on war and/or revolution. Many of those sympathetic to the revolutionary forces have suggested that the PCE policy of militarization and centralization—putting the war first and foremost—undermined working people's enthusiasm for the struggle and left them feeling as though there were little to fight for. Goldman put what she termed the Communist "betrayal" in the starkest terms: "I only know I must cry out against the murderous gang directed from Moscow that is not only trying to squeeze the life out of the revolution and the CNT-FAI. It has and is deliberately sabotaging the antifascist front. I do not know of any other such instance of betrayal. Judas betrayed only Christ. The Communists have betrayed a whole people."[61]

Others have criticized the CNT policy of collaboration with the government, and suggested that any effort to fight a revolutionary war by conventional means was doomed to failure. Anarchists and others should have engaged in guerrilla warfare, rather than accepting the PCE policy of militarization.[62] Much of her private correspondence suggests that Emma Goldman was sympathetic to such criticisms of the CNT, although she publicly defended its actions as the best of the "reprehensible" choices available. In fact, she wrote often to comrades in Europe and the United States, urging them to temper their public criticisms of CNT policy.[63] Interestingly, Mariano Vázquez and Pedro Herrera (heads of the CNT and FAI, respectively), wrote to her in January 1938, asking that she tone down her own criticisms of the behavior of the Communist party and the government: "To talk always about the bad attitude and actions of the communists and the Negrín government," they wrote, may create "an atmosphere of indifference. . . . The international proletariat will ask itself: 'Why should we give aid to the Spanish antifascists if its government engages in persecutions . . . worse than any other bourgeois government?' "[64]

Finally, those sympathetic to the PCE position have argued that the odds against the Republic were so great that the POUM-CNT-Left Socialist position of revolution *and* war was fanciful: it was necessary to mobilize all resources for the war if there was to be any hope of defeating the rebel forces.[65] In fact, at the end of the war, Vázquez wrote to Emma Goldman that, if the CNT had committed any mistake, it was that of being "too revolutionary." "If, on the 19th of July, instead of the collectives and the Revolution, we had concentrated on a bourgeois Republic, international Capitalism would not have been frightened and, instead, would have decided to aid the Republic. . . . Precisely what was needed was not to make the Revolution before winning the war."[66]

Nevertheless, it is far from clear that the counterrevolutionary policy of the PCE and the government made the definitive difference in the actual outcome of the war. In fact, none of these positions gives sufficient weight to the international context. Franco and the rebels could count both on the direct support of Hitler and Mussolini and on the indirect support of the United States, Britain, and France, which refused to intervene on the side of the Republic and looked the other way when domestic corporations sold strategic goods to the rebels. On the Republican side, Soviet aid was, of course, crucial. But even aside from the price the Republicans paid for it—in strategic or in monetary terms—it could not match the aid pouring into the rebel camp. In many respects, the Spanish Civil War was effectively decided in the international arena, though it was the Spanish people who bore the physical and emotional brunt of the fighting—and of the years of repression that followed.[67]

In sum, revolution and war offered women and men dramatically new opportunities for social participation, in many cases contributing to a vastly broader sense of their own capabilities and of the possibilities of social change. Nevertheless, the long-term effects of the war itself undermined many of these gains. In addition to the shortages of food and raw materials, and the economic and social dislocations caused by the war, the continuing "civil war within a civil war" set limits to the social revolution.

Especially in the early months of the war, many organizations and individuals envisioned the creation of a truly revolutionary, egalitarian society. Those goals animated the activities of anarchist movement organizations in general and of Mujeres Libres in particular. But the wartime situation also constrained what they would be able to accomplish. In the remaining chapters, I explore how Mujeres Libres developed out of this larger revolutionary context and, in turn, both shaped and was shaped by it.

# IV

## THE FOUNDING OF
## MUJERES LIBRES

Social revolutionary activity reached its peak in antifascist Spain in the first months of the Civil War, flourishing in ground that had been prepared by the anarchist and socialist movements during the preceding seventy years. Mujeres Libres was born of that preparation and of the social turmoil of the Republic. Although the national federation was not formed officially until 1937, a journal first appeared in May 1936. Publication of the journal was preceded by over two years of active organizing among anarchist women, particularly in Madrid, Barcelona, and their surrounding areas. The founders of Mujeres Libres were all militants in the anarcho-syndicalist movement. Yet they found the existing organizations of that movement inadequate to address the specific problems confronting them as women, whether in the movement itself or in the larger society. This chapter explores their experiences in the movement, in preliminary organizing efforts, and in establishing an organization to struggle directly for women's emancipation.

### The Anarcho-Syndicalist Movement and
### the Subordination of Women

All those compañeros, however radical they may be in cafés, unions, and even affinity groups [FAI], seem to drop their costumes as lovers of female liberation at the doors of their homes. Inside, they behave with their compañeras just like common "husbands."[1]

Despite the strong attachments and sense of community that women activists developed through their involvement in unions, ateneos, and youth groups, even the most activist women reported that their male friends did not always treat them with respect. Experiences varied, but the message was the same: for all their commitment to equality, the boys/men would not treat the girls/women as their equals. "It's true that we have struggled together," Enriqueta recalled saying to her male comrades in the Juventudes and the ateneo, "but you are always the leaders, and we are always the followers. Whether in the streets or at home. We are little better than slaves!"[2]

Those women who were active members of CNT unions or who participated in ateneos or in FIJL groups were always a minority. Their efforts to incorporate other women into the activist core never seemed to get very far, whether because of the sexism of the men, the diffidence of the women, or some combination of the two. A few of their stories may help to recall the atmosphere of the time.

Azucena Fernandez Barba, granddaughter of Abelardo Saavedra, had grown up in a household with two parents deeply committed to the movement. She and her sisters and brother helped found the ateneo Sol y Vida in Barcelona. But, as she reported her experiences, "inside their own homes, [men] forgot completely about women's struggle":

> It's the same as—to use an analogy—a man who is obsessed with playing cards. They go out to play cards, and they do it regardless of what's going on in the house. The same with us, only it wasn't cards, but ideas. . . . They struggled, they went out on strike, etc. But inside the house, worse than nothing. I think we should have set an example with our own lives, lived differently in accordance with what we said we wanted. But no, [for them] the struggle was outside. Inside the house, [our desires] were purely utopian.[3]

Pepita Carpena, who had long been active with the CNT and Juventudes in Barcelona, described one of her experiences with a compañero from Juventudes that was typical of many I heard:

> I'll tell you a story because, for me, what has always been my saving grace is that I'm very outgoing, and I'm not bashful about responding to people who give me a hard time. . . . One time, a compañero from the Juventudes came over to me and said, "You, who say you're so liberated. You're not so liberated." (I'm telling you this so you'll see the mentality of these men.) "Because if I would ask you to give me a kiss, you wouldn't."
>
> I just stood there staring at him, and thinking to myself, "How am I going to get out of this one?" And then I said to him, "Listen, when I want to go to bed with a guy, I'm the one that has to choose him. I don't go to bed with just anyone. You don't interest me as a man. I don't feel anything for you. . . . Why should you want me to 'liberate myself,' as you put it, by going to bed with you? That's no liberation for me. That's just making love simply for the sake of making love. No," I said to him, "love is something that has to be like eating: if you're hungry, you eat, and if you want to go to bed with a guy, then . . . Besides, I'm going to tell you something else. Perhaps you'll get angry at me." (This I did just to get at

him, no?) "Your mouth doesn't appeal to me. . . . And I don't like to make love with a guy without kissing him."

He was left speechless! But I did it with a dual purpose in mind . . . because I wanted to show him that that's not the way to educate compañeras. . . . That's what the struggle of women was like in Spain—even with men from our own group—and I'm not even talking about what it was like with other guys.[4]

The claim that concern with male-female equality did not carry over well into intimate personal relationships was widespread among the women with whom I spoke. But what bothered many of them equally was that many men did not seem to take women seriously even in more "public/political" contexts. Pura Pérez Benavent Arcos, for example, who had attended the rationalist school run by Puig Elías in the barriada of El Clot in Barcelona and joined Juventudes there, noted that when girls went to meetings of the Juventudes, the boys would often laugh at them even before they spoke! Pura got to know Soledad Estorach in Barcelona and told her of her experiences. Soledad apparently wouldn't believe how bad it was and went herself—only to be laughed at in similar ways.[5]

These attitudes and behaviors reflected some of the variety of views on women's proper place in society and in a revolutionary movement that had been developed over time within the Spanish anarchist movement. As we have seen, these views ranged from a Proudhonian acceptance of women's secondary status to a Bakuninist insistence that women were the equals of men and ought to be treated as such in all social institutions. Although the latter position had been adopted by the Spanish anarchist movement as early as 1872, women's actual contributions to the social struggle were rarely acknowledged, and the CNT was lax, at best, in its efforts to organize women workers. The situation was worse at home. Virtually all of my informants lamented that, no matter how militant even the most committed anarchists were in the streets, they expected to be "masters" in their homes—a complaint echoed in many articles written in movement newspapers and magazines during this period.

Apparently, the belief that woman's proper role was to be mother and wife was shared by at least some anarchist women. Matilde Piller, for example, writing in *Estudios* in 1934, argued that woman's emancipation was incompatible with her role as mother: "One cannot be a good mother—in the strict sense of the term—and a good lawyer or chemist at the same time. . . . Perhaps one can be an intellectual and a woman at the same time. But a mother? No."[6] That view was surely a common one among men. In 1935, for example, in an article lamenting the lack of interest by women in their own emancipation (and defending the movement against women's claims that it was not doing enough to address women's subordination), Montuenga asserted that "woman . . . will always be the beautiful side of life, and that is what . . . she ought to be: the lovable compañera, who fortifies and soothes us in the struggle of life, and a loving mother to our children."[7]

Nevertheless, the official view of the CNT was that women were the equals of men and ought to be treated that way in the home and in the movement. The Zaragoza Congress of May 1936 clearly articulated the egalitarian position. In the "Dictamen sobre 'Concepto confederal del comunismo libertario,'" the most complete spelling out of the con- structive vision of the CNT at that time, we find, "since the first goal of the libertarian revolution consists in assuring the economic indepen- dence of all people, without distinction by sex, the interdependence (in the sense of economic inferiority) created between men and women under the capitalist system will disappear with it [capitalism] . . . [in a libertarian communist society] the two sexes will be equal, both in rights and in obligations."[8]

However, acceptance of the view that women were exploited econom- ically, and that women's subordination ought to be a focus of anarchist revolutionary attention, did not signify agreement about the nature of the exploitation or how it would best be overcome. Many argued that women should contribute to their emancipation by supporting male revolutionaries. Some, probably reflective of the majority within the movement, denied that women were oppressed in ways that required particular attention. Federica Montseny acknowledged that "the eman- cipation of women" was "a critical problem of the present time." But she argued that women's oppression was a manifestation of cultural factors (including women's poor sense of self) that would not be re- solved through organizational struggle.[9] Paralleling the arguments of Emma Goldman, she insisted on the *internal* nature of the struggle: only when women came to respect *themselves* would they be able to effec- tively demand respect from men. She agreed with other anarchist writ- ers, both male and female, that the appropriate goal was not equality with men under the present system, but a restructuring of society that would liberate all. "Feminism? Never! Humanism always!"[10]

Feminism, of course, represented yet another perspective on how best to achieve equality for women. Although feminism was quite late in taking root in Spain (the first independent feminist organization, the Asociación Nacional de Mujeres Españolas, was not founded until 1918 and had little, if any, impact on working-class women),[11] feminist analyses of women's subordination and strategies for emancipation attracted a great deal of critical attention from anarchists. Federica Montseny was perhaps the most outspoken Spanish anarchist critic of feminism. Feminism, she argued, advocated equality for women, but did not challenge existing institutions: "Its only ambition is to give to women of a particular class the opportunity to participate more fully in the existing system of privilege." Privileges were unjust, however, and "if they are unjust when men take advantage of them, they will still be unjust if women take advantage of them."[12]

Furthermore, Spanish feminists had claimed (along with feminists elsewhere) that women were more peaceful than men and that, given the opportunity, they would govern more justly than men. But Montseny and other Spanish anarchists roundly criticized this perspective: "Neither cruelty nor sweetness is the patrimony of one sex. . . . The force of authority and domination makes men haughty and irritable. And the same causes will produce the same results [in women]."[13] Women were not by nature more peace-loving than men, any more than men were by nature more aggressive than women. Both temperaments were the products of social conditioning. The only way to end the domination of men over women was as part of a larger struggle to end all forms of domination. Feminism was too narrowly focused as a strategy for women's emancipation; sexual struggle could not be separated from class struggle or from the anarchist project as a whole.

A small minority within the movement as a whole also argued that women faced sex-specific forms of subordination that needed particular attention. Many of these (both men and women) insisted that the struggle to overcome that subordination had begun to be addressed within the CNT, FAI, Juventudes, ateneos, and other movement organizations, and that the struggle needed to continue in those contexts. Those who held this view interpreted the movement's commitment to direct action and spontaneous order to mean that, since it was in these organizations that the dilemmas were experienced, these organizations were the places in which the struggles could best be worked through to their logical conclusion. Thus, Igualdad Ocaña, who was well aware of the ways women's contributions had been devalued within movement organizations, nevertheless insisted that "we are engaged in the work of creating a new society, and that work must be done in unison. We should be engaged in union struggles, along with men, fighting for our places, *demanding* to be taken seriously."[14] They opposed separate organizations for women to address such problems, and found support for their position in the anarchist emphasis on the unity of means and ends.

Those who opposed autonomous women's organizations argued that anarchism was incompatible not just with hierarchical forms of organization, but with any independent organization that might undermine the unity of the movement. Since the aim of the anarchist movement was the creation of an egalitarian society in which men and women would interact as equals, the struggle to achieve it should engage men and women together as equal partners. They feared that an organization devoted specifically to ending the subordination of women would emphasize differences between men and women rather than their similarities, and would make it more difficult to achieve an egalitarian revolutionary end.

### Organizing Women: First Steps

Slowly, women in a variety of movement contexts began to discuss the specific subordination of women within the movement and to take steps toward organizing to overcome it. In some Catalan industrial villages, women's groups began forming even in the last years of the dictatorship. In Terrassa, for example, a group of women workers, all of whom were members of the clandestine CNT textile workers' union there (the CNT was illegal during the dictatorship of Primo de Rivera), began meeting in 1928 in the *centro cultural y cooperativista* of the FAI. Their purpose was to become comfortable with speaking in a group and to discuss among themselves those issues (work or salaries, for example) that they might wish to raise in union assemblies. It was as a result of these meetings, reported Teresina Torrelles, a member of the group, that the union included in its demands, as early as 1931, the right of women to equal salary with men for equal work and eight weeks of paid maternity leave. Although this group hardly had the resources to "prepare" women fully, it did contribute a great deal to working women's *ideological* development. When the war and revolution began in 1936, the women of Terrassa were ready to act: they set up a clinic and a school for nurses in the first days of the struggle.[15]

In Barcelona, a group known as the Grupo Cultural Femenino, CNT, began to form late in 1934 in the aftermath of the abortive October revolution.[16] This organization brought together women involved in CNT unions in order to foster a sense of solidarity and to enable them to take more active roles in the union and in the movement. Lucía Sánchez Saornil, a writer and poet, and Mercedes Comaposada, a lawyer, undertook a similar task in Madrid. Lucía had been active in movement circles in Barcelona and had the idea to start an organization to educate women. She took the idea to a number of unions, but they seemed totally uninterested. So she left Barcelona and went to Madrid, where she met Mercedes Comaposada.[17]

Mercedes herself had begun her initiation into leftist politics at an early age. Her father had migrated to Barcelona from rural Aragon in his early teems to escape extreme poverty, learn a trade, and find a job. He became a shoemaker, but mostly he was a "cultural worker." He taught himself French and German, and was the Spanish correspondent for *L'Humanité*. Mercedes recalled that he would get up at 4 or 5 A.M. to study, and would tease his children by asking them how they could sleep so long. There were always people in and out of the house: "My poor mother was a victim. . . . She had no control over who would be there or when."

His activities, and his example, left a deep impression on her: "My father, who was a Socialist, left me with a very strong sense of humanity. I went to an *escuela graduada,* which was very special at the time. I had a wonderful teacher. One day, the teacher took me aside and said, 'Some day you'll hear that your father is in jail. I want you to know that if he is, it is *not* because he's a thief, but because he really cares about workers!' "

Mercedes learned to type when she was twelve, and she went to work for a film company, where she learned editing and mounting. "They were all in the CNT, so I joined, too. My first union card was in the cinema!" During 1916–1917, she studied in Madrid. It was then, apparently, that she began taking conscious note of the plight of women, as well as of working people: "I was living in Madrid, where the condition of women was *very* bad—much worse than in Catalonia. And I was very impressed with the CNT. It was so direct, so sensible. And they were working with a proletariat that was—if you'll excuse the expression, I don't mean it in a derogatory way—less prepared than that of the UGT. So I joined."

In 1933, while she was studying law in Madrid, Mercedes was invited by Orobón Fernández to teach the workers. At that meeting, which Lucía Sánchez Saornil also attended, Mercedes was confronted by the negative ways in which even CNT militants viewed women. She and Lucía were both frustrated and appalled.[18]

> Lucía and I left and went outside. We had an immediate understanding. For months, we'd meet along the Parque del Retiro, sit on the benches, talk, walk some more, etc. Then, in 1935, we started sending out notices. Lucía was working for the railway union and had access to a list of all the anarcho-syndicalist–affiliated "women's groups" (both those operating within unions and those outside). We wrote to all the groups on that list, and to any others we knew of. We asked them what issues were important to them, what they'd like to hear about, etc. And of course, our great joy was the responses. They were enthusiastic; they came from all over, including Asturias, the Basque country, Andalusia . . . and there were always more.[19]

These two women, together with Amparo Poch y Gascón, were to be the initiators of Mujeres Libres and the editors of its journal. Although they differed in personal style and background, all were deeply committed both to the movement and to the enculturation of women. In fact, all were educated women—a characteristic that distinguished them from the overwhelming majority of their Spanish sisters—and they sought ways to share the fruits of that education with other women. At eighty-eight years of age, Mercedes still exudes a desire to educate and to communicate the value and the breadth of culture and the possibilities available to women.

As for Lucía Sánchez Saornil (who disappeared somewhat mysteriously after the war), virtually everyone recalled her as a real firebrand. She was a small woman with a powerful presence as an orator, who reminded them—physically and in personality—of Louise Michel, the heroine of the Paris Commune. Although she was very diffident, Lucía possessed a rare ability as a speaker and organizer. She was always the one to sum up discussions in meetings, and she had a real authority about her, without being authoritarian.

The third member of the trio was the physician, Amparo Poch y Gascón. Mercedes recalled that, while she and Lucía always saw eye to eye politically, Amparo was a bit different. She had been a *treintista*, a member of the more reformist faction of the CNT, which separated from the mainstream of the organization in 1932. The two groups were reunited just before the war began.[20] But she, too, was a woman of enormous energy with an extraordinary capacity for work. Soledad lamented, in fact, that she never got to know Amparo very well and has little recall of her face because, on those few occasions when she saw her, Amparo had her head buried in work![21] A physician, committed to breaking through the barriers of shame and ignorance about sexuality that had long kept women subordinate, she had written many educational articles and pamphlets advocating greater sexual freedom for women and challenging monogamy and the sexual double standard. Apparently, she lived out those beliefs. One of her co-workers recalled with a smile that, along with her capacity for work, Amparo had a tremendous capacity for love. She had had many lovers (sometimes, they thought, more than one at a time!) and often teased others about being sexually monogamous: "Don't you get bored," Amparo would ask, "of always breaking bread with the same person?"

Lucía and Mercedes were instrumental in beginning Mujeres Libres in Madrid. Amparo joined them on the editorial board of *Mujeres Libres* and later became active in Barcelona as the director of Mujeres Libres' education and training institute, the Casal de la Dona Treballadora. All three were spurred to action by their prior experiences in male-dominated organizations of the anarcho-syndicalist movement. But the groundwork for the organization was also being laid by women around the country, many of whom were virtually unaware of one another's existence.

In Barcelona, for example, Soledad Estorach, who was active both in her ateneo and in the CNT, had also found existing movement organizations inadequate to engage women workers on equal terms with men.

> In Catalonia, at least, the dominant position was that men and women should both be involved. But the problem was that the men *didn't know*

*how* to get women involved as activists. Both men and most women thought of women in a secondary status. For most men, I think, the ideal situation would be to have a compañera who did not oppose their ideas, but whose private life would be more or less like other women. *They* wanted to be activists twenty-four hours a day—and in that context, of course, it's impossible to have equality. . . . Men got so involved that the women were left behind, almost of necessity. Especially, for example, when he would be taken to jail. Then she would have to take care of the children, work to support the family, visit him in jail, etc. *That,* the compañeras were very good at! But for us, that was not enough. That was not activism![22]

The first anarchist-affiliated women's group began to form in Barcelona late in 1934, building on the experiences that Soledad and other women activists had had with activism in mixed groups. As she reported:

What would happen is that women would come once, maybe even join. But they would never be seen again. So many compañeras came to the conclusion that it might be a good idea to start a separate group for these women. . . . In Barcelona, . . . the movement was very large and very strong. And there were lots of women involved in some branches, in particular—for example, textiles and clothing makers. But even in that union, there were few women who ever spoke. We got concerned about all the women we were losing. Late in 1934 a small group of us started talking about this. In 1935, we sent out a call to all women in the libertarian movement. We couldn't convince the older militants who had places of honor among the men—old-timers such as Federica or Libertad Ródenas—to come along with us, so we focused mainly on the younger compañeras. We called our group Grupo Cultural Femenino, CNT.[23]

The responses to the call in Catalonia were similar to those Mercedes and Lucía received in Madrid—enthusiasm from some and ambivalence from others, both women and men. Many in movement organizations feared the development of a "separatist" group. Others framed their objections in the form of a claim that the women were in danger of falling into "feminism," by which they meant a focus on access to education and professional jobs. These types of issues, of course, had long been the concern of middle-class feminists, in Spain as elsewhere, but they had been rejected by anarchists as irrelevant to the concerns of working-class people, women as well as men, and as reinforcing structures they were committed to overthrowing.

The charge of "feminism" mystified most of these anarchist women. As Soledad explained,

Most of us had never heard of "feminism" before. I didn't know that there were groups of women out there in the world organizing for women's

rights. There were some one or two within our group who had heard of
feminism—they had been to France. But I didn't know that such things
even existed in the world! We didn't import this from elsewhere. We
hadn't even realized it existed.

Knowing that their agenda was not "feminist" in this derogatory sense,
they ignored the criticisms and went about their business as best they
could. Early in 1936, they held a meeting in the Teatro Olimpia, in the
center of Barcelona, to publicize their activities and provide an opportunity for new women to join. Although the meeting was virtually
ignored by the anarchist press, the hall was packed. The gathering
provided the basis for a regional organization that included both various neighborhood associations in Barcelona and organizations from
surrounding towns and villages.

It was not until later in 1936 that the groups in Barcelona and Madrid
discovered one another's existence. Mercedes Comaposada recalled that
Lola Iturbe first mentioned to her that there was a group in Barcelona.
But the person who really got them together was a young man named
Martínez, the compañero of Conchita Liaño (who was later to become
the secretary of the Catalan regional committee of Mujeres Libres).
Martínez told Mercedes she must go to Barcelona to meet "those
women." In September or October, she visited Barcelona and attended
a regional meeting of the Grupo Cultural Femenino to talk about the
work of Mujeres Libres. The groups had begun with somewhat different
foci. The Barcelona group wanted to encourage greater activism on the
part of women who were already members of the CNT, whereas Mujeres
Libres in Madrid wanted, in Mercedes' words, "to develop women who
could taste life in all its fullness. . . . Women with a social conscience,
yes, but also women who could appreciate art, beauty."[24] Nevertheless,
the Catalan women soon recognized their affinities with Mujeres Libres,
and voted at that plenum to affiliate and to change their name to
"Agrupación Mujeres Libres." Thus was begun what was to become a
national federation.

During these early months, the groups engaged in a combination of
consciousness-raising and direct action. They created networks of
women anarchists who attempted to meet the need for mutual support
in union and other movement contexts. They attended meetings with
one another, checking out reports of chauvinist behavior on the part of
their male comrades and strategizing about how to deal with it.

Aside from these forms of mutual support, the most concrete activity
in which the Barcelona group engaged during this period was the
establishment of *guarderías volantes* (flying day-care centers). In their
efforts to involve more women in union activities, they had met repeatedly with the claim that women's child-care responsibilities prevented
them from staying late at work, or going out at night, in order to

participate in meetings. They decided to address this problem by offering child-care services to women who were interested in serving as union delegates. Members of the group went to women's homes to care for children while the mothers went to meetings.

Of course, as Soledad noted with a typical gleam in her eye, the project was not simply designed to provide a service: "When we got there, we'd do some 'propagandizing.' We'd talk to them about comunismo libertario and other subjects. Poor things, they'd be at meetings, and then come home just to get lectured at by us! Sometimes, by then, their husbands would be home, and they'd join in the discussion."[25]

By the time the revolution began in July 1936, both the Grupo Cultural Femenino in Barcelona and Mujeres Libres in Madrid had been meeting for some time. They had established a network of women anarchist activists and had begun their work of consciousness-raising. They were well prepared to participate in the revolutionary events of July and to "retool" to educate themselves and other women for the work of constructing the new society.

### The Organization "Takes Off"

While individual groups were meeting in Catalonia and in Madrid, many of these same women were carrying on further organization in the pages of the anarchist press. *Tierra y Libertad*, *Solidaridad Obrera*, and *Estudios*, in particular, printed numerous articles concerned with "the woman question." Mercedes Comaposada, Amparo Poch y Gascón, and Lucía Sánchez Saornil were frequent contributors.

The debates reached a peak of intensity late in 1935, when Mariano Vázquez, secretary of the CNT, published two articles in *Solidaridad Obrera* on the role of women in the anarcho-syndicalist movement. Lucía Sánchez Saornil responded with a five-part series entitled "La cuestión femenina en nuestros medios" (The woman question in our media), followed by "Resúmen al márgen de la cuestión femenina: Para el compañero M. R. Vázquez" (A summary on the woman question: for Compañero Vázquez), in which she developed the rationale for what was to become *Mujeres Libres*—both the journal and the organization. This exchange merits discussion in some detail here because it set the terms of the debate in the anarchist movement and press at the time of the founding of Mujeres Libres.[26]

Vázquez's initial article seemed sympathetic to the problems women faced within the anarchist movement. It began by asserting that women were historical actors, though they had often been forgotten and their contributions ignored. In contemporary Spain, women were effectively slaves of slaves; men seemed to think they dominated women by right. Why did women allow this, he asked? Because of their economic dependence on men. To overcome it, he said, it would be necessary for women to join together with men to transform society. In struggling to create a new society that would guarantee economic independence to *everyone*, women would also liberate themselves from male tyranny.

Lucía began her response with the claim that most anarcho-syndicalists seemed barely interested in encouraging the full participation of women. Many contexts for organizing women existed: factories, schools, ateneos, homes. That so few women had been recruited to the movement indicated lack of interest on the part of the men. The real propagandizing about women had to be done among men, not among women: "Before you can reform society, you had better reform your homes." Furthermore, those anarcho-syndicalists who did attempt to organize women did so from the point of view of the movement, rather than from that of women.[27] If women were to be recruited into the movement, they had to be approached on their terms, not on men's, and treated as equal and capable comrades.

Later articles developed the theme of what we now term woman's "personhood" and addressed women's economic subordination. Lucía challenged the notion that woman's proper role was mother and wife. Women earned lower salaries than men (and undercut salaries for all workers), she insisted, because men—including men of the CNT—treated them as inferior.[28] In addition to economics, Lucía took on her generation's equivalent of "sociobiology." Women, she argued, had been reduced to *nacer, gestar, morir* (to be born, to be pregnant, to die). "The concept of mother is absorbing that of woman, the function is annihilating the individual." By contrast, she insisted, anarchists ought to recognize that mother is to woman as worker is to man: "For an anarchist, the man always comes before the worker, the woman before the mother. Because, for an anarchist, before and above all is the individual."

The final article in the series addressed the sexual question, chiding anarchist "Don Juans" who seemed to interpret increased sexual freedom as license to dominate women.[29] If anarchist ideas about sexuality and free love were to be communicated to young people—and they certainly should be—that task should be done by people who fully understand their significance and do not use the occasion simply to increase the possibilities of their own sexual conquests.

Meanwhile, on October 10, Vázquez had responded to Lucía's first three articles with his "Avance: Por la elevación de la mujer." While agreeing with her that too many men were tyrants at home, he insisted that women were equally to blame in not claiming their rights. Furthermore, while it might be true that men did not treat women as equals, it was "only human," he argued, to want to hold on to privilege. Men should not be expected to give up their privilege voluntarily, any more than we expect the bourgeoisie to voluntarily cede its power over the proletariat.[30] Just as anarchists had always argued that "the liberation of workers must be the work of the workers themselves," they ought to take up the cry that "the emancipation of women must be the work of women themselves!"[31] In furtherance of this goal, he proposed that *Solidaridad Obrera* should take a cue from the bourgeois press and dedicate one page each week to women.

Lucía's response was sharp. She attacked those anarchist men who seemed to have no patience for women. It was not sufficient to say that "revolution is around the corner, we have no time to organize women." It may be valuable to wait for the revolution, "but it's even better to go in search of it, creating it minute by minute in the minds and hearts of people." "Preparing" women for social revolution is part of making that revolution. The recruitment of women should be a major, and not a secondary, concern of those who wish to bring about the social revolution. But she saved her true fire for Vázquez's analogy of the bourgeois and the proletarian. First, she argued, it was not sufficient to say that "it's only human" for men to want to hold on to their privilege—especially if you are asking women for *their* support! Second, of course, these were not *any* men, they were supposedly anarchist men, committed to equality and nonhierarchy. "It may be 'very human' [for them to want to preserve their privileges], but it can hardly be called 'anarchist'!" Further, the analogy was flawed. The interests of bourgeoisie and proletariat were fundamentally contradictory, but those of men and women were not. "Since they [men and women] are different, their characters complement one another and form a totality together. . . . There will be no harmony in the future life if all of these elements do not enter proportionally into its creation."

In short, what was at stake, she argued, was not simply the emancipation of women, but the creation of a future society for both men and women. In that task, both men and women must participate as equals. Women had already begun to claim their full rights and personhood; it was time for men to recognize the importance of that struggle and to meet women on terms of equality.

Finally, she rejected Vázquez's suggestion that *Solidaridad Obrera* devote a page to women each week, and she stated in print, for the first time, the idea that was to be *Mujeres Libres:* "I am not taking up your suggestion about a women's page in *Solidaridad Obrera*, however interesting it might be, because I have larger ambitions. I have a plan to create an independent journal that would be directed exclusively to the ends you have proposed."

Her vision, which served as a blueprint for Mujeres Libres' activities in the years to follow, obviously struck a responsive chord in her readers. The series of articles, and the letters she and Mercedes sent to activists around the country, generated much support. By April, they had sent notices of the forthcoming appearance of *Mujeres Libres* to the anarchist press as well as to unions, ateneos, and groups of Juventudes around the country, and they had begun the process of organizing supporters to serve as reporters and to take responsibility for distribution of the journal. The letters they received in response from both men and women demonstrated great enthusiasm for the project. Many indicated that they had been waiting for this moment since Lucía's announcement of her plan the previous fall in the pages of *Solidaridad Obrera*.[32] The first issue of *Mujeres Libres*, published on May 20, 1936, was sold out almost immediately. A second issue appeared on June 15. Altogether, fourteen issues were edited, though the last one was at the printer's when the battlefront reached Barcelona, and no copies of it survive.[33]

As the editors described it to potential contributors and subscribers, the journal was to appear monthly, addressed to working-class women—whose education had long been neglected by the movement— aimed at "awakening the female conscience toward libertarian ideas."[34] They saw its mission in both political and cultural terms. Importantly (a matter stressed in virtually every communication), the journal was not to identify itself as anarchist "because of the fears that word could raise among most women in this country. . . . [But it] would take upon itself to initiate them into discussion of social problems and, at the same time, raise their cultural level."[35] Nevertheless, Lucía constantly reminded her correspondents, although the word *anarchist* would not be used, any knowledgeable person reading the journal would easily recognize "the libertarian orientation of all its content."[36]

A number of features of this correspondence seem worthy of mention, particularly since it raised issues that were to be with the journal and the organization throughout the coming years. First, the editors seem to have relied on existing movement networks to spread the word about the forthcoming publication of the journal. Almost all correspondents indicated that they had heard about the journal in the anarchist press or from flyers distributed at union halls, ateneos, or meetings of Juventudes. Many such letters came from men, especially members of local Juventudes, who placed substantial orders from their communities.

Yet, although they may have depended on movement organizations for communication, the editors repeatedly emphasized that they were independent of these organizations, financially and otherwise, and were undertaking this project on their own. Thus, for example, Lucía thanked María Luísa Cobos especially for volunteering help with sales and distribution "because . . . the journal is not receiving subsidy or economic support from anyone, and we are editing it entirely on our own." Often, the pleas took on a tone of greater urgency. Lucía began a letter to compañeros of the Juventudes in Soria by apologizing for the delay in responding to their offer of support and noting that "you can imagine how hard we are working to organize this all by ourselves, without help from anyone."[37]

Not surprisingly, most of the requests for material help went to men and to movement organizations. They were the people who could have been expected to have financial means (however minimal) in Spain at the time. Both men and women volunteered to serve as distributors, using whatever resources they had. For example, Lucía asked Diego Abad de Santillán (a well-known writer and anarchist theorist, member of the regional committee of the CNT and of the editorial board of the anarchist journal, *Tiempos Nuevos*) to use his connections with *Tiempos Nuevos* to arrange for the distribution of *Mujeres Libres* in Barcelona.[38]

They expressed gratitude to men and women, local syndicates and Juventudes from around the country for all the help they had proffered. Some letters, however, also expressed the editors' frustration with the lack of attention from the major anarchist media, particularly *Solidaridad Obrera*—a pattern (support from local groups but not from the major organizations) that was to plague Mujeres Libres throughout its existence. On May 28, 1936, Lucía wrote a sharp letter to the director of *Solidaridad Obrera*, complaining that he had ignored the inaugural issue of *Mujeres Libres*. Although its editors had sent paid announcements of *Mujeres Libres'* appearance, as well as two copies of the first issue, in the hope of receiving a review or at least a mention in the newspaper, the major daily newspaper of the anarcho-syndicalist movement had given them no notice whatsoever.

> We are not, after all, unknown to you; we are compañeras who have been putting what abilities we have at the service of the organization and the idea, and we don't think you've been acting in accordance with [the] solidarity [expected of movement comrades]. In the name of the simple decency to be expected among comrades, since we are working for a common cause, and not for anyone's particular interests, the least you owe us is to tell us if you think our work is not worthwhile—not this absurd silence.[39]

In other respects, however, those early months were a time of great excitement and satisfaction. Mujeres Libres received letters from all around the country—letters written by women who were enthusiastic about the journal though often barely literate themselves. Although Castilian Spanish is almost totally phonetic, many of those letters revealed a lack of familiarity with written language. Many had multiple spelling errors and little sense of proper sentence construction. It seems, from this small sample, at least, that Mujeres Libres *was* reaching those it was directed toward—that is, clearly not the best educated women in Spain.

It is also clear from this correspondence that *Mujeres Libres* was meant to awaken women—and men—to the realities of what women were doing and might do within a larger framework of anarchist understandings of the nature of social change. So, for example, Lucía requested Josefa de Tena, who had agreed to report news from Mérida, to send information about a women's strike in the area. She asked de Tena to provide information about the background, demands, and size of the strike and also to try to get pictures ("one of the interior of a workshop involved in the conflict, another of a group of compañeras, if possible at a meeting").[40] Similarly, in a letter to María Luísa Cobos, outlining what they would like from her as a reporter for Mujeres Libres in Jérez de la Frontera (a town in Andalusia), Lucía noted,

> We have a great interest in fostering mutual understanding between women in cities and in the countryside, providing ways for each to learn about the conditions under which the other lives. To this end, you could send us a report that covers the following points: What is the most important agricultural work in the area, what kinds of labor does it require, at what times of the year are these tasks performed and, very specifically, what roles do women take in each of these tasks?

Again, they requested pictures to accompany the story.[41]

Finally, it is important to note that many of the letters were from men—among them such anarchist luminaries as Eduardo Morales de Guzmán and Mariano Gallardo, both frequent contributors to *Estudios* and outspoken supporters of women's emancipation—who volunteered not just to distribute copies, but to contribute articles. To each, the editors responded that they appreciated the support, but that they had committed themselves to a magazine written and produced entirely by women. To Morales Guzmán, for example, Lucía wrote,

> We received your work, which we are returning to you, because we have adopted the rule that the magazine will be produced exclusively by women. We believe that the orientation of women is something that must be left to . . . women . . . and that however much you [masc. plur.] do, with whatever goodwill—and we recognize that you are among those who have given this most attention and goodwill—you don't manage to find quite the right tone.[42]

Many of these themes and concerns were reflected in the contents of the first issue of the journal, which appeared in May 1936. An editorial introducing the new magazine stated that its aim was "to encourage social action by women, providing [women] a new vision that avoids the contamination of their hearts and minds by masculine errors. By masculine errors, we mean all those current notions of life and relations; [we term them] masculine errors because we reject all responsibility for past events in which woman has not been an actor, but a silent witness." Rather than affixing blame for the past, however, the editors insisted that their concern was with the future. Nor were they interested in a "declaration of war" between the sexes: "No, no. Mutuality of interests, easing of anxieties, eagerness to join in the struggle for a common destiny."

This approach, they insisted, was not "feminism," which would be simply the obverse of the masculinism they opposed. Rather, their goal was an "integral humanism," to be achieved by a proper balance of masculine and feminine elements in society. Not surprisingly, the attempt to articulate just what those "masculine" and "feminine" elements were resulted in some of the same confusions and stereotyping to which many contemporary U.S. feminist analyses have also fallen prey. They went on to argue, for example, that "an excess of the masculine virtues of boldness, roughness, and rigidity has given life that brutal quality by which some are nourished by the hunger and misery of others. . . . Woman's absence from History has resulted in the lack of appropriate understanding, consideration, and feeling, which are her virtues, the counterweight of which would provide the world the stability it so lacks." While the terms were stated somewhat more crudely, the claim that women's behavior was different from men's, and that both perspectives were necessary for a proper balance in the world, has been echoed in our own time by Carol Gilligan, among others; it forms an important part of the arguments of some feminist peace groups, as well as of theorists of the "maternal thinking" school.[43]

The final paragraphs of this editorial validated the editors' claims that the content of the journal would be clearly libertarian. The editors stated that *Mujeres Libres* aimed to make woman's voice heard and "to prevent woman, who yesterday was subject to the tyranny of religion, from opening her eyes and falling victim to another tyranny—no less refined, and even more brutal— . . . that of politics." The analysis reads almost like a primer in the anarchist approach to social change, asserting, for example, that politics—and all power—corrupts, and offering as an alternative the strategy of direct action: "MUJERES LIBRES strives for this ultimate end by the free and direct action of multitudes and individuals. We must build the new world by proceeding in new ways."

Articles in the journal addressed the stated intentions of the editors. This first issue presented articles offering a mix of cultural and political commentary, as well as pieces on child care, health, and fashion. All assumed an audience of working-class women, aware of their class position and of the social and economic disabilities that characterized it. And each assumed that readers would want to know both how to operate within that context and how to change it. In short, the orientation of the journal was neither to deny class differences nor to encourage resignation to them. Whatever the subject at hand, articles pointed out possible routes to change at both the individual and the communal levels.

A number of the pieces were explicitly political commentaries: a letter from Emma Goldman describing the openness of Welsh workers to anarchist ideas; a critique of the failure of both the League of Nations and international workers' organizations to take effective action against the Italian invasion of Abyssinia; and an analysis of law as inimical to the fluid nature of life and as specifically subordinating of women (an analysis that could be termed "pure anarchist" in its tone and content, but that never mentioned the word).

In addition, the journal printed a number of articles on cultural themes: a discussion of Pestalozzi's educational theories and their appropriateness to the education of working-class children; a review of Charlie Chaplin's "Modern Times," by Mercedes Comaposada, which highlighted its anticapitalist themes; an essay extolling the value of sports and exercise for health and vitality; and an article by Lucía Sánchez Saornil on the life of agricultural laborers in Castile (an article introducing primarily urban readers to the nature of life in rural areas).

And, finally, there were articles on topics of the sort one would expect to see in women's magazines, though always with a critical/political slant. "Vivienda" by Luisa Pérez discussed the necessity of home hygiene—the value of indoor bathrooms and gas (at that time considered unnecessary luxuries for working-class apartments), proper arrangements for garbage disposal, and the role of spitoons in spreading disease. An article by Amparo Poch described the proper care of newborn babies, mixing instructions on how much a child should sleep and how to wash and care for a baby with discussions on the importance of love and attention for proper growth and development.[44] The magazine even had an article on fashion: "the aesthetics of dressing." It noted that middle- and upper-class women seemed to be freer to choose practical clothes, while working-class women, who could least afford them, remained loyal to traditions that required major expenditures and were neither comfortable nor attractive.

Most striking about the content of the journal was the attempt to address women readers "where they were" and also to use every possible opportunity for political and cultural consciousness-raising. It would have been possible for a woman not affiliated with the anarchosyndicalist movement, and with little class consciousness, to pick up this journal and begin reading it as another magazine devoted to women. Yet, it was surely different from most: insisting on the importance of woman's personhood and her experiences and potential as an historical actor, while at the same time speaking to her immediate concerns as wife and mother. The editors succeeded in striking a tone that was both respectful of their readers and, at the same time, educational. It contained none of the "blaming the victim" quality so common among articles in mainstream anarchist journals lamenting the lack of women's participation in the movement, and none of the condescension so typical of middle-class (even middle-class feminist) women's magazines when they dealt with topics related to working-class women.[45]

Finally, *Mujeres Libres* was well received by many individuals and groups within the movement. In the months that followed, *Acracia* (the journal of the CNT in Lérida) and the *Boletín de Información, CNT-FAI*, reprinted editorials from *Mujeres Libres*, mentioned specific articles, and in other ways encouraged their readers to read and support the new magazine. During May and June, the editors received numerous letters of support and encouragement from male as well as female anarchists, thanking them for raising important issues and praising the quality of the articles. Many of these letters included contributions for subscriptions or support.[46] Thus, while the appearance of the journal may not have been greeted with the enthusiasm and financial support that the editors had hoped for from other movement organizations, neither did it fall on deaf ears. *Mujeres Libres* found an enthusiastic audience.

The course of development of both the journal and the organization changed sharply after July 1936. The Civil War and the months of increasing agitation leading up to it between February and July 1936 offered many new opportunities to women at the same time that it set limits on what they would be able to accomplish. Mujeres Libres' own development could not help but be affected by these events.

On the most immediate level, those women who were most involved both in Mujeres Libres in Madrid and in the Grupo Cultural Femenino in Barcelona joined their male comrades in the streets in response to the rebellion. They supplied food to the militiamen, set up popular dining rooms, and began to organize daily life in the "rear guard." Soon thereafter, the women's groups began to re-form and to redirect their activities. Soledad Estorach, Pepita Carpena, and others traveled through Catalonia and Aragón, helping to establish rural collectives. Many went along with representatives of the CNT and FAI to areas near the battlefronts, with makeshift loudspeakers, calling on peasants and rural laborers to "come over to our side." Others organized convoys of food and supplies to send to Madrid. Mujeres Libres groups formed throughout the Republican zone. With the specific goal of empowering women to overcome their triple servitude—"the enslavement of ignorance, enslavement as producers, and enslavement as women"—they developed literacy programs and, together with unions, co-sponsored apprenticeship training.

The changes brought on by war and revolution were quickly reflected in the tone and content of the journal. Mercedes Comaposada described the transformation in an article published in *Tierra y Libertad* in May 1937: "that calm 'magazine of orientation and social documentation' did not disappear: it was transformed into a livelier journal, which, in tune with current circumstances, offers constructive criticism and an orientation for now and for later."[47] Issue number 5 ("Día 65 de la Revolución"), responding to the new reality and published in October 1936, reflected this transformation. The journal continued to carry articles presumed to be of interest to women, though many were oriented to the wartime situation: a criticism of political parties for staging marches of children in uniforms, discussions of ration lines, stories of militiawomen at the fronts and women at work in factories. There were, in addition, articles devoted to political consciousness-raising: reports of the early days of the struggle in Barcelona, of the expropriation of buildings and establishment of collectives in Torrassa, and a variety of articles explicating the "revolution *and* war" position of the anarcho-syndicalist movement.

The editors acknowledged the changed context and its implications for the journal. "Although we might have preferred to work in more tranquil times," the world had changed. In consequence, "we pledge . . . to adjust our tone and expression to the speeded-up rhythm in which life unfolds." Before, it was necessary to search out women in their homes and convince them of the necessity of engaging in social life, but the war had made that need patently obvious. Women *had* engaged; they had answered the call. "But this response is only an instinctive one, not a self-conscious one. Our task now . . . is to convert that instinct into consciousness." Most dramatically, perhaps, the editors identified their goals with those of the anarcho-syndicalist movement:

> To be an antifascist is too little; one is an antifascist because one is already something else. We have an affirmation to set up against this negation . . . [that] can be condensed into three letters: CNT (Confederación Nacional del Trabajo), which means the rational organization of life on the bases of work, equality, and social justice. If it weren't for this, antifascism would be, for us, a meaningless word.[48]

Even at this early date, it is possible to see some striking differences in the tone and approach of *Mujeres Libres* compared to that of other journals addressed to women at the time. In its issue of October 1936, *Mujeres*, the journal of the Spanish Communist party (PCE), identified itself with "Women Against War and Fascism," an early popular front organization for women. In contrast to *Mujeres Libres'* revolutionary vision, *Mujeres* stated that the primary responsibility of women in Madrid was to take the place of men at the workplace so the men could go off to fight and to "learn to bear arms if it should be necessary."[49] An article by Dolores Ibarruri (La Pasionaria) argued that "victory will make work available to everyone: men and women." But the dominant theme of her article was that women's work must be understood as a contribution to the war effort. "It is necessary to prepare women so that if all men have to take up arms, they can assure the continuation of public life in Madrid and the production of what is necessary for war and the provision of basic necessities."

Consistent with the Popular Front strategy advocated by the PCE, the focus of virtually all the articles in *Mujeres* was on winning the war. The sole article not directly related to the war or the defense of Madrid was entitled "Preparemos la nueva generación: Lo que era la maternidad y lo que debe ser." ["Let us prepare the new generation: What maternity was, and what it should be."] This article focused on overcoming women's fears of maternity hospitals, discussing the changes that had been brought about as a result of a lay takeover of these institutions, and encouraging women to go to hospitals, rather than to give birth at home.

*Companya,* a magazine directed to women and published by the PSUC (the Catalan Communist party) beginning in March 1937, addressed somewhat more explicitly women's particular subordination *as women,* and argued that "the work of women's emancipation belongs to the woman." But its formulation of the process of emancipation and its discussion of women's roles still put primary emphasis on the importance of women's participation to the war effort.[50]

By the fall of 1936, within months of the outbreak of the war and the accompanying social revolution, Mujeres Libres had begun to establish itself as an independent organization, with goals and programs that differentiated it both from other left-wing women's organizations and, to some extent, from other organizations of the anarcho-syndicalist movement. While the founders of the journal saw their programs and policies as consistent with the theory and goals of the larger anarchist movement, they believed that, left to its own devices, the movement was incapable of mobilizing women effectively for the social revolution and the reconstruction of society.

What was necessary was an organization run by and for women, one committed to overcoming women's subordination in all its facets, whether in their homes, in the workplace, or in the anarcho-syndicalist movement itself. The programs they developed, prefigured in Lucía Sánchez Saornil's articles in *Solidaridad Obrera* in October 1935, were to be created and implemented by women, for women. These included classes to overcome ignorance and illiteracy, industrial and commercial apprenticeships, as well as consciousness-raising groups, designed to empower women and to instill in them the knowledge and confidence they would need to participate as full citizens in a revolutionary society. These programs were to be organized in a federated, nonhierarchical way that, in structure as well as program, would exemplify women's capacities to act autonomously to contribute to social transformation.

*Milicianas* on guard duty.
*Photo courtesy of Sara Berenguer.*

Cristina Piera with her two sons, Rugelio (L) and
Enrique (R) Cassañes, 1981.

Enriqueta (Fernandez) Rovira, 1981.

Ana Delso, 1989.

Sara Berenguer, March 1936.
*Photo courtesy of Sara Berenguer.*

Azucena (Fernandez) Barba, 1981.

Pura Perez Benavent (R) with a *compañera*
from Mujeres Libres, Eucarena García, 1942.
*Photo courtesy of Pura Arcos.*

Sara (Berenguer) Guillén, Amada de Nó, and Conchita Guillén, 1988.

Soledad Estorach, 1982.

Dolores Prat, 1988.

Cover of *Mujeres Libres* issue
"8th month of the Revolution."
Caption reads "By work and
with arms we women defend
the people's freedom."

"Liberatorios de Prostitución"
from *Mujeres Libres*, "65 Days
of the Revolution."
*Photo courtesy of Federico Arcos.*

# V

## EDUCATION FOR EMPOWERMENT
### PREPARATION AS REVOLUTION

The demands of confronting both revolution and war led Mujeres Libres to develop a set of programs with two separate but related goals: *capacitación*, "preparing" women for revolutionary engagement, and *captación*, actively incorporating them into the libertarian movement. This dual orientation was expressed clearly in its statement of purpose:

> (a) to create a conscientious and responsible female force [originally, a "revolutionary force"] that can act as a vanguard of progress; and (b) to this end, to establish schools, institutes, conferences, special courses, etc., designed to empower women and emancipate them from the triple enslavement to which they have been, and continue to be, subject, the enslavement of ignorance, enslavement as a woman, and enslavement as a worker.[1]

*Capacitación* is a word that has no exact English equivalent. Some combination of consciousness-raising and empowerment (in the sense of developing and feeling confident in one's own abilities) is probably the closest we can get. It signified Mujeres Libres' commitment to enable women to overcome their subordination and to recognize and act on their potential. *Capacitación* was Mujeres Libres' appropriation of the concept of preparation to the specific situation of women in Spain. It is best understood to refer to the *content* of the organization's activities—activities designed to overcome women's illiteracy, to prepare them to participate actively and effectively in the work force, to provide them with information about themselves as women (e.g., on motherhood, child care, sexuality), and, ultimately, to enable them to experience themselves as competent historical actors.

*Captación*, a goal which took on ever greater importance as the counterrevolution grew in strength, referred to the organizational and ideological context of *capacitación*. I have already noted that one concern of those who established Mujeres Libres was the dearth of women activists; they had committed themselves to encouraging female militancy in the CNT and FAI. Increasing women's participation in movement organizations was important to them precisely because they saw in the libertarian movement the best hope for change that would benefit women as well as men. As the Civil War dragged on, Mujeres Libres' concern with *captación* came to signify not just a commitment to the greater involvement of women in the CNT but also a competition with the Asociación de Mujeres Antifascistas (and the Communist and Socialist parties) for the loyalties of newly mobilized women.

Mujeres Libres rejected both feminism (by which they meant treating men as the enemy and striving for "equality for women within an existing system of privileges")[2] and the relegation of women to a secondary position within the libertarian movement:

> We are aware of the precedents set by both feminist organizations and by political parties. . . . We could not follow either of these paths. We could not separate the women's problem from the social problem, nor could we deny the significance of the first by converting women into a simple instrument for any organization, even . . . our own libertarian organization.

> The intention that underlay our activities was much broader: to serve a doctrine, not a party, to empower [*capacitar*] women to make of them individuals capable of contributing to the structuring of the future society, individuals who have learned to be self-determining, not to follow blindly the dictates of any organization.[3]

In practice, however, as the somewhat defensive tone of the preceding quotation suggests, these goals were sometimes in tension. For example, both the CNT and FAI (whose financial and moral support Mujeres Libres desperately needed) were more interested in captación than in capacitación. They would have been more than willing to support Mujeres Libres' efforts to organize women into unions, for example, but they were less than enthusiastic in their support for broad-based programs of capacitación. These movement organizations never accepted capacitación as an independent goal that required organizational autonomy. Yet, from Mujeres Libres' point of view, captación without capacitación made no sense, because women were not yet prepared to enter the movement as equals.

Anarchism provided the basic grounding for Mujeres Libres' analysis and programs. Its aim was an egalitarian, nonhierarchical society in which people respected themselves and were respected by others. However, given the relative neglect with which women and women's issues had been treated within the anarcho-syndicalist movement, Mujeres Libres' main concern was to address those aspects of the societal system of inequalities and hierarchies that specifically affected women. Treating women's subordination as part of a larger system of hierarchies located its project firmly within an anarchist framework, while a focus on the specific gender consequences of those inequalities differentiated Mujeres Libres from the mainstream of the movement at the time.

Organizational autonomy was crucial to this vision. Women needed a separate organization, Mujeres Libres argued, not because men could not be trusted and not because men might be less than fully committed to women's emancipation, but because, in the end, only through their own self-directed action would women come to see themselves as capable and competent, able to participate as equals in the movement. As Lucía Sánchez Saornil had written in 1935: "I believe it is not the place of men to establish the role of women in society, however elevated that might be. The anarchist way . . . is to let the woman act on her own freedom, without either guides or enforcement; to let her move in the direction that her inclinations and abilities direct."[4]

This chapter explores the nature and functioning of Mujeres Libres' programs of *capacitación*—specifically, its efforts to adapt anarchist principles of preparation to the particular situation of women in Spain. Key to understanding these programs was Mujeres Libres' analysis of women's difference, both the nature and sources of women's subordination to men in Spanish society and the particular contributions women could make to the revolution and to the construction of a new society. Although these views were rarely spelled out in any direct way, much can be pieced together from an examination of Mujeres Libres' writings and programs.

Mujeres Libres focused on the links among economic, cultural, and sexual subordination. We can find in its writings an analysis of women's subordination that runs something like this: Women who stayed at home were economically (and therefore sexually) dependent on men. That dependence contributed to, and was reinforced by, their lack of education which, in turn, contributed to a societal devaluation of women and a lack of self-respect on the part of women themselves. The situation was scarcely different for those women who were paid for their labor, whether in domestic service or in factories. Their low salaries were "justified" on the grounds that they were secondary workers, not supporting a family. The low salaries, in turn, contributed to women's subordinate status and lack of self-respect. Finally, the combination of economic subordination and relative cultural backwardness made women particularly vulnerable to sexual exploitation—whether in marriage or outside it.[5]

Consistent with anarchist analyses of relations of domination and subordination, Mujeres Libres never attributed women's subordination to any single factor. Education would be crucial to overcome women's cultural subordination, but it would not be sufficient in itself to make women full participants in the economy or society. Jobs, too, would be essential, but work alone would not overcome cultural and sexual exploitation. Consequently, effective programs of capacitación would have to focus on overcoming each aspect of women's "enslavement" and their interactions. Activities would have to be directed to many fronts at once.

Mujeres Libres' position on what women specifically had to contribute either to the revolution or to the new society was ambiguous. While most of its activities and propaganda focused on overcoming the subordination that prevented women from taking their places alongside men in creating the new society, some writings explicitly stressed women's difference from men and the importance of incorporating women—with all their differences—into the revolutionary process. An editorial celebrating the founding of the National Federation of Mujeres Libres in August 1937, for example, stated:

> In identifying its goals with the CNT and the FAI, [Mujeres Libres] has gathered the most genuinely Spanish and the most authentically revolutionary and enriched it with the best of its own, specifically feminine, characteristics. . . . Mujeres Libres desires that in the new Society, the two angles of vision—masculine and feminine—will converge, to provide the equilibrium necessary. . . . There cannot be a just society unless masculine and feminine are present in equal proportions.[6]

Here, the writer seems to be arguing for the incorporation of the unique perspective women bring to political/social life, foreshadowing Carol Gilligan's recent call for listening to woman's "different voice." But exactly what that perspective was remained elusive. The question of what feminine characteristics are and what women have to offer to society, a focus of debate and discussion among contemporary feminists,[7] was also raised by the members of Mujeres Libres. As we will see, ambiguity about what constituted woman's nature was evident in many of Mujeres Libres' programs.

## Education Programs

Education formed the center of Mujeres Libres' programs of capacitación and took primary place in discussions of its accomplishments. Education was essential to releasing women's potential and enabling them to become fully contributing members of the movement and the new society: "Culture for culture's sake? Culture in the abstract? No. Capacitación of women with one immediate and urgent end: to help to win the war. To empower [capacitar] woman to free her from her triple enslavement: her enslavement to ignorance, her enslavement as a producer, and her enslavement as a woman. To prepare her [capacitarla] for a new, more just social order."[8]

Educational programs were among the first activities Mujeres Libres organized, and they had a number of components. Most basic and widespread was a crusade against illiteracy. Embarrassment about "cultural backwardness" prevented many women from active engagement in the struggle for revolutionary change. Literacy was to be a tool to develop self-confidence and further participation.[9]

In addition to classes in basic literacy, institutes in cities and towns offered more technically oriented classes and programs in "social formation"—by which they meant an orientation to the social and political world. In the fall of 1936 Mujeres Libres in Barcelona offered intensive courses in general culture, social history, economics, and law in its offices in the Plaza de Cataluña. At the end of that year, the Agrupación had an Instituto Mujeres Libres at a site in the Calle Cortes; a few months later, the Casal de la Dona Treballadora opened its doors. By October 1937 the Casal de la Dona advertised courses in the following areas:

> Elementary Classes (Illiterates and three grades): Reading, writing, arithmetic, geography, grammar, and natural phenomena
> Classes Complementary to Elementary Education: World history, French, English, Russian, typing, and stenography
> Complementary Professional Classes: Nursing, child care, skills (mechanics, electricity, business), sewing, agriculture, and aviculture
> "Social Formation": Union organization, sociology, economics, and general culture.[10]

No matter what the level of the course, the material discussed included a new understanding of what it meant to be a woman. Courses in "social formation" were a must for would-be activists. As new members of the organization, Pepita Carpena, Conchita Guillén and Amada de Nó all studied with Mercedes Comaposada during 1937–1938. The essence of the course was that women had to take responsibility for their lives: "There has to be equality between the compañero and the compañera, that is, independence, personality. The compañera is capable of developing herself in her own way, without her compañero telling her what to do. They explained that the woman has to take her own initiative and independence."[11]

Mujeres Libres also offered courses in elementary education, with a goal of preparing a new generation of teachers to educate children for a new society. Finally, there were courses and programs in agriculture and aviculture. Mujeres Libres established farm schools for girls who had come to the city from rural areas to engage in domestic service, aimed at teaching them skills that would enable them to participate more effectively in collectivized farming in their native villages.

In large cities, Mujeres Libres organized both on a citywide basis and in neighborhoods. Neighborhood centers offered night courses, so that women who worked during the day could attend. In urban neighborhoods and rural villages, basic literacy classes were the most common offering, supplemented by courses in elementary education, mechanical skills, child care, and nursing and medical assistance. These allowed the women who "graduated" from them to teach in new schools or to work in hospitals and clinics, whether at the front or in their barrio. As the war created more and more refugees, Mujeres Libres groups formed in the areas where refugees were gathering and offered extensive educational programs to serve the needs of both adults and children.[12]

The goals of Mujeres Libres' educational programs went beyond simple transmission of skills. In July 1937, the Catalan Generalitat had established an Institut d'Adaptació Profesional de la Dona [Institute for the Professional Training of Women], with the participation of both the UGT and the CNT. Formed when the Generalitat took control over the Escuela de Adaptación Profesional de la Mujer (a joint venture of Mujeres Libres and the CNT in Barcelona), the Institute aimed to provide women with the skills they would need to enter the work force and replace men who had gone to the front.[13] Apparently, this Institute complemented the "Escola Profesional per a la Dona," created in 1883 to provide training for working-class girls entering the textile industry. Its program had expanded dramatically after July 1936, when the Generalitat included a wider range of courses.[14]

But Mujeres Libres saw this new institute as offering only a partial response to women's needs: "Those institutes cannot achieve their ends without a prior preparation, not just in the sense of facilitating the acquisition of basic knowledge and understanding, but also of spiritual and social formation."[15] Mujeres Libres' aims were broader. As Soledad explained, "The professional training schools [run by the Generalitat] opened their doors to women and gave them *technical* training to allow them to take over the jobs of men. But we [in the Casal] joined technical training with a kind of social preparation. It was more like a kind of school for activists."[16] Mujeres Libres, of course, was not the only organization to attempt to use training programs for broader political purposes. In fact, as we will see in chapter 6, one of its main complaints about the Escuela de Adaptación Profesional de la Mujer was that it was being used for propaganda purposes by other organizations.

These programs of direct educational services reached many thousands of women; between 600 and 800 women were attending classes each day at the Casal de la Dona in Barcelona in December 1938.[17] Beyond this, Mujeres Libres' programs of press and propaganda spread its message even more widely, supplementing the journal with books and pamphlets on a variety of topics, from child-rearing to biographies of revolutionary women (see Appendix B). Within the first months of the revolution, Mujeres Libres in Barcelona established a kiosk on the Ramblas to make these publications more easily available to potential readers.[18] It also mounted public expositions to highlight the activities and achievements of women during the revolutionary period.

Finally, both nationally and regionally, Mujeres Libres established committees focused on culture and propaganda to spread the message in person as well as in writing. A group in Barcelona made regular radio broadcasts. Others traveled through the Catalan countryside to speak to those who might not be reached by written or radio propaganda. After she completed her course with Mercedes Comaposada, for example, Pepita Carpena became a regular participant in propaganda tours as a member of the Catalan Regional Committee of Mujeres Libres, responsible for culture and propaganda. On the local level, individual agrupaciones agreed to establish circulating libraries.[19] In November 1938, a budget of the Regional Committee of Mujeres Libres of Catalonia showed that of the twelve members of the Committee, seven had posts related to culture and propaganda.[20] The pattern was similar elsewhere in the country.

The work was clearly satisfying and exciting. Pepita's description of her experiences on propaganda trips communicates her enthusiasm:

> We would call the women together and explain to them . . . that there is a clearly defined role for women, that women should not lose their independence, but that a woman can be a mother and a compañera at the same time. . . . Young women would come over to me and say, "This is very interesting. What you're saying we've never heard before. It's something that we've felt, but we didn't know." . . . The ideas that grabbed them the most? Talk about the power men exercised over women. . . . There would be a kind of an uproar when you would say to them, "We cannot permit men to think themselves superior to women, that they have a right to rule over them." I think that Spanish women were waiting anxiously for that call.[21]

In many ways these talks were as important for those who delivered them as they were to the listeners. Sara Berenguer Guillén, Conchita Guillén, and Amada de Nó, for example, made their first appearances on a public rostrum as speakers for Mujeres Libres, urging others to study and prepare themselves. The exhiliration and sense of accomplishment they felt was palpable, even as they described these activities fifty years later.

Cultural work was critical because, if Mujeres Libres aimed to create a "conscientious responsible [revolutionary] force," that force would have to be educated. Programs had to proceed on a number of levels simultaneously. Even while women were taking classes to develop their skills and self-confidence, they were participating in organizational activities that necessarily took those skills and confidence for granted. Since virtually all the activists were self-taught within the libertarian movement, Mujeres Libres had to put into practice anarchist theory about direct action and "learning by doing." The range of its accomplishments is eloquent testimony to the possibilities of such an educational approach.

### Employment and Apprenticeship Programs

Closely connected to programs of general culture and education were activities and projects designed to facilitate women's entry into the work force as skilled workers at decent pay, which meant, in effect, training women for jobs that had previously been perceived as men's work. The apprenticeship programs that formed the core of this component of Mujeres Libres' agenda were usually joint ventures with local unions. The working out of the relationship was difficult, reflecting all levels of disagreement about women's subordination and the understanding of women's difference.

> The *secciones de trabajo* [labor sections] were probably the most important activities. We started in that area immediately, because it was essential to get women out of the home. Eventually, there were Mujeres Libres groups in almost all the factories. Many of them probably focused on issues that had little to do with women's emancipation, but they did provide a way for women to talk about factory issues. . . . We had to be careful not to take over the job of other organizations, especially the unions, [and] not to foment male-female antagonism.[22]

While union cooperation with these programs was based primarily on a desire to fill the factory jobs left vacant when men went to the front, Mujeres Libres' commitment to women's participation was based as well in the belief that decently paid work, under reasonable working conditions, was as much a woman's right as a man's, whether in wartime or in peace. "We are not talking about the incorporation of women into work either as a gift or as a necessity," asserted an article in 1938. "Work is a right that women won in the first days of bloody struggle."[23]

> In conjunction with education, work was the key to women's self-development. We wanted to open the world to women, to allow women to develop themselves in whatever ways they wanted to. . . .
>
> The first thing was to get women out of the house. It's true that even women who worked were not entirely independent economically—that would have been impossible, given the situation of the working class in those years. But getting women out of the house to do paid work *does* make a difference. It enables them to develop a *social sense*. Also, hus-

bands had a certain respect for their wives when they worked, too. So we saw it as important to get women out of the house, even if they wouldn't be fully independent economically.[24]

Mujeres Libres addressed women and work in two different, though related, ways. Articles in the journal analyzed the history of work and of women's participation in the work force; organizational programs addressed the specific needs of women in the wartime and revolutionary situation.

Most of Mujeres Libres' theoretical writings treated work in the historical context. Work had traditionally been conceived, Mercedes Comaposada wrote, as either a punishment, a necessity, or some combination of the two. People worked in order to survive. But with the advent of capitalism, the punitive aspects of work took on even greater force. Capitalism (and scientific management) achieved industrial progress at the cost of "forgetting the human being." Revolutionary change would have to address the spiritual, as well as the physical, damage caused by dull, repetitive work.[25]

A number of articles explored how the ideology of what we now call "separate spheres" and the expectation that woman's place was in the home differentially affected rural and urban, working-class and middle-class women. With industrialization, for example, many rural working-class women had migrated to the cities, hoping to support themselves by domestic service or factory work. But they encountered "just a more elevated form of slavery." Middle-class women were also affected by industrialization and by the rising expectations that followed World War I. Many took jobs in offices or shops, but for them, too, the promise of "wealth through employment" was often more a dream than a reality.[26]

Although *Mujeres Libres* was critical of the conditions of work—for both women and men—under primitive, feudal, and capitalist conditions, writers set forth a vision of what work would mean and how it would be experienced in the new society. First, work was a necessary and indispensable part of life. Humans had the capacity to use technology to lighten the burden of labor, structuring production so that machines would be at the service of people, and the exploitation of some by others would end.[27] Labor should be the expression of human capability and creativity, a prerequisite for freedom: "Work is creation, or it is nothing; creation is progressive enlightenment [*superación*], and the aim of enlightenment is freedom."[28] The vision of work as part of a fulfilled life was especially important for women—who, until then, had been deemed unfit for productive labor. Mujeres Libres insisted that work contributed both to general social progress and to women's emancipation more specifically, enabling women to be—and to experience themselves as—productive members of the society.[29]

A second aspect of this vision was that women should be treated as equals in the work force—with equal access to jobs and equal pay for the work they did. Mercedes Comaposada went so far as to argue that *all* salary differentials (including those between manual and "technical" laborers) ought to be eliminated immediately.[30] To the degree that woman's exploitation was rooted in her economic dependence, it would be overcome only when she became independent—or at least equally dependent with men! "Equal pay for equal work" was thus an immediate necessity. In a discussion at a plenary of the libertarian movement in October 1938, Mujeres Libres challenged the unions that "if they did not want to agree that women who do the same jobs as men should receive equal wages, they should say so clearly."[31]

But if women were to participate fully as workers, they needed preparation, the meaning of which varied somewhat with the circumstances. In the early months of the struggle, the organization encouraged women to get involved in whatever ways they could, arguing that lack of preparation ought not stand in the way of women's working.[32] During the course of the war, however, as the fronts advanced and foreign orders fell, jobs became scarcer. While Mujeres Libres still insisted on the incorporation of women into the work force, it placed even greater emphasis on the importance of education. "Mujeres Libres does not make demagogic promises or false appeals. Mujeres Libres does not assure you an immediate placement. [But] Mujeres Libres offers you the possibility of preparing yourselves to serve our struggle effectively."[33] Still, at the final stages of the war, Mujeres Libres continued to argue that work was women's right, a right exercised dramatically in their enthusiastic and voluntary incorporation into the workforce in the early days of the revolution. "Woman has put all her faith in the revolution. Let her not be defrauded by atavistic egoisms."[34]

Although the majority of articles argued that work was women's right, some suggested that women's work in the paid labor force was only temporary, a necessity of war.[35] Even these, however, insisted that women must learn to think and act collectively: "The woman must produce for the collectivity, she cannot return to egoistic, domestic, familial production." Another article criticized those who viewed their incorporation into the paid labor force as a personal, individual triumph: "This is not the time to strive for individual gains, nor those of a sex; we are dealing here with the defense of our very way of life, with the collective defense of a people. No one can think, when she takes up a piece of equipment at work, that she is resolving some personal situation."[36]

The ambiguity of these views on women's incorporation into the labor force was related to Mujeres Libres' understanding of women's "difference." Some writings emphasized women's specifically feminine qualities—"they knew how to stamp the coarse atmosphere of war with the delicate smoothness of their feminine psychology"—or focused on the variety of ways women might contribute to the war effort: "At the fronts, some [women] fight, others stand in wait for those who fight. In the rear, they work ceaselessly and contribute to the growth of that culture which, until now, the women's movement has so lacked. Woman is redeeming herself."[37] At other times, Mujeres Libres seemed less concerned with the specifically "feminine," and focused more on overcoming that which prevented women from full incorporation as equals in the work force. Although Mujeres Libres' programs of capacitación seemed to take for granted that women would work—to support themselves, their families, and the war effort—some articles in the journal continued to address women primarily as mothers or "support personnel." Clearly, the question of what was woman's "nature," and what could be expected of her, was far from resolved.

The apprenticeships and other work-related programs that Mujeres Libres developed reflected both the exigencies of the war situation and these ambiguities surrounding women's subordination in the workplace. The majority of its programs consisted of technical or skills training, but training was always accompanied by "social formation," directed to other dimensions of subordination.

Beginning at the local level and then spreading ultimately to regional and national units, Mujeres Libres organized secciones de trabajo, labor sections with responsibility for specific trades or industries, which cooperated with relevant CNT unions. By July 1937, for example, Mujeres Libres in Madrid was running a mechanics school, sewing classes, training programs for domestic servants and clerical workers, a workshop for women in the textile trades, and schools for drivers and metalworkers. Mujeres Libres in Barcelona had secciones de trabajo in transport, metallurgy (preparation for work in factories producing war materiél), public services, textiles, domestic service, health, commerce, and clerical work.

Most local unions were apparently eager and enthusiastic participants in these programs. Pura Pérez Arcos, for example, who took a course in transport and was among the first group of women licensed to drive trams in Barcelona, described the Transport Workers' Union as "fantastic": "They took people on as apprentices, mechanics, and drivers, and really taught us what to do. If you could only have seen the faces of the passengers [when women began serving as drivers], I think the compañeros in Transport, who were so kind and cooperative toward us, really got a kick out of that."[38]

Mujeres Libres prepared women for work in rural areas as well, most notably by establishing experimental stations for agriculture and aviculture to provide women with the knowledge they would need to participate in rural production. Agricultural experiment stations existed in Barcelona, Aragon, and Valencia, and women came to them from many surrounding communities.[39]

The secciones de trabajo encouraged women to become more involved in their workplaces, in both rural and urban contexts. They made frequent educational visits to factories.

> Groups of us would go to collectivized factories, and stop the lines for fifteen or twenty minutes, sometimes up to an hour, and talk to the workers, have little classes. This, of course, we did only with the approval of the workplace council; so we had the assistance of the unions. We did this throughout Barcelona—in war industries, textiles, transport, light and power, metallurgy, and wood—and also in some pueblos. Some days we went to as many as fifty different places![40]

The purpose of these visits—as of those to rural collectives—was twofold, reflecting a commitment to both capacitación and captación. They aimed to talk to women about their responsibilities at work (social formation) and also to encourage women to affiliate with Mujeres Libres and to join unions. One further goal was to assure that Mujeres Libres would have representation in all factories and on all union committees.[41]

Finally, the secciones de trabajo concerned themselves with child care. If women were to be incorporated into the workforce, they would have to be relieved of child-care responsibilities during work hours. Responsibility for child care belonged to the community as a whole. In its first congress, Mujeres Libres called for the establishment of child-care centers in factories and workshops with rooms for nursing, and committed itself both to setting up such centers and to writing about them, so that groups around the country would have guides to their establishment.[42]

### Consciousness-raising and Support of Women's Activism

Through all of these educational programs, Mujeres Libres attempted to raise consciousness about women's activism. Virtually every issue of the journal had at least one article on women as social-political activists or on the exploits of exceptional women, whether in contemporary Spain or in other historical and geographical contexts.[43] In attempts to reach both unaffiliated women and anarchist men with its message, Mujeres Libres published columns in other anarchist periodicals, such as *Acracia, Ruta, CNT* and *Tierra y libertad*, dealing with women's participation in the revolutionary struggle. A number of other booklets and pamphlets, as well as pictorial expositions in Madrid and Barcelona, highlighted the achievements and activities of women.

In addition, Mujeres Libres actively supported women's participation in military aspects of the struggle. The journal ran articles about militiawomen at the front and about those few women who held significant military positions. At least some of these women soldiers evidently valued the support. Amada de Nó recalled sitting in the local Barcelona office of Mujeres Libres when "a very good-looking soldier" came in and asked if this were the office of Mujeres Libres. When she replied that it was, the soldier said "he" wanted to sign up. At first, Amada thought it was a joke or someone wanting to harass them. Then she realized the soldier was a woman, Mika Etchebéhère, one of the few women who actually held a command position in the Republican army![44] Mujeres Libres in Madrid set up a shooting range and target practice for those women "disposed to defend the capital," and Mujeres Libres in Catalonia established a section of "war sports," which provided "premilitary preparation for women so that, if it should be necessary, they could intervene effectively, even on the battlefield."[45]

Mujeres Libres insisted that women's activism should not be seen as an anomaly. Women belonged in the public arena: "It is a very widespread but wrongheaded belief that intellectual and spiritual activities kill woman's feminine and maternal character. The opposite is more likely. Pursuits that explore life's ideals give more tenderness, kindness, feeling, and generosity to a woman than the vulgar preoccupation with material things."[46]

Some argued that women's activism had a character quite distinct from that of men. Federica Montseny, in her sole contribution to *Mujeres Libres*, argued that women were notable for "the collective force of a sex, sacrificing themselves, struggling as do the women workers in munitions factories in Spain, defying death during many hours of the day," rather than for individual acts of heroism. Woman's particular contribution to the struggle, in Montseny's view, was her "heroic resignation" to the dislocations of war and revolution.[47]

Not all writers argued in this vein, however. Equally common was the sort of claim, made by Aurea Cuadrado in the same issue of the journal, that women were capable of the same levels of self-mastery and self-development as men. Pythagorean women in ancient Greece, she argued, "occupied prominent positions in public halls, in the legislature, and in both private and public life." Spanish women should expect no less, but with one important difference: "If the norm of the ancient Pythagoreans was self-mastery, creating an aristocracy to which the slaves did not have access, the self-mastery of the contemporary woman must be based on the hope of nurturing an aristocratic spirit that will relegate all memory of slavery to oblivion." This insistence on the need for spiritual development, in addition to cultural capacitación, was an important part of Mujeres Libres' message, one manifest particularly in the writings of Mercedes Comaposada and Lucía Sánchez Saornil.[48]

Finally, Mujeres Libres attempted to articulate a sense of what life might be like for fully self-conscious, self-empowered women. Women's situation differed from that of men: Although men and women should engage together in the struggle to overcome relations of domination imposed on them from outside (primarily by capitalism), women had an additional struggle for their "interior liberty," their sense of self. In this they would have to struggle alone and, all too frequently, against the opposition of their male comrades or family members. Nevertheless, "when you have achieved your goal, you will belong only to yourselves. . . . You will become persons with freedom and equality of social rights, free women in a free society that you will build together with men, as their true *compañeras*. . . . Life will be a thousand times more beautiful when the woman becomes a really 'free woman' [mujer libre]."[49]

The importance of this approach cannot be overemphasized; it was one of the ways Mujeres Libres differed most dramatically from other women's organizations in Spain at the time. Many of the organization's publications appealed to women to educate themselves and to join the work force as their contribution to the war and revolutionary effort—a perspective shared by organizations such as the AMA and the women's organization of the POUM. *Mujeres* and *Companya*, for example, journals published by groups affiliated with the PSUC (the Communist party in Catalonia) during the war, contained frequent appeals to women to work to replace men at the front, but they did not locate those appeals in the context of a larger campaign for capacitación or women's self-development for her own sake. An article by "La Pasionaria," for example, in the first issue of *Companya*, noted that "we have an inexhaustible source of human reserves; but we must prepare them, organize them, empower them [*capacitar-les*] for the war." Mujeres Libres' insistence on women's emancipation as an end in itself was unique. In fact, as we will see, the contention that women's emancipation was a goal to be valued even apart from the revolutionary situation often set Mujeres Libres at odds not only with other women's organizations but with many colleagues in the libertarian movement.

### Motherhood

Many articles in the journal took issue with the identification of women with motherhood, and insisted that women had an identity and social function independent of their (potential) status as mothers. Nevertheless, the organization's programs were based on the presumption that motherhood was the reality for many, if not most, Spanish women. As Mercedes Comaposada explained:

One thing we wanted to make very clear was that the woman is an *individual*, and she has value and worth even apart from being a mother. Yet, at the same time, we wanted to make sure there was a place for mothers. . . . What we wanted, at the least, were *madres conscientes* [self-conscious mothers]. People should be able to choose whether and when and how to have children and to know how to raise them. . . . And they shouldn't have to be one's own children—there is need to take care of other people's children, of orphans, and the like.[50]

A commitment to the "woman as person," not just as mother, was evident in virtually all Mujeres Libres' literature. Beginning with Sánchez Saornil's concern that "the concept of mother is absorbing that of woman, the function is annihilating the individual,"[51] Mujeres Libres' writers insisted that developing oneself as a person was a woman's first priority. It might be true, Pilar Grangel argued, that women must give birth to children if there is to be a next generation. But women can not do it alone; they need the assistance of men and, more importantly, the self-confidence and intelligence to orient themselves and their children to the world. She placed reproduction third on the list of women's social responsibilities, after work and the development of a social conscience.[52] As one issue of *Mujeres Libres* proclaimed on its cover, "She is not a better mother who holds her child close to her heart, but she who helps to make the world a better place for him [*sic*]."

Related to this perspective was Mujeres Libres' insistence that motherhood was not something that "comes naturally"—except in the biological fact of bearing children. Much of women's socialization—a socialization that oriented her to be a *mujercita* [a doll baby] and to devote her attention to making herself attractive to men—was, in fact, inimical to good mothering. To be a mother, one must learn to pay proper attention to the needs of a child. One could not be a mujercita and a mother at the same time. The other side of this claim was the insistence that women needed to *learn* to be proper mothers (as men needed to learn to be proper fathers)—how to feed and care for their children, how to facilitate their growing into strong, independent persons as adults.[53]

Despite this insistence that women were not "born to mother," Mujeres Libres expressed a range of views on the naturalness of maternal feelings to women. Amparo Poch y Gascón dedicated her book *Niño* "to all those women who love their children or others' children; that is to say, to all the women of the World." Etta Federn's *Mujeres de las revoluciones* made frequent reference to maternal feelings on the part of the revolutionary women she described, even though most of them did not have any children of their own.[54]

Mujeres Libres' programs to educate women about child care took the form of written materials and "hands-on" activities. Many issues of the journal contained articles on aspects of proper child care, written either by Amparo Poch or by "Florentina" (Carmen Conde). In an effort to reach a wide range of women, Poch y Gascón also contributed articles to a variety of general distribution anarchist newspapers. In the context of providing medical and health information, an overview of the basic stages of child development, and a review of what to expect from your child at what ages—a kind of simplified Dr. Spock—Poch y Gascón presented what was, in effect, an anarchist approach to child-rearing. She insisted, for example, that parents must let their children develop in their own way: "Repression [of habits such as thumb-sucking] must have a limit if you don't want the child's personality to be entirely lost. . . . Remain attentive so that the soul and mind of your child retain their own character, the stamp of his or her own personality. Allow your child to create and follow his or her unique path, free from coercion."[55]

Mujeres Libres' attempts to respond to women's health-care needs and to educate them about proper motherhood went beyond the written word. In the first days of the revolution, for example, Teresina Torrelles and other activists from Mujeres Libres in Terrassa established a school for nurses and an emergency medical clinic to treat those injured in the fighting. They worked together with Dr. Juan Paulís, author of *Las obreras de la aguja*, a physician with a social conscience who had long been a member of the CNT. Teresina and the others became, in her words, "instant apprentices" in those first few days. They took sheets and mattresses from their own houses and outfitted the clinic through a combination of donations and requisitions from the local government.

Within a short time, they created the first maternity clinic there, also under the direction of Dr. Paulís. Despite her lack of experience in the medical field (but probably because of her extensive experience as an organizer and activist in the CNT and in the women's group in Terrassa), Teresina was named administrator. On the first day she reported:

> I went to the operating room, and looked around. I put things in their places, and saw what we needed. And then I went to City Hall and said, this and this is what we need. . . . They either gave it to me or arranged for me to get it. If we needed alcohol, for example, I went to the pharmacy and got it, with money they gave me, because we had nothing, not even disinfectant.

The job was a difficult one; not everyone was eager for this new system:

> The midwives—there were twelve of them—went on strike. They refused to work for us. . . . When they returned to work, they would eat first and give the women who had given birth what was left over. I said, "This cannot be." So I took the food and took it around to the patients, and what was left, I took to the kitchen for the nurses and midwives. . . . We

used diapers with buttons, instead of pins, because Dr. Paulís said that the pins weren't safe for the babies. I had to arrange that, too. . . .

I remember how many times fathers would come up to me in the clinic to request something, and I would say, "Please, here all of us are equals." And they would say to me, "Here, you really have made the revolution." I had such satisfaction from this. Because I administered the whole thing without any education. . . . What I believed, that's what I put in practice there. . . . And that's what I can tell you of what I did for the revolution. The rest, I did what everyone else did. But this, this was something I did.[56]

In Barcelona, Mujeres Libres ran a lying-in hospital, Casa de Maternidad, directed by Aurea Cuadrado, which provided birth and postnatal care for women and their babies and offered a class on conscious motherhood, dealing with such topics as child and maternal health, birth control, sexuality, and eugenics. As part of its educational program, the hospital (together with *Mujeres Libres*) ran a veritable campaign about breast-feeding, trying to convince women of the superiority of breast milk over cow's milk. *Mujeres Libres* no. 7, in fact, reported that the hospital would not allow women to leave the hospital with their babies until they had·breast-fed them![57] Cuadrado's aim was to enable women to overcome the ignorance and the prejudices of the "society of the past," and to give them a start on developing the "equilibrium necessary for intelligent mothering." She hoped that, once in possession of more information about their bodies and sexuality, women would take control over other aspects of their lives, "develop their capacity for maternal love, raise their moral level, and generate a feeling of social solidarity."[58]

Dr. Paulís, who had directed the clinic and the nursing school in Terrassa, later went to Barcelona and collaborated with Mujeres Libres and health-care unions there to establish the Instituto de Puericultura y Maternología Luísa Michel (the Luisa Michel Institute of Maternal and Child Care) in February 1938. The Institute provided medical services for mothers and children, maternity counseling and financial assistance, programs to train child-care workers, and a child-care center (for the children of working mothers, particularly in the needle trades). This center had two units, one for children between three and twenty-four months, and one for children aged one to five years, as well as a library and a program of medical check-ups for children attending rationalist schools.[59]

While this Barcelona program was, no doubt, the most extensive, Mujeres Libres worked with health-care unions in other towns and cities to meet the health needs of women. Nursing education programs were probably the most common form this cooperation took. Since, in the prewar period, nursing care had been a monopoly of the church, the need was certainly great. Not surprisingly, a considerable number of the women I interviewed had served as nurses at some time during the war.

## Child Education

Women had been given the primary responsibility for raising children. That responsibility, Mujeres Libres argued, required that women educate themselves in order to raise their children properly. But it also required that women struggle to see that children had the best education possible.

Mujeres Libres' attitudes toward children were expressed almost as often through pictures as through words. Issue after issue of the journal contained pictures of children—playing, exploring, working; hopeful and sad; in schools or out in the world. The captions and articles that accompanied such pictures emphasized a number of characteristics of children that formed the basis of virtually all Mujeres Libres' programs in the field of education. Children were naturally enthusiastic and open, constantly taking in information from the world around them; adults (and especially teachers) ought to guard against doing anything to dull that youthful enthusiasm. Children were the hope of the future; they should never be made to feel ashamed of themselves or their bodies; they should be allowed to remain open to all points of view.[60] Children should never be used for propaganda purposes: the vision of young children marching through the streets in uniform—even those of workers' organizations—was an abomination. "Children cannot, and ought not, be either Catholics, socialists, communists, or libertarians. Children ought to be only what they are: children." Finally, a child's curiosity and adventurousness ought to be encouraged as much as possible. Rather than punishing a small child for breaking something valuable, adults should keep valuables in a place where children cannot reach them.[61]

Mujeres Libres' philosophy of education drew on anarchist theory and practice, and was consistent with these views of childhood. Education ought to be viewed as a process of development and exploration, rather than as one of repressing a child's instincts and inculcating obedience and discipline. Children learn best when they feel good about themselves, others, and the world. The best education, therefore, would orient the child to the world, facilitating the child's learning from others and from his or her environment. Furthermore, it would engage children as fully as possible (taking advantage of all the senses), encouraging them to develop and value their own abilities as well as to cooperate with others. Education, that is, should be active, noncompetitive, and as nondirective as possible, relying heavily on children's natural curiosity.[62]

Respecting children and educating them well was vitally important to the process of revolutionary social change. Ignorance made people particularly vulnerable to oppression and suffering. More importantly, education prepared people for social life. Authoritarian schools (or families), based on fear, prepared people to be submissive to an authoritarian government. Different schools would be necessary to prepare people to live in a society without domination.[63]

Teachers needed to be specially trained to prepare children for a more egalitarian world. They would have to think of themselves as artists, able to spark creativity in others: "Let no one without imagination, without intuition, without inspiration become a teacher!"[64] And these new teachers must be taught new principles of education:

(1) Pedagogy must be considered an art, based in creativity.
(2) Education is about a teacher's discovering in every child and at every moment the living truth that each child and each moment has to offer.
(3) There is no doctrine so perfect as to be legitimately imposed on a child.
(4) A teacher should not love "children in the abstract," but each child in his or her particularity, and should attempt to learn from each child.
(5) A teacher should teach according to the capacities and abilities of each particular student.
(6) A teacher should avoid competition and external rewards and punishments.
(7) Classes should be small (ideally, no more than ten children per teacher).[65]

## Sexuality

I noted in chapter 1 that Spanish anarchists had devoted considerable attention to sexual liberation, for both women and men. They advocated increased information about sex and sexuality, greater sexual freedom, and the abolition of legal and religious marriage in favor of "free love," by which they meant voluntarily contracted relationships that could be terminated at the will of either partner. Some small percentage of anarchist militants had attempted to live by these precepts even in the prerevolutionary period. But the advent of the Civil War and the social revolution made it possible for much larger numbers of people to live according to new sexual norms. The revolution allowed for the implementation of new public policies in the arena of sexuality, particularly in Catalonia. For example, decrees of the Generalitat legalized abortion for "therapeutic, eugenic, or ethical reasons," simplified divorce procedures, and made birth control information and devices more readily available.

We might expect that Mujeres Libres would have devoted considerable attention in its writings and in its programs to the sexual liberation of women. Many women who were later to be active in the organization had been among those writing (in the prewar years) in favor of greater sexual freedom. For example, between 1932 and 1935, Amparo Poch y Gascón wrote a number of articles and an educational pamphlet that discussed women's sexuality, emphasized the importance of sexual expression for women as well as for men, criticized monogamy and the sexual double standard, and advocated education about physiology, sexual pleasure, sexual functioning, and contraception. Many of her arguments paralleled those of earlier anarchist writers, particularly her insistence that sexuality was an important aspect of human identity and development. As a result of both social convention and uncaring husbands, she had written, women were denied the natural right to satisfy their bodily needs and desires. They must be given access to the information they needed about themselves, their bodies, and their sexuality so that they could develop themselves fully as persons. Further, since sexual expression was an important aspect of women's lives, rather than simply a means of satisfying male desire or of creating children, women needed information about, and access to, contraception—not exhortations to sexual abstinence.[66]

Little of this explicitly "pro-sex" writing was to be found in *Mujeres Libres*, however. Nor did education about sexuality loom very large in its programs or in the journal. While some articles advocated the abolition of the sexual double standard, none dealt explicitly with women's sexuality or sexual liberation. The majority of articles related to sexuality concerned prostitution, analyzing its causes and efforts to eliminate it. Nevertheless, the view of sexuality as an important constituent of human personhood, and of sexual expression as a normal and necessary aspect of human life, did find voice in some of Etta Federn's sketches in *Mujeres de las revoluciones*. For example, during the course of an explication of Alexandra Kollontai's views on free love, she stated that Kollontai "struggled against the false but widely held belief that sexual satisfaction without love is a symptom of moral perversion—especially in the case of a woman. . . . The double standard with respect to masculine and feminine sexuality, which reigned even among revolutionaries, was the object of her vehement and forceful struggle."[67]

Essays about sexual issues were generally more subdued in *Mujeres Libres;* "free love" did not appear in its pages at all. The journal did nevertheless contain a few articles explicitly critical of marriage, es-

pecially the so-called *casamientos a la libertaria*—the practice of replac-
ing church- or state-sanctioned weddings with those performed by
unions or revolutionary organizations. A number of Mujeres Libres'
writers found this a practice ripe for ridicule. *Mujeres Libres* no. 7, for
example, printed a "Proposal for the creation of a marriage factory (see
Appendix C), gently poking fun at the practice of union organizations'
formalizing marriages.[68] As secretary of the Building and Wood-Trades
Union in Barcelona, Sara Berenguer Guillén often drew up such documents. But her most intriguing memory was of a couple who returned,
some months after their "marriage," to request a divorce. She replied
that, as they were not legally married, they needed no divorce; they
could simply part company and go on with their lives. But the couple
refused, and in the end, Sara drew up a document of divorce, which was
duly witnessed by members of the union.[69]

Lucía Sánchez Saornil was rather less gentle in an article she wrote,
"La ceremonía matrimonial o la cobardía del espíritu" ("The Marriage
Ceremony or Spiritual Cowardice"), which appeared in *Horas de revolución*. It was ridiculous and hypocritical, she insisted, to engage in such
practices: "If we spent all those years asserting that the free consent of
both parties is sufficient for union between them, and that a wedding
certificate was nothing other than a contract of sale, how can we explain
these absurd ceremonies in union organizations. . . ?" The practice was
doubly reprehensible, she continued, because most of those ceremonies
simply imitated religious rites and because, like church and state weddings, they represented the inappropriate intervention of the public
into what should be private relations between people.[70]

Most of the attention Mujeres Libres devoted to issues of sexuality
focused on the relationship between economic and political exploitation and women's sexual subordination, a relationship made manifest
in prostitution. Both Mujeres Libres and other organizations of the
libertarian movement engaged in extensive campaigns against prostitution, which they saw as emblematic of human relations under capitalism.[71] But while mainstream movement organizations focused
mainly on unionizing prostitutes or on exhorting women not to engage
in the profession (or men not to patronize them), Mujeres Libres focused
its attention more on what it took to be the causes of prostitution,
especially the economic and political exploitation of women.

The first issue of the journal to appear after the outbreak of the Civil
War asserted that eliminating prostitution, "the greatest of slaveries,"
ought to be Mujeres Libres' first priority. Prostitution was not "their
problem [speaking of the prostitutes], but ours, that of all women and
all men." The labeling of some women as "dishonorable" was what
allowed other women to label themselves "honorable." Furthermore,
since prostitution was a result of women's economic exploitation, it
would not be sufficient to prohibit its practice. Instead, women would

have to be trained to support themselves in other ways. Accordingly, Mujeres Libres announced its intention to establish a network of *liberatorios de prostitución*, (retraining centers for prostitutes) which would involve "(1)medical-psychiatric research and treatment, (2) psychological and ethical programs to develop in the students a sense of responsibility, (3) professional orientation and capacitación, and (4) moral and material assistance whenever they need it, even after they have left the liberatorios."[72]

The CNT and the anarchist press applauded the plan, even if they were more inclined to view prostitutes as victims who needed to be rescued. However, at the same time there were some groups within the movement who insisted that prostitution could not be eliminated; at best, prostitutes could be protected from exploitation via unionization. In the early days of the revolution, there were attempts to organize prostitutes into a *sindicato de amor* [love union]. Most of these attempts were short-lived, however, and within a few months to a year, articles appeared in the anarchist press ridiculing the notion of unionization of prostitutes and, instead, calling on men not to patronize prostitutes.[73] Overall, the anarchist movement seems to have been rather lax on this point: both articles in *Mujeres Libres* and interviews with participants noted that anarchist men were much less likely to live up to their ideology in this respect than in many others.[74]

As an organization of and for women, Mujeres Libres directed its projects *to* women, particularly to those women most vulnerable to the sexual and economic exploitation considered to be the root of prostitution. Although war conditions prevented the project of liberatorios de prostitución from getting off the ground in any formal way, Mujeres Libres appealed to prostitutes to abandon their occupation and join the movement. Pepita Carpena recalled one prostitute who responded to the appeal, joined Mujeres Libres, attended classes, and eventually became a member of Pepita's cadre of traveling speakers and cultural workers.[75]

Despite the difficulties of the wartime situation, Mujeres Libres insisted that any program to eliminate prostitution must address the economic exploitation that was its source. *Mujeres Libres* no. 9, for example, noted that prostitution had worsened and suggested that the root of this increase was twofold. Many young women who had been domestic servants in the cities were thrown onto the streets without work once their former employers fled the republican zones. Second, young men had greater access to money to pay prostitutes. Women had become the "blind playthings of historical process." In such a context, revolution alone—without specific attention to "the sexual problem"— would not be enough: "We insist that the only way to resolve the social problem is through economic and political equality, aspects of an empowerment of women [*capacitación femenina*] that can endow women with a sense of responsibility and obligation. Any institution for the capacitación of women is, more than a liberatorio, a *preventorio* of prostitution."[76]

Further, prostitutes were not to be identified only with women who sold their bodies on the streets or in brothels. Mujeres Libres insisted, as Emma Goldman had some years earlier, that all women who depended on men were in some sense prostitutes. "A woman who lives in economic dependence receives a payment [for sex], even if it be from her legal husband. . . . All that propaganda, all those actions, in favor of the family, of that fictitious 'homey warmth,' keep woman in her eternal position: distant from production and without any rights." Only full economic equality between men and women, allowing women access to paid productive work on terms equal to those of men, could address and eliminate the true causes of prostitution.[77]

Mujeres Libres provided information on sexuality and encouraged women to take advantage of educational programs and other services available in hospitals. A number of articles in the journal spoke proudly of the accomplishments of Federica Montseny in the Ministry of Health and Public Assistance or those of Aurea Cuadrado in the Casa de Maternidad in Barcelona. The programs cited included those providing information about eugenics, contraception, and euthanasia, in addition to basic information about sexuality and procreation.[78] Mujeres Libres also took pride in the legalization of abortion in Catalonia (by decree of the Generalitat) and in the increased contraceptive options available to women as a result.[79]

Compared to its programs in the fields of literacy, work, motherhood, and education, those related to sexuality (and, in particular, sexual freedom) seem rather limited, both in scope and in result. For all of the anarchist movement's discussion of the importance of sexual liberation to full human emancipation, Mujeres Libres devoted virtually no attention to it as a goal. How can we explain the relatively narrow range of its programs in this area?

First, we must take note of the difference between written materials and day-to-day activities. Along with other movement organizations, Mujeres Libres frequently sponsored talks and educational sessions on sexuality and contraception. Julia Mirabé reported that doctors affiliated with the FIJL and Mujeres Libres "arranged to get us silver gadgets [obviously some sort of IUD]. Every six months, you would go, and they'd take out the mechanism and boil it, they'd examine you, and put it back in, and you wouldn't get pregnant."[80] Sexual practices among activists in Mujeres Libres, as among female movement activists more generally, were considerably more liberated than traditional Spanish culture allowed. For some, being part of the revolutionary culture meant that they were free to "unite" with their compañeros without either church or state sponsorship. For others, the new mores provided a way out of a conventional marriage. Sara Berenguer Guillén, for example, recalled that, almost on the eve of the revolution, a young teacher had asked her father for her hand. Sara admired his learning, but was not in love with him. Nevertheless, she said, had it not been for the revolution, she would almost certainly have married him. In fact, she did not. Later, she met and freely united with the young man who was to be her lifelong companion, Jesús Guillén. Similar stories of sexual openness, experimentation, or, at the very least, the relaxation of previously existing strict standards of behavior were common among activists.

The relative silence of Mujeres Libres on this issue reflects both factors internal to Mujeres Libres and the dynamics of the broader cultural context. Spanish anarchist calls for greater sexual openness had always gone hand in hand with a certain puritanism. As one activist remarked, "We were always very puritanical, worse than the Christians in some ways. . . . Take free love, for example. Compañeras virtually never had more than one compañero at once; the rest was theory."[81] Most men apparently interpreted free love to mean freedom for them, but not for their compañeras. Those women who did attempt to take free love seriously—whether by having more than one lover at a time or by leaving a lover when the relationship no longer felt satisfying—often faced social ostracism, even among their friends and comrades from the movement. Men may have talked about free love, but most men ridiculed or denigrated those women who practiced it.[82]

This puritanism was certainly evident in my recent conversations with many of the women of Mujeres Libres as well as with anarchist men. A surprising number expressed discomfort with what they saw as the frivolousness of the modern feminist movement, with its focus on "sexual freedom, lesbianism, love, and abortion." Both Suceso Portales and Pepita Carpena noted that Mujeres Libres did not focus attention on sexual preference or homosexuality, even though Lucía Sánchez Saornil was a lesbian, an aspect of her life she made no effort to hide from others in the movement. Everyone ought to be able to love whomever she or he wanted, they argued, but one's sexuality was hardly a "political" issue, one on which the movement should feel called to take a stand.[83]

Mujeres Libres attempted to teach women about sexuality and sexual pleasure by training nurses and midwives and offering courses to provide women with information about their bodies. However, its programs were clearly limited by prevailing attitudes toward sexuality. Given continued male dominance, Mujeres Libres may have hesitated to advocate greater sexual freedom for women, for fear that men would use the changed ideological climate to take advantage of women. Overall, many of the women indicated that issues of sexuality (beyond prostitution, pornography, or abortion rights) were "private," to be negotiated by women in their relationships, not issues to be the focus of a movement. "What is there to talk about?" one woman replied to my question about sexuality. "It's something between individuals." Mujeres Libres, as they saw it, aimed to empower women so that they could fend for themselves in the context of their relationships (or non-relationships).

In addition, the wartime situation placed limits on Mujeres Libres' accomplishments in this field. Surely, liberatorios de prostitución would not be high on the priority list of a movement that was already short of workers, funds, and facilities. Since so much of Mujeres Libres' funding came from movement organizations, without their support it would have been able to accomplish very little. More important, perhaps, were the dislocations caused by the war. Refugees were constantly pouring into the major cities from areas taken by Franco's troops. Increasingly, Mujeres Libres' limited resources were needed for basic education and for shelters for newly homeless women and children. The constant influx of people (including young women) also made it difficult to develop and maintain any long-term coordinated effort against prostitution.

Mujeres Libres may have toned down some of its radicalism on sexual questions in recognition of the difficulties of the wartime situtation. Although there were some articles in the early issues of *Mujeres Libres* criticizing the practice of casamientos a la libertaria, none appeared after the first few months of the war. One woman's reactions to them, looking back on those years, may be instructive:

> Some of us looked askance at the "marriages" that took place in unions then. But when I think back on all that now, I react somewhat differently. After all, there were these young people who had just gotten together, and the boys were going off to the front, perhaps not to return. How could you criticize a poor young woman who wanted some formal recognition of that union, some piece of paper signed before her compañero went off to the front?

Finally, Mujeres Libres may have limited the expression of its sexual radicalism in order to avoid alienating the women it hoped to attract. While programs devoted to literacy, job-training, child care, and motherhood would certainly have been radical in their context, all could be explained in terms of the needs of the war and the construction of the new society. None of these directly challenged male authority in the household, although, of course, any and all programs to empower women ultimately posed a challenge to male authority. Each of the programs made a contribution to the larger social effort while empowering women. On the other hand, programs focused on women's coming to a sense of their own sexuality might have seemed more threatening, especially to working-class women. They could not so easily be justified in terms of contribution to the larger social whole. In short, it may be that Mujeres Libres' initial commitment not to operate from an explicitly anarchist stance found its clearest expression in the limits of its programs on sexuality.

### Refugee and Social Service Programs

Finally, Mujeres Libres devoted attention to the support services traditionally performed by women and women's organizations in times of war. These programs fell into two major categories: (1) refugee programs providing shelter, schools, and other services for the growing numbers of adults, old people, and children displaced as the frontlines receded, and (2) assistance to combatants, including visits to soldiers at the front or in hospitals, washing or mending clothes, etc.

Work with refugees was a source of considerable pride to Mujeres Libres. In the major cities, refugees were aided by the large organizations, such as SIA (Solidaridad Internacional Antifascista, a kind of anarchist Red Cross). However, many refugees did not make it to the major cities, remaining instead in smaller towns or villages. There, Mujeres Libres cooperated with SIA to provide services both to refugees (adults and children) and to the wounded.[84]

As the war dragged on, articles in *Mujeres Libres* listing the activities of various groups around the country made increasing mention of refugee work, including appeals to women to welcome the refugees. Given the shortages of food and other necessities, one can imagine that villagers would not have been too eager to take in extra people, particularly those with many mouths to feed but few hands to work. Providing schools for the refugees was an important aspect of this project. Anna Delso, for example, noted that once she and her younger siblings moved to the Catalan town of Vilanova i la Geltrú in November 1936, she spent virtually all her time establishing and then teaching in a school for forty refugee children.[85] *Mujeres Libres* no. 11 reported that the 127th brigade of the 28th Division (what was left of an anarcho-syndicalist–based militia) had, with the assitance of Mujeres Libres, established a nursery school serving seventy refugee children.

Traditional women's support work also formed a part of Mujeres Libres' program. Virtually every agrupación had at least some members (if not a full sección) dedicated to solidarity work, assisting combatants and wounded soldiers. One aspect of this work in Barcelona was setting up and running a "soldier's place": the local transit workers' union provided the building, Marianet (national secretary of the CNT) provided the beds, and they scrambled around to buy or borrow whatever else they needed. Conchita Guillén recalled that the three speeches she gave as a member of the propaganda committee toward the end of

1938 involved encouraging women to be strong in the rearguard in order to strengthen the men who were at the front.[86]

Of course, Mujeres Libres was hardly alone in doing support work: AMA and other women's groups made such support work a raison d'être of their organizations. Mujeres Libres mobilized groups of women to make periodic trips to the battlefronts, to bring the men fresh clothes, hot food, and—perhaps most important—company. Since many of the women of Mujeres Libres were militants in one of the other anarchist organizations, they sometimes traveled under different sponsorship. Amada de Nó, who was a representative of her *barrio* to the local committee of Mujeres Libres in Barcelona, recalls going to the front on a mission sponsored by SIA, along with Lucía Sánchez Saornil (then the general secretary of SIA), Soledad Estorach, Libertad Ródenes, and Conchita Liaño. Although all were members of Mujeres Libres, they traveled not as Mujeres Libres, but as women of the CNT.[87]

Of course, as might be expected, Mujeres Libres' intentions in sending women to the fronts were not always coincident with the soldiers' expectations. Educational work among both women and men was constant. In her capacity as SIA representative, for example, Sara Berenguer Guillén had many dealings with militiamen, and corresponded with many soldiers as a way of keeping up their morale. More than once she had to fend off marriage proposals from young men who misinterpreted her letters as evidence that she had a romantic interest in them!

Nevertheless, she, Pepita Carpena, and Conchita Guillén spoke enthusiastically of their trips to the front to visit soldiers. Sara described one such trip, organized through SIA. "There was a group of young women factory workers who . . . wanted to do something for the soldiers. They said, 'Why don't we all contribute something—maybe twenty-five pesetas, or something—and we'll buy supplies through SIA and take them to the front.'" Since Sara was then working for SIA, she served as the delegate of the SIA National Council for the trip. "We rented two buses, loaded them up with the material and with all the girls from the factory. Two CNT militants accompanied us: Expósito, a teacher in a rationalist school, and Saturnino Aransáez." One of the buses broke down en route near a military encampment. Convinced by Sara of the need to get moving as soon as possible (since they were carrying goods for the anarchist 26th Division and the soldiers would likely be moving their position fairly soon), the mechanics worked well into the night and repaired the axle. The girls got back onto the bus and arrived at the camp of the 26th Division early the next morning.

> The girls were exhausted from lack of sleep, so they went to the dining room to nap, resting their heads on the tables. When the soldiers came in and saw the girls there, they started to make advances. Meanwhile,

Saturnino, Expósito, and I had gone off to find the company commanders to arrange for the day's events. When we came back, we heard the girls screaming and crying. The soldiers had disappeared as soon as they saw us! We asked the girls what had happened, and they explained. . . . I said to them, "Look, they didn't know how to act, but maybe it's not all their fault. Maybe, before we got here, another group of women had been here, from who knows where, for other purposes, and the soldiers figured, well, all women are alike. So let's tell them why we're here." . . . That's what they did, meeting with the soldiers in groups of two or three, and it all worked out fine.[88]

As women of Mujeres Libres, they wanted not just to visit and cheer the soldiers but also to educate. Mujeres Libres was always quick to point out that it understood this solidarity work within a larger political context. As Lucía Sánchez Saornil expressed it in July 1938, referring to Mujeres Libres' goal of creating a "conscientious and responsible female force": "This feminine force that we wish to create and that we are creating has, of course, a purpose and a political destiny much greater than sewing uniforms for militiamen or visiting the sick. . . . These are immediate needs, required by the circumstances. . . . Our organization has other more far-reaching goals that inform its principles and that must, at all times, guide its actions.[89]

It is evident from my conversations with some of those who were young "recruits" to Mujeres Libres that, although this solidarity work often took on a life of its own, the ultimate goals never were far from sight. Young women like Conchita Guillén and Sara Berenguer, who were only sixteen when the war broke out and who had had little personal exposure to anarchist ideals and activities in the years before the war (they described themselves as "novices, who knew nothing about nothing"), became totally caught up in Mujeres Libres in the final months of the war. Their understanding of the larger issues of capacitación and their insistence that Mujeres Libres enabled women to "respect themselves and be respected" come through clearly in all their conversations.

# VI

## SEPARATE AND EQUAL?
### DILEMMAS OF REVOLUTIONARY MOBILIZATION

Given Mujeres Libres' dual commitment to education and activism, we might expect it to have been welcomed with open arms by the CNT and FAI, its "brother" organizations in the libertarian movement. Mujeres Libres shared much with these organizations. Virtually all its militants were also activists in at least one of the others. Mujeres Libres' apprenticeship programs and programs of *formación social* prepared women to assume active roles in production and CNT activities. The anarchist/libertarian orientation of Mujeres Libres' cultural and educational programs addressed many of the goals of the FAI (and of the FIJL).

Nevertheless, these libertarian movement organizations never treated Mujeres Libres as a fully equal partner. In addition, Mujeres Libres' relationships with nonlibertarian women's groups were also strained, due to the greater financial and political power of the Communist party and its affiliated organizations. Examination of Mujeres Libres' relations with women's groups outside the libertarian movement and with other organizations within it can provide insight into the nature of Mujeres Libres' project and the "separate and equal" status it struggled to achieve within the libertarian community.

### Relations with Other Women's Organizations

Mujeres Libres' relations with nonlibertarian women's organizations were a product of its attitude toward feminism and of its role in the libertarian movement. As I have argued, Mujeres Libres rejected existing feminist ideology and political organizing. It insisted that women's subordination would be overcome not by a narrow struggle for voting rights, or even for equal pay at the workplace, but only through a movement with clear social and educational goals. In its view, political organizing (i.e., organizing without a social/educational and class dimension) would only perpetuate the subordination of working-class women.[1]

One purpose for which Mujeres Libres was founded, then, was to meet those women's needs which existing movement organizations had neglected. Nevertheless, as the civil war within a civil war progressed, Mujeres Libres' activities took on a further dimension and purpose: to compete with socialist organizations for the allegiance of the Spanish working woman. In a retrospective justification of its activities, Mujeres Libres argued to the libertarian movement:

> With the advent of the Republic in Spain, there began a veritable contest of captación among the political parties. . . .
>
> It was then, in view of the danger these events posed for the libertarian tendency and for the society as a whole, that a group of compañeras conceived the idea of creating a journal, managed and directed by our women, that would begin to work among the feminine sectors of our country, introducing among them . . . an inclination toward libertarian tendencies. This journal was the magazine *Mujeres Libres*, which appeared in May 1936.[2]

Of course, some libertarian women's groups (those in Terrassa and in Barcelona, for example) existed even *before* the journal began to be published. Mercedes and Lucía had sent letters to many of those groups in an effort to begin a network as early as 1935. But since those groups were explicitly rooted in the libertarian movement, they may not have fit the broader scenario Mujeres Libres was attempting to sketch out in these memoranda.

In fact, it is not at all clear that competition with socialist organizations was a primary goal at first. However, once the various leftist parties launched women's organizations, the captación piece of Mujeres Libres' agenda intensified, particularly the competition with the AMA.

In the prewar period, most other leftist organizations and parties, while committed in theory to overcoming the subordination of women, had tended to adopt the traditional Marxist perspective that the subordination of women was secondary to the divisions of a class society. Consequently, the most effective way to overcome that subordination was to organize women into working-class organizations to struggle jointly for an end to class oppression. In general, they denied what Mary Nash has termed the "specificity of women's oppression," and argued that "the emancipation of woman would be achieved exclusively through her incorporation into the class struggle."[3] Many of the organizations developed "women's sections," aimed at mobilizing women to participate in their activities.

Left-wing and dissident socialist organizations differed slightly in their orientation. They addressed the need for equality between men and women in the workplace and at home, and actively supported programs of cultural preparation. Nevertheless, their strategy was politically similar to that of PSOE, PCE, and PSUC: both the BOC and the POUM created "women's sections" to attend specifically to the mobilization of women into those parties.[4]

With the advent of the war, the strategy of the Marxist parties changed. They established separate women's organizations, among them Dona a la Reraguarda and the Asociación de Mujeres Antifascistas, and journals specifically oriented to women (e.g., *Mujeres* and *Companya*). These focused not on overcoming women's subordination, but on mobilizing women to contribute to the war effort. In neglecting to address the specificities of women's subordination, these socialist and communist organizations differed significantly from Mujeres Libres.

The AMA, in particular, represented itself as a nonpartisan organization, concerned with mobilizing women for the struggle against fascism. Its formal objectives were (1) to contribute to the struggle against fascism and in favor of peace, (2) to defend culture and women's right to an education to overcome their enslavement to ignorance, (3) to defend civil rights and equal justice, and (4) to incorporate women fully into the political and social life of the country.[5] Despite this stated concern with cultural subordination, however, its war-related activities soon overshadowed these gender-specific goals.

It was in this context that Mujeres Libres took issue with the AMA. Mujeres Libres was deeply committed to the *revolutionary* struggle: not just to winning the war but also to societal transformation. The AMA marginalized that struggle, downplaying both women's particular subordination and issues of broader social transformation. It focused instead on mobilizing women for work. In Mujeres Libres' view, the political effects of this supposedly nonideological mobilization effort were clear: it would reinforce the ideological dominance of the group already holding effective political power, the Communist party.

A concern with the political implications of the AMA's alleged nonpartisanship was at the forefront of Mujeres Libres' dealings with that organization. These implications were perhaps clearest in the syndical context. Over and over again, in circulars and letters to the CNT, Mujeres Libres emphasized the dangers of the AMA's "winning the battle" at workplaces. As male workers (most of whom, at least in Barcelona, had been members of the CNT) went off to the fronts, they were increasingly replaced by women. But would these women be affiliated with the CNT and continue the anarcho-syndicalist tradition in the workplaces? Or would they be "nonpolitical" women, trained in Generalitat programs, who, in joining the workforce as unaffiliated workers, would undermine, if not reverse, the gains made by generations of CNT organizing?[6]

In short, Mujeres Libres interpreted AMA's "nonpartisan" work as deeply political and as a direct challenge to the unions. Mujeres Libres saw its own programs of apprenticeship and capacitación as efforts to compete with AMA at the workplace: "The primordial preoccupation of Mujeres Libres was to preserve the syndical strength on which our libertarian movement rests."[7] The aim was to develop a revolutionary social consciousness that would enable women to join in the union-based struggle at the workplace and withstand the ideological influence of the Communist party in technical training programs.

This competition with AMA for the loyalties of women in factories, however, formed only a small part of Mujeres Libres' broader concern with developing a female force that was oriented toward revolutionary social transformation in all its dimensions. The other major context in which the competition revealed itself was in Mujeres Libres' response to the AMA's calls for the "unity" of all women and women's organizations (including republicans, socialists, and communists, along with Mujeres Libres) under the umbrella of the AMA.

Consistent with the position of the larger libertarian movement, Mujeres Libres vociferously opposed all calls for "feminine unity" that denied the important ideological and political differences among the groups. It insisted on the need to maintain an independent *libertarian* women's presence in a true coalition, in which each group would maintain its identity and autonomy. Such a coalition could draw strength from the variety of perspectives, rather than attempting to present a unified—and not coincidentally nonrevolutionary—common front. From the first, Mujeres Libres expressed deep distrust of the motives and intentions of the AMA and other "unity" organizations, emphasizing the political and ideological context in which these calls for unity were taking place. For example, in response to an invitation to attend the congress of the "Unió de Donas de Cataluña" in November 1937, Mujeres Libres issued a critique of the congress's statement of goals. I reproduce part of that response here, to provide a sense of its tone and intensity:

> 1º *To contribute to antifascist unity:*
>    Response: End the persecutions against antifascist organizations that are not represented in the government. . . .
> 2º *To work for equality of salary with men:*
>    . . . the problems of working-class families will not be resolved by equality of salaries. . . .
> 5º *To save our country from the fascist invasion.*
>    From the two invasions: that which is being fought at the fronts, and that which is operating in the rearguard. . . .
> 6º *To emancipate women for work, teaching them new skills.*
>    For Mujeres Libres, this is a fact that has been a reality for some time, and not a point to attract people to a congress.[8]

Many of the critiques Mujeres Libres circulated could have been meant for the education of its own agrupaciones (local groups) and CNT unions as well as for the AMA. After it had been rejected repeatedly by the national and regional committees of Mujeres Libres, the AMA began approaching individual agrupaciones to participate in its conferences and activities. A circular from Mujeres Libres' national committee to locals, dated May 23, 1938, warned them specifically not to be taken in by AMA propaganda.[9]

Mujeres Libres insisted that true unity must recognize diversity.[10] As Lucía Sánchez Saornil wrote, in response to an invitation from the AMA: "Mujeres Libres is not interested in 'feminine unity,' because that does not represent anything. We have called a thousand times for political and syndical unity, the only kind of unity that truly contributes to the cause . . . As long as differences [of politics and strategy] among the tendencies exist, a fusion of groups is impossible, because it is incompatible with human variety."[11] It was important that each organization should retain its "character and personality" and continue its work to further the war effort, the revolution, and women's emancipation. "Women's interests," Mujeres Libres argued, were neither so "clearly defined nor so universally agreed upon that, in themselves, they could form the basis for a single organization." True antifascist unity would require not the merging of all into one, but a recognition of the diversity of political views and a willingness to accept the autonomy of perspective and action of all the groups in the coalition. Mujeres Libres was not about to sacrifice its principles of direct action and spontaneous order to some vague and counterrevolutionary notion of "feminine unity."

## The Libertarian Movement

This insistence on autonomy and on the recognition of diversity among women's groups paralleled Mujeres Libres' claims for organizational autonomy and the recognition of diversity within the larger libertarian context. Mujeres Libres had been prepared for a struggle with women's groups allied with other organizations, but it was not prepared for the resistance it encountered within the libertarian movement. Though aware of the sexism of men in movement organizations and of the failure of those organizations to deal adequately with women and women's issues, Mujeres Libres planned to work closely with both the CNT and the FAI on the local, regional, and national levels. It expected to be welcomed into the libertarian "family." On the local level, this expectation was partially fulfilled, but at the level of national organizations, Mujeres Libres was consistently disappointed.

Part of its disappointment may, in fact, have been a consequence of the confusion evidently generated by its simultaneous insistence on inclusion and autonomy within the larger movement. Until its establishment as a national federation in August 1937, Mujeres Libres had consisted of a series of more or less independent agrupaciones. Mercedes Comaposada recalled that, at various times during the first half of 1937, she and Lucía had traveled to Valencia (the seat of the national government and the national committees of libertarian movement organizations) to request official recognition and support for Mujeres Libres.

> One time I had with me all sorts of pamphlets and records of all the different kinds of work we had done. I asked Marianet, "Why don't you recognize us as an organization?" And he said, "How can we recognize you as an organization? We know what you're doing, and you're doing it well. But until you come to us with an *organization*, that is, committees, regional committees, a national committee, people who are ready to serve in positions of responsibility, etc., there is nothing we can do."[12]

That conversation and others like it provided an impetus for calling a first national conference in August 1937, which brought together representatives of ninety local groups and established Mujeres Libres as a national organization.

The conference established a federal structure with provincial, regional, and national committees, a form of organization designed to provide maximum flexibility. Not coincidentally, it was a form based on the model of the CNT and the FAI, with which the members of Mujeres Libres were thoroughly familiar. In addition, the conference followed "accepted federal procedures" as these had been developed over the years in the CNT and the FAI. For example, rather than naming specific individuals to particular tasks, the conference named delegations (by locality), and the delegations, in turn, designated the individuals who would participate in the particular committee.[13] These practices clearly located the organization within the larger libertarian community.

Mujeres Libres identified itself ideologically with the goals and methods of the CNT and the FAI. At the same time, it jealously guarded its autonomy. Its initiators chose "Mujeres Libres" (free women), rather than "Mujeres Libertarias" (libertarian women), as its name, for example, to make clear that it had ideological connections to the libertarian movement, but was not a subsidiary organization.[14] The tension was also evident in the debate over the design for what was to be Mujeres Libres' membership card. After some discussion of the compañeras' "special fondness" for red and black (the colors of the CNT and FAI), it was agreed that the membership card should carry those colors—but not the letters "CNT-FAI." Although "we are a related organization, we are not a dependent of the others." Similarly, the official banner would be blue (for "optimism") with white letters, but would also carry a black-and-red stripe.[15]

The complexity of Mujeres Libres' own goals with respect to autonomy and inclusion was apparent. At the first meeting, the assembly voted to invite the relevant committees of the CNT and the FAI to send delegates to meetings of the regional and national committees of Mujeres Libres—in a nonvoting capacity—and to request that Mujeres Libres be permitted to send delegates (again, with no voting privileges) to meetings of the parallel committees of the CNT or FAI. The conference decided *not* to request that representatives from Mujeres Libres be accorded voting rights in the meetings of these other organizations because (a) they already had influence in those organizations through membership in unions (in the case of the CNT) and participation in anarchist agrupaciones (in the case of the FAI and FIJL); and (b) they did not want to run the risk of being bound by decisions taken by those organizations with which they might disagree. The scenario the conference discussed was: "Let us suppose, for example, that the CNT National Committee—which we would belong to—should decide, in opposition to our opinion, that our organization had lost its reason for existence and agreed, by majority vote, to dissolve it. What would be our position?"[16] In short, Mujeres Libres wanted to be included in congresses and in the deliberations that took place during them, but not to lose its independence.

Over the course of the next eighteen months, while insisting that it was "an integral part of the libertarian movement," Mujeres Libres continually asserted its autonomy. "Mujeres Libres," one statement argued,

> could have converted itself into an appendage of the union movement with respect to feminine preparation, transforming women into a receptacle of anarcho-syndicalism. . . . It could have converted itself into an annex or a "Women's section" of the FAI . . . but it didn't do this either. . . .
>
> Since those of us who were its "prime movers" were anarchists, we could not accede to a situation in which, within this specific organization, there would be individuals without a social formation; nor could we, as anarchists, convert those individuals into blind instruments [in the service of the movement] without contradicting our own anarchist principles.[17]

Despite its frustrations with movement organizations, Mujeres Libres continued to communicate its expectations for support and acceptance. It invited the FAI and CNT to send representatives to its congresses, hoping to demonstrate its membership in the libertarian community and to win legitimacy within it.[18]

The struggle for full organizational recognition was relentless. Representatives of Mujeres Libres often joined representatives of CNT and FAI when a car went out to the countryside on propaganda trips, marking shared goals and purposes in a symbolic way. Mujeres Libres further insisted that when the libertarian movement held rallies, a speaker from Mujeres Libres should be on the podium, along with those from the CNT, FAI, and FIJL. Announcements of such rallies in the press indicate that they were often successful. In preparation for the events commemorating the first anniversary of the death of Durruti, for example, the national committee of the CNT sent a circular to all the regional committees with instructions that, at each event, there should be five speakers, one from Mujeres Libres, one from SIA, one from FIJL, one from the CNT, and one from FAI.[19]

Nevertheless, I could find no other circulars from the National Committee following up on this one nor any documents of those organizations that mentioned either Mujeres Libres or SIA along with FAI and CNT as *equivalent* organizations. Further, Sara Berenguer Guillén reported that, when plans were announced for the second anniversary commemoration, there were no representatives from Mujeres Libres on the list of speakers. According to Sara, Soledad Estorach raised a fuss with the Catalan regional committee, demanding that representatives of Mujeres Libres also take part in the meetings. She succeeded in convincing the committee, but then they had to come up with speakers to go to rallies in towns and cities throughout Catalonia. Sara and Amada de Nó were among the young women who represented Mujeres Libres at some of these gatherings. Sara was to go Hospitalet and Granollers, though she was not able to speak at the former because the highway had been cut by fascist bombs and the event was cancelled. Amada went to Gerona. To deal with her nervousness, she memorized an article Soledad had written for a newspaper and recited it en route.[20]

Within this complex and often confusing context, Mujeres Libres did receive some recognition and support from other movement organizations. Much of the anarchist press seems to have been at least supportive, and at times enthusiastic, about Mujeres Libres' work and accomplishments. *Acracia*, the anarchist daily in Lérida, referred to the work of Mujeres Libres with some regularity, usually in the most laudatory of terms.[21] *Tierra y Libertad, Solidaridad Obrera, Tiempos Nuevos*, and a variety of other periodicals also made frequent reference to the work and activities of Mujeres Libres.

Locally, Mujeres Libres received help from individual CNT unions. Many locals participated actively in the apprenticeship programs and readily opened the doors (and temporarily stopped the assembly lines) of collectivized factories to Mujeres Libres' teams of speakers. There were also examples of direct support. When Pepita Carpena's compañero was killed at the front, the metalworkers' union, of which he had been a member and with which she had been involved since her youth, paid his weekly salary to her, so that she could continue her work with Mujeres Libres. Some local unions and many soldiers at the front also sent regular contributions to Mujeres Libres in support of its work.[22] At least in some communities, Mujeres Libres seems to have achieved the recognition it desired: being included *as an organization* as part of the larger libertarian movement. Minutes of meetings of the local federation of ateneos libertarios in Madrid, between July 1937 and April 1938, for example, report the attendance of Mujeres Libres, the local FAI, the local federation of CNT unions, and the local federation of the FIJL.[23]

Mujeres Libres sent a steady stream of requests for financial and other substantive assistance to the CNT and FAI at the national and regional levels. It appealed to them as "one more member of the libertarian family" in need of financial support to carry out work that was critical to all libertarian organizations. Mujeres Libres requested financial support and facilities for regional congresses (one held in Barcelona in February 1938, another held there in October 1938), for publications and propaganda work, for maintaining offices, and for salaries for members of the regional committee. Both the CNT and the FAI, particularly in Catalonia, seemed quite prepared to provide meeting space, food, and support for these conferences. In addition, between July and October of 1938, both the Catalan Regional Committee of the FAI and the National Committee of the CNT offered small but regular subventions to Mujeres Libres, which subsidized the printing of issue no. 13 of *Mujeres Libres*.[24] While the financial contributions usually fell short of what Mujeres Libres had requested, rarely was the organization turned away empty-handed.[25] Although little of the correspondence among the organizations indicates that Mujeres Libres was treated as an *equal* member of the libertarian family, it was certainly treated as a member, even if as a younger and perhaps immature sister.

Mujeres Libres nevertheless expressed frustration at not being treated with respect and seriousness by members of these organizations. All too often, individual compañeros referred to Mujeres Libres in sexually degrading or derogatory ways: calling them Mujeres Liebres, for example. ("Liebre" means hare; the term was obviously one of opprobrium, implying that they jumped from bed to bed like rabbits. This labeling of female activists as sexual deviants was not unique to Spain.)[26] Mujeres Libres repeatedly appealed to both the regional and national committees of the CNT and the FAI, asking them to "rein in" the hostility of their local groups and encourage them to provide direct support.[27]

Mujeres Libres also sought support from regional and national organizations of the libertarian movement. For example, in 1937, Mujeres Libres requested of the National Committee of the CNT that local unions regularly allow women time for extra apprenticeship training sessions in workshops and factories. But the CNT did not respond positively. Consequently, many training opportunities were taken over by the government, and the AMA and socialist unions were taking ready advantage of them. Mujeres Libres later requested that women identified by Mujeres Libres as potential militants be allowed an hour and a half off with pay, a few times a week, so that they could attend classes in "general culture and social preparation." This arrangement, they argued, would be in the interest of the movement, as well as of individual women, and would help to counter the effects of government (and communist-dominated) programs.[28] At this same time, the secretariat of the UGT in Barcelona was attempting to pressure its local unions to be more accepting of women workers trained in the Generalitat-sponsored institute.[29] Mujeres Libres' concern that other organizations were taking better advantage of the training programs thus seems well founded.

Mujeres Libres repeatedly requested financial assistance at both the regional and national levels. Noteworthy is a March 1937 letter to the Peninsular Committee of the FAI, in which Mujeres Libres identified itself as "Agrupación Mujeres Libres, FAI." The letter detailed some of its goals and activities, reporting that it had five hundred members, but was in desperate financial need. The Catalan Regional Committee, however, writing in response to this letter, met Mujeres Libres' request for eight thousand pesetas with a grant of only five hundred pesetas to support its work.[30] Three months later, Mercedes Comaposada, writing for the Secretariat of Propaganda of Mujeres Libres, again addressed the Peninsular Committee of the FAI, noting that Communist-sponsored organizations (all of which were receiving substantial financial assistance from both the Party and government ministries) were "making headway among women in the UGT and even in the CNT." In a statement that reveals a great deal about the way Comaposada thought Mujeres Libres was being perceived by the libertarian movement, she concluded, "Mujeres Libres arose in opposition to this, with the aim of educating the women our movement is so in need of—and not, as some compañeros misunderstand us, with intentions of separatism or of feminist agitation."[31]

Mujeres Libres frequently compared its position in the libertarian movement to that of AMA in the communist camp. One circular noted that, in addition to offering substantial financial support, a UGT transport workers' union had even presented a car to the AMA's Sección de Propaganda. "Comparing this with our own economic impotence brought tears of rage to our eyes. What we could do with even half of what they have! Just with what they spend on posters!"[32]

Emma Goldman took up the cause during one of her visits to Barcelona. Since Mujeres Libres had refused to dissolve itself into AMA, she wrote to Mariano Vázquez: "They receive no aid whatsoever, while the

Communist women not only receive aid, but are also collecting money outside the country from women in factories. . . . Mujeres Libres is being left behind on all fronts."

> You must know that I have struggled for the emancipation of women for some years, so it is natural that I should be interested in Mujeres Libres. I am very surprised that our organizations CNT, FAI, and even the Juventudes have done so little to help them, and have shown so little interest. Don't you think, dear compañero, that it would also be in the interest of the CNT and of the FAI to assist Mujeres Libres as much as you can?[33]

Vázquez was quite defensive in his response, insisting that the CNT was "just as concerned about Mujeres Libres as you are" and that the libertarian movement had provided whatever assistance it could to Mujeres Libres—although, since it did not have the backing of a strong international organization, its financial capabilities were far inferior to those of the Communists. "I must, therefore, reject totally your claim that the CNT has not done everything possible for Mujeres Libres. It is true that the CNT has not been able to give it [Mujeres Libres] the millions that other organizations and parties can give to their women's organizations. And we have not done so, because we don't have them [the millions of pesetas]."[34] The CNT's resources *were* inferior to those of the Communist party. Nevertheless, as we will see, budgetary considerations were not the only factor in these decisions. The question of the autonomy of Mujeres Libres seems, in fact, to have been much more significant.

## The Women's Secretariats of the FIJL

Questions of autonomy and inclusion came clearly to the fore in Mujeres Libres' relations with the FIJL. When the FIJL established a *Secretaría Femenina* (women's bureau) at the end of 1937, Mujeres Libres found itself in a directly competitive relationship. Pepita Carpena, who had long been a member of both Juventudes and of the CNT, and who had originally refused to join Mujeres Libres on the grounds that she saw no need for the separation of men and women in the struggle, described her reaction:

> I was active in the Juventudes. . . . They called a meeting and put forward the proposition to establish a Secretariado femenino inside the FIJL. It seems that the compañeros had this idea from the Communists, who were becoming quite powerful, and had established "women's sections" everywhere. Now, I had been committed to the emancipation of women from the beginning. But I accepted the prevailing view that the struggle should be carried out equally by men and women. So I didn't like this business of a "women's bureau" in the FIJL at all. . . . I said that I was totally opposed. Nevertheless, even though my group accepted the proposition, I

was named delegate from my Juventudes group to the Local Federation
of Juventudes. . . . So, I had to go to the meeting and announce that we
accepted the proposition. But I decided then (and told them) that, since it
seemed to me counterproductive that the FIJL should have a Secretariado Femenino, I was leaving, and from then on, I would carry on my
militancy in Mujeres Libres.[35]

The Secretaría was meant to counter the efforts of the Communist-
sponsored Asociación de Jóvenes Antifascistas, the Asociació de la Dona
Jove (young women's organization), and the Unión de Muchachas (girl's
union) to engage in propaganda and political work among young people
and, further, to provide programs of captación and capacitación for
young women.[36]

Pepita viewed the creation of a special women's section in the FIJL as
an abandonment of what she took to be the longstanding anarchist
principle that struggles should be carried on jointly. She also saw it as a
negation of the work Mujeres Libres was already doing. Why create a
special women's department in the FIJL, she wondered, when there was
already a libertarian group devoted to educating and preparing women
of all ages?

Pepita's concerns were shared by others, both within and without
Mujeres Libres. In the months after the decision was taken, the Secretariado Femenino sent out a stream of announcements addressing these
concerns—explaining its goals and insisting that it meant neither to
deny the significance of, nor to compete with, Mujeres Libres. However,
since it defined its purpose in almost exactly the same terms as Mujeres
Libres—the capacitación and education of young women—and since
the activities it proposed to undertake—schools, apprenticeship programs, journals, discussion groups—were virtually identical, the argument was a difficult one to sustain.

Its *Circular no. 3* of November 1937, for example, argued that "there is
no duality of functions, nor is there any basic competition between
Mujeres Libres and Juventudes Libertarias." Mujeres Libres, the document asserted, was valuable as an organization, but one directed to the
needs of *adult* women. The Secretariadas Femeninas, on the other hand,
would address *young* women, challenging their marginalization and
assuring that there would be women in the organization to replace the
men who were constantly being called away. The language is virtually
identical with that of Mujeres Libres, the sole difference being the claim
that Mujeres Libres addressed adults whereas the Secretariado
Femenino would be oriented to young people.[37] But since so many of
the activists in Mujeres Libres were young people (Pepita, Soledad,
Sara, Conchita, and many of their friends were in their mid to late teens
at the beginning of the revolution), it seemed to many in Mujeres Libres

that the Secretarías Femeninas would simply be duplicating its work and draining the movement's scarce resources.

The Secretariado was well aware of this sentiment, and apparently devoted as much energy to discussions of how to deal with Mujeres Libres as it did to dealing with the AJA and other Communist-affiliated youth organizations. Relations with Mujeres Libres were strained, at best. The Secretarías frequently referred to Mujeres Libres as a "young" or "immature" organization, one with little success in organizing women—although they did acknowledge that Mujeres Libres' "weakness" might be due to its precarious financial condition. They were well aware of Mujeres Libres' opposition to the existence of the Women's Bureau: "Its position with relation to our Secretariats is of opposition. They believe that they should be the only ones in the libertarian camp to win over [captar] women—and the ones to distribute the activists they don't need to their sister organizations."38

Of course, Mujeres Libres did not see its role as "distributing excess militants" to other organizations. It saw itself as preparing women to participate in whatever libertarian movement organization they might choose. What these passages and other documents reveal is a strong sense of organizational rivalry.39 Mujeres Libres saw the creation of the Women's Bureaus as redundant. The Women's Bureaus, for their part, wanted Mujeres Libres to become a "dependent" organization of the Libertarian movement: "all of us orient its [Mujeres Libres'] work, and we should have the responsibility for its development and activities and for providing it with economic means."40

In October 1938, the Secretariado Femenino prepared a report of its activities for presentation to the National Plenary of the FIJL, in which it reiterated earlier claims that Mujeres Libres was acting improperly in attempting to incorporate both young and adult women in its programs, and raised with the congress whether it might wish to bring to the forthcoming joint congress of the libertarian movement a resolution that Mujeres Libres be an organization for adult women only. Further, the report revealed that the Peninsular Committee had experienced considerable difficulties in convincing some of its own regional committees of the need for a Women's Bureau. Apparently, both the Local Federation of Barcelona and the Catalan Regional Committee had rejected the proposal for a bureau, arguing that "a number of the tasks we set out were being addressed already by Mujeres Libres, and that there was no reason for us to put ourselves in competition with them."41

The report may be even more important, however, for what it revealed about the frustration of the Secretaría with its position in the FIJL. Despite the earlier claims that Mujeres Libres had been largely ineffective in achieving its goals (and that the Women's Bureaus were much better placed to engage effectively in this work), what is evident is a sense of frustration with how little the Secretarías had accomplished in the past months. They referred to a number of problems, including the claim that the position of the Secretaría within the FIJL severely limited its freedom of action. It was time, they insisted, either for a recommitment or a reorientation: "Either we recognize 'the special characteristics of women' and create an organism with sufficient independence of activity to address them; or, on the contrary, we deny the existence of 'special characteristics' and stop bothering with this problem any more, dissolving the Secretarías Femeninas."[42]

Thus, despite the organizational competition with Mujeres Libres, the women who participated in the Women's Bureaus apparently had experiences that validated Mujeres Libres' insistence on the importance of autonomy. The Women's Bureaus adopted goals very similar to those of Mujeres Libres, but attempted to achieve them within the FIJL. The Bureaus' complaints about their treatment by other organs of their own movement, the lack of support they received, and their need for greater independence seem to justify Mujeres Libres' own position vis-à-vis the movement as a whole. Nevertheless, the Bureaus never offered public support for Mujeres Libres' view.

### The Libertarian Movement Congress, October 1938

After many months of informal approaches to specific organizations and movement leaders for moral and financial support, Mujeres Libres formally requested organizational recognition at the joint National Plenary of Regionals, CNT-FAI-FIJL in October 1938. That congress, which took place in Barcelona and lasted two weeks, was the first national meeting to bring together representatives from the three major movement organizations.

Mujeres Libres had not received an official invitation to attend. In the past, members of Mujeres Libres had often participated in meetings of movement organizations as members of those organizations. But with a few minor exceptions they had never attended *as* representatives of Mujeres Libres. This time, however, Mujeres Libres wished to attend as an organization. It assembled a delegation of fifteen women who presented themselves at the congress, seeking accreditation as delegates of Mujeres Libres and formal recognition of Mujeres Libres as a fourth constituent branch of the libertarian movement.

Pura Pérez Arcos traveled from Valencia to Barcelona to serve as a Mujeres Libres delegate:

> We sailed from the port of Alicante on the afternoon of October 7, in a small English boat. The group included people from Madrid, Valencia, and a variety of places in Andalusia. Our tiny Mujeres Libres delegation was inspired by the great hopes and expectations we had of the Congress. . . . To make a trip in those days was very risky, and we all knew it.

The harbors were being bombarded every night, and we were totally illegal travelers on this British boat, which had to sail right by Franquista ships. We were due to arrive the next morning, but as we neared the harbor, we could hear the explosions of the fascist bombing of the port. The captain headed north, and we sailed around all that day and night, finally arriving in Barcelona, exhausted and hungry, on the morning of the 9th. We were tremendously excited, and ready to argue the case for Mujeres Libres on the floor of the congress. But they would not even allow us into the meeting![43]

The delegate accreditation committee (comprised of the secretaries of the three major organizations) brought the issue of Mujeres Libres' attendance to the full congress for decision. Interestingly, in addition to the delegation from Mujeres Libres, there was another person present who had requested permission to join in the proceedings: Emma Goldman, the official representative of the CNT in London. The assembly readily agreed to allow her to sit in on the meetings as an observer, given her "special character." But the matter of the delegation from Mujeres Libres was not so easily resolved. After much debate the assembly agreed that "Mujeres Libres should attend only [the discussion of] that point which affected them directly." Consequently, while some of the would-be delegates were able to stay through the meeting as delegates from other organizations, Mujeres Libres' delegation was present only for the congress's eighteenth and nineteenth sessions (October 25 and 26, 1938), to participate in the discussion of the fifth point of the agenda, "How to assist the work of auxiliary organizations of the libertarian movement."[44]

Mujeres Libres had attempted to lay the groundwork for its attendance and proposal in the preceding months. In January it circulated a document entitled "Some Considerations from the National Committee of Mujeres Libres to that of the CNT about the Political Importance of the Former." In September it sent a nine-page statement to the national and peninsular committees, reviewing its history and accomplishments and emphasizing its work of captación vis-à-vis the AMA.

In its presentation at the congress, Mujeres Libres discussed the particular disabilities confronting women in Spain, the need to counteract "political" forces (that is, the Communist party and the AMA), and the importance of a separate libertarian organization to meet these needs. Its statements repeatedly emphasized both the libertarian character and commitments of Mujeres Libres, and the necessity for its autonomy within the context of the larger movement.

The only way to serve both aspects of our movement, the syndical and the specific [anarchist], was by maintaining the autonomy of the new organization. That autonomy would permit us to work with the female sector in the pure territory of ideological and professional capacitación, providing

women opportunities . . . to engage in an apprenticeship in self-determination, accustoming them to study and confront political problems.

   Only . . . the independence [of this female force] creates the possibility
of its being useful in either an ideological or syndical sense. . . .

   This is why Mujeres Libres has insisted on being . . . a movement that is
politically autonomous, protecting its ability to determine its own ends,
while its Statutes and Declaration of Principles guarantee its libertarian
essence."[45]

The delegates, however, did not understand Mujeres Libres' insistence
on both membership and autonomy. And the parliamentary situation in
which Mujeres Libres found itself did not make the job of explaining it
any easier. Officially, Mujeres Libres was attending the meeting only as
an "auxiliary" to the movement.

The resulting situation made Mujeres Libres' task particularly difficult, and it provided many opportunities for parliamentary maneuver-
ing to those who opposed granting Mujeres Libres equal and autonomous organizational status. Mujeres Libres presented cogent and
powerful arguments in support of its claims, but these were effectively
marginalized in the debate. The assembly never addressed Mujeres
Libres' request directly because others argued that the question of
Mujeres Libres' status had never appeared on the agenda of the call to
the meeting and that, given the rules of the organization (according to
which, delegates could only vote on the basis of prior instructions given
them by the bodies that had elected them), the assembly was not
empowered to make a decision. In the end, the assembly refused to vote
on Mujeres Libres' proposition, agreeing instead to a two-part alternative proposal: (1) that since the delegates did not bring directions
from their organizations, a proposal should be drawn up which could be
circulated to all the national and regional committees and be discussed
by the locals; and (2) that since Mujeres Libres was in need of both
moral and financial assistance, unions should encourage their female
members to join Mujeres Libres and should commit themselves to
supporting Mujeres Libres financially, whenever possible. Despite Mujeres Libres' complaint that the proposal solved nothing, it passed
unanimously.[46] Mujeres Libres did draw up a two-page summary of its
arguments, including a formal request that it be accepted as a fourth
branch of the libertarian movement, which was circulated to national
and regional committees shortly after the congress.[47] But, because of
the rapidly deteriorating war situation, no further plenary was held,
and the motion never came to a vote. Mary Nash has written of this
meeting that Mujeres Libres' bid for recognition "was rejected on the
grounds that a specifically woman's organization would be a source of
disunity and inequality within the libertarian movement."[48] Nevertheless, apart from the parliamentary maneuvers, Mujeres Libres' proposal
was never formally rejected.

A study of the debate at the congress and of the documents Mujeres Libres circulated before and after it reveals a great deal about the position of Mujeres Libres within the movement, both organizationally and ideologically. Organizationally, Mujeres Libres analogized its situation to that of the AMA in other political movements and to that of the FIJL within the libertarian movement. Mujeres Libres pointed to the support the FIJL was receiving from the CNT and FAI, despite the fact that it was an organization devoted "only" to young people, and argued that Mujeres Libres ought to be accorded comparable support and recognition for its work in mobilizing women. Ideologically, Mujeres Libres insisted that libertarians ought to recognize that the specific needs of women would require particular ideological, as well as organizational, attention.

The analogy with the Juventudes did not serve Mujeres Libres well, at least in part because the status of the FIJL was also ambiguous. At one point in the debate, for example, delegates argued that, since the FIJL was only an auxiliary organization, Mujeres Libres should be considered in the same category. Representatives of the FIJL objected to this characterization, noting that the FIJL had been invited to the congress. Later in the debate, however, others commented that, although the FIJL was present as a result of a fait accompli, there was no reason to "repeat the same mistake" with Mujeres Libres.[49]

In the end, the FIJL and Mujeres Libres were treated very differently. The FIJL had been invited as an organization; its secretary sat as one of the three members of the credentials committee, and its delegates participated with voice and vote in all the debates of the congress. Further, the congress approved a proposal to provide the FIJL with regular and substantial financial assistance. It is true that, even within the debates about that proposal, representatives of the FIJL chafed at what they regarded as insufficient recognition of their own autonomy and achievements as an organization. Nevertheless, FIJL succeeded in asserting its own definition of its mission and goals and received widespread support, both financial and moral, for its activities and for its status as a constituent organization of the libertarian movement.[50]

There was no such support for Mujeres Libres. One after another the delegations indicated that, although they were willing to provide moral and material support to Mujeres Libres, they opposed granting the organization equal status as a fourth branch of the movement. A number of different arguments were adduced: (1) that anarchism (and syndicalism) admitted of no differences by sex, and, therefore, that an organization oriented only to women could not truly be a libertarian organization; (2) that Mujeres Libres was causing confusion because it was engaging in work that should be done by unions; and (3) that Mujeres Libres should not be functioning as an autonomous organization, but should be operating within the unions and cultural centers.

In its responses, Mujeres Libres attempted to meet all these objections. Its initial presentation to the congress addressed the question of
autonomy, stressing the uniqueness of women's situation in Spain, the
need for an organization to address it, and the demonstrated failure of
the CNT, FAI, and FIJL to meet that need. Mujeres Libres' speakers
expressed anger at being asked constantly to justify themselves and to
prove their worth and commitment. They argued that the organization
was working both within and outside the unions and that the work of
capacitación and captación required a much broader and multifaceted
approach than any of the existing organizations were equipped to do.
Further, Mujeres Libres was representing women and their interests in
the workplace: for example, struggling for equal pay for equal work, a
goal which unions had not defended with appropriate vigor. Speakers
repeated that Mujeres Libres was not a separatist organization, and
that it had intervened in opposition when it had heard of women's
efforts to establish separate women's unions, arguing that the women
ought to join with men in existing union organizations. Finally, they
argued that anarchism and syndicalism were not the exclusive province
of men: as compañeras, they had a right—and a responsibility—to
propagate libertarian ideas and practices: "Our self-determination cannot be opposed on the grounds that Anarchism doesn't admit of sex
differences, because then it would be necessary to conclude that, as of
now, our Libertarian Organizations are not deserving of that name
because, whether by choice or by necessity, its militants are almost
exclusively men!"[51]

My own sense, confirmed by interviews with participants, is that the
key issue was autonomy. The fact that it was an organization of *women*
would not necessarily have been sufficient to deny recognition. After all,
the FIJL was an organization of only young people. The Women's Bureaus were set up with an even narrower purview: young women.
Where Mujeres Libres truly differed from the FIJL was in its insistence
on autonomy. It claimed the right to define its priorities; it would
organize its programs not just to mobilize women *[captar]*, but also to
educate and empower *[capacitar]* them. Mujeres Libres' demand for
autonomy in setting its goals and priorities seems to have been the
"sticking point" for other movement organizations.

Despite its frustration with the decision (or, more accurately, non-
decision) of the Congress with respect to its status as an organization,
Mujeres Libres took the delegates at their word on the question of
financial and moral support. In the weeks following, Mujeres Libres
corresponded with the regional and national committees of both the
FAI and the CNT, reminding them of the resolutions passed at the
meeting and requesting financial assistance—requests which apparently met with some success.[52]

It is also clear, however, that even in the aftermath of the Congress they felt a lack of moral as well as of financial support. In December 1938, for example, the Ministry of the Interior attempted to dispossess Mujeres Libres of the building on the Paseo Pi y Margall in Barcelona that housed the Casal de la Dona Treballadora and to turn the building over to the Bank of Spain. After repeated, though unsuccessful, attempts to have the decision reversed, Mujeres Libres agreed to move if the Ministry found them a suitable replacement building. But the Ministry was unresponsive, sending police to evict them. Mujeres Libres requested assistance from the FAI, CNT, and FIJL in Barcelona. The FAI responded, arranging special meetings between representatives of Mujeres Libres and of the Bank of Spain, and calling on Federica Montseny to intervene with the Ministry of the Interior, which she did. FAI representatives supported Mujeres Libres' decision to remain in the building and to engage in passive resistance to eviction until a suitable replacement site should be found.[53] But Mujeres Libres received little support from the CNT, and expressed disgust with the CNT's attitude, characterizing it as "rather timid, and little inclined to support a firm position on our part." "It is a pity," Lucía wrote to the National Committee of the CNT, "that you compañeros have always had so little time to acquaint yourselves with the valuable work of Mujeres Libres and that the consequence of this is the little interest you have shown in responding to our plea."[54] Mujeres Libres was still a long way from being fully accepted by other libertarian organizations.

Nevertheless, it had made considerable progress. Conchita Guillén mentioned one poignant detail that may shed some light on the relations between Mujeres Libres and other organizations in the last days of the war.

> On the very day of the evacuation of Barcelona [January 24, 1939], when the fascists were practically at the gates, we were called to a meeting of the libertarian movement: CNT, FAI, JJLL, and Mujeres Libres. Jacinta Escudero and I attended as delegates of the Local Federation of Mujeres Libres. It was a meeting of some importance, because it was a crucial moment: we had either to resist, or to abandon [Barcelona]. . . . We put ourselves at the disposition of the movement; they thanked us, but said it would be a useless sacrifice, since they had no strength at all, and we all should get out as quickly as possible.[55]

The first time that Mujeres Libres was called, as an organization, to a meeting of the libertarian movement was to be, in fact, its last. Even so, Conchita's memory of the event was clear and strong: for once, they were accorded the status as equal members of the movement that they had struggled so long to achieve.

# CONCLUSION
## COMMUNITY AND THE EMPOWERMENT
## OF WOMEN

> One can talk for a long time about
> experiences such as those we lived.
> The most important thing, though,
> is not having made the revolution,
> but having continued the struggle in
> the years since, each in his or her
> particular setting, or in many
> settings at once, without trumpet or
> drum.
>
> —Anna Delso

As women whose particular needs had been neglected by the larger society and by their libertarian comrades, the women of Mujeres Libres had a special commitment to the creation of a society that recognized and valued diversity. Empowerment would come through the struggle for the anarchist vision of coordination without hierarchy, diversity without inequality, and individuality with collectivity.

However short-lived the revolution in which Mujeres Libres played so important a role, the experience of participating in it had a dramatic and long-lasting impact on the lives of the women active in the organization. Women who were only in their teens and early twenties at the time of the revolution reflected years later that those events changed their lives dramatically. The energy, enthusiasm, and sense of personal and collective empowerment that they experienced stood as markers for them of what life could be and of what people could achieve, if they worked together with commitment and hope. The most rewarding aspect of engaging in this study was the contact with people, both women and men, who retained that vision through years of exile and/or oppression. Surely one of the reasons they were able to do so was that, for them, social revolution had not been simply a vision or a hope; they had actually *lived* a change in their daily life.[1]

I wish to explore the implications of Mujeres Libres' activities for some of the central issues confronting contemporary feminists and social change activists—questions of empowerment, the incorporation of diversity, and the meaning and nature of political and social participation. The women of Mujeres Libres addressed women's difference from men within the context of a working-class movement. Contemporary feminists and participatory democrats are striving to create a society that can address differences of class, racial-ethnic community, sexual orientation, age, and physical abilities, as well as of gender. Mujeres Libres' experience, however, has much to teach us about empowerment and changing consciousness, about the relation between individuals and communities, and about the meaning of difference.

### "Cowards Don't Make History": A Legacy of Empowerment

Do you live in a town where women are relegated to a position of insignificance, dedicated exclusively to housework and the care of children? No doubt, many times you have thought about this with some disgust, and when you've noticed the freedom that your brothers or the men of your households enjoy, you have felt the hardship of being a woman. . . .

Well, against all this which you have had to suffer comes Mujeres Libres. We want you to have the same freedom as your brothers . . . we want your voice to be heard with the same authority as your father's. We want you to attain that independent life you have wanted. . . .

But realize that all this requires your effort: in order to achieve them, you need the assistance of others. You need others to be concerned with the same things as you, you need to help them, as they will help you. In a single word, you must struggle communally.[2]

Both feminists and communalists have recognized that it is difficult for isolated individuals to feel strong and powerful. As Marge Piercy wrote, "Strong is what we make / each other. Until we are all strong together, / a strong woman is a woman strongly afraid."[3] In developing a sense of connection with others, subordinated people often overcome the sense of powerlessness that can inhibit social change.

Thoroughly rooted as it was in the communalist anarchist tradition, Mujeres Libres insisted that the process of individual empowerment was, at base, a collective one. Along with contemporary feminists, Mujeres Libres recognized that people do not exist as social isolates. They live in families and communities, and their sense of self derives from the relations they have with others in those communities. Truly egalitarian communities respect the diversity and individuality of their members, and only when we live and work in such communities can we come fully to a sense of our own powers and capacities.

Mujeres Libres was founded because too few women had experienced empowerment within the existing organizations of the Spanish anarchist and anarcho-syndicalist movements. It aimed to become a "community of empowerment" for working-class women and, at the same time, an organizational context for women's empowerment within the libertarian movement as a whole.

The organization clearly contributed to the empowerment of many of its members, both those who had little prior involvement in the anarchist and anarcho-syndicalist movements and those who had been activists in them. Each experienced the fears—and the pride—of having "to do for oneself" that went along with being an activist in a group of women dependent only on themselves. The sense of community they developed and shared with others through the years transformed them. Having lived through those times, and having planned and organized new arenas of social life, they came to know a much wider range of their own capacities. The community of other women with whom they shared those activities became a primary source of validation of their new sense of self. Continued connection with other Spanish libertarians and with women of Mujeres Libres in the years since the war helped to keep alive not only the memory of their activities together, but the reality of their personal transformations.

The long-range impact of the experiences varied greatly with the individual and with the social and political contexts that they found or created for themselves.[4] The empowerment each of these women experienced was connected not only to what she personally had achieved but, more importantly, to the community of activists, male and female, with whom she lived and worked—both during the revolution and in the years of exile and repression that followed it. This finding should hardly be surprising. Contemporary feminist theorists have placed increasing emphasis on the importance of relationships among women. Some have argued that women's networks provide important supports for women in their families, workplaces, and communities, and enable them to engage in what is commonly recognized as "political action."[5] Others have focused on the ways women's location within networks of friends, family, and associates and their particular relationship to social institutions define the ways women experience themselves in the world to the extent that women may develop psychological orientations, patterns of moral reasoning, and criteria for action that differ significantly from prevailing (male-defined) norms.[6]

Attention to context, a defining characteristic of what we might term a "feminist world-view,"[7] was also an important element of the Spanish anarchist orientation. Many of Mujeres Libres' programs had a strong "consciousness-raising" component, which enabled the participants to locate their experiences in a social context and to build solidarity with others on the basis of shared perspectives. As in consciousness-raising (CR) groups in the early days of the contemporary women's movement in the United States, the realizations an individual woman experienced empowered her because they were validated by the experiences of others.

Consciousness-raising groups, of course, are not the only contexts in which consciousness changes. As Marx insisted, consciousness changes in and through struggle. Traditionally, Marxists have interpreted that to mean that truly revolutionary consciousness—in other words, that based in class—is born out of conflict at the workplace, when workers come to recognize themselves as engaged in a common struggle against the bourgeoisie. Spanish anarchists criticized the economic mono-causality of this analysis while retaining the emphasis on struggle and activity as the prime generators of radical consciousness. General strikes in both rural Andalusia and industrial Barcelona (discussed in chapter 2) demonstrated that consciousness of oppression can derive from a variety of experiences in different contexts and that community-based networks can be as important to consciousness-change as factory-based struggle. Ateneos and rationalist schools also provided contexts for people to test out new cultural visions, new understandings of themselves, and new relationships to the world.

Spanish anarchists recognized, and Mujeres Libres drew on the rec-ognition, that radicalization is born of action. People develop new senses of themselves by breaking with traditional molds, taking on roles and moving in areas previously closed to them. When those who cross the boundaries of what is considered appropriate behavior do so in the context of a supportive group, they can become empowered—and come to question the appropriateness of those boundaries in the first place. The women who participated in the general strikes and "women's war" in Barcelona in the first decades of this century, for example, did not necessarily leave their neighborhoods in protest against high food prices *because* they were challenging conventional understandings of "women's place." However, movement out of their neighborhoods and into more public/governmental arenas opened new perspectives and provided the grounds for the development of a critical consciousness. The women who went to work in factories during the Spanish Civil War did not do so *because* they were challenging the sexual division of labor, but because they needed income to support their families while their husbands, brothers, or fathers were at war and because jobs had to be done. But the process of working in factories—and meeting with other women in similar circumstances—had radicalizing effects. Women who become involved in community-based struggles in their neighborhoods often follow a similar process. While they may join in protests out of their understandings of traditional women's role to protect their fam-ilies, the process of engaging in action can itself be politicizing.[8]

The development of a "critical consciousness" is an active process, one that involves both "participation in social struggle and the design of change. Collective confrontation with structures of authority and/or the creation of some new social-political reality in the interstices of existing power relations generates changed consciousness and energizes continued action (resistance)."[9] I would emphasize here the importance of *collective* confrontation. Radicalization seems to require—or at least be enhanced by—the existence of a community of others with whom one shares the experience and which then continues to validate the new sense of self (though, of course, not all experiences of commonality are radicalizing in a progressive sense).[10] It is that community which Mujeres Libres provided to its members, and it is that sense of community among contemporary feminists (and those of the "first wave" as well) which has been crucial to feminist consciousness-change.

The experience of consciousness-raising and of empowerment through shared experience is not the only parallel between contemporary feminism and Mujeres Libres. Another side of the recognition of the importance of community is the insistence that we can devise ways to overcome oppressive relations only by taking account of the familial, work, and other relationships in which all of us are embedded. Feminist theory and practice have begun to make clear that the "social glue" holding many societies together is not a formal structure of authority but, rather, patterns of human relationships rooted in common needs. Communities—and even political movements—succeed not because of hierarchical lines of command, but because groups of people build the day-to-day connections that sustain them.[11] The affinity groups of the FAI, the ateneos, the agrupaciones in which Mujeres Libres structured itself were more or less egalitarian collectives, in which everyone could feel part of the community. The interpersonal connections on which those structures were based (and which they fostered) in turn sustained the group and its members. The emphasis in feminist theory on the importance of mutually supportive relationships is strikingly similar to the Spanish anarchist insistence that the ideal society is one based on, and regulated through, relationships of mutuality and reciprocity, rather than of hierarchy and dominance.

Nevertheless, the women of Mujeres Libres were also aware of the ambiguous nature of communities. Specifically, communities that ignore or deny differences can perpetuate relations of hierarchy and domination despite an ostensible commitment to equality. Mujeres Libres' criticisms of the failure of anarchist organizations adequately to address women's uniqueness parallels the criticisms that working-class and ethnic minority women have leveled against U.S. feminist movements. Networks may be crucial to the creation and maintenance of communities. But if the communities are truly to be egalitarian and transformative, those networks must include the previously dominated, as well as the previously dominant, members of the minority and the majority.

Thus, finally, another aspect of anarchist and feminist attention to community as a context for empowerment is a focus on the interrelationship of community and individuality. As Martin Buber once noted, a person needs "to feel his [sic] own house as a room in some greater, all-embracing structure in which he is at home, to feel that the other inhabitants of it with whom he lives and works are all acknowledging and confirming his individual existence."[12] For Buber, the essence of true community was the strengthening of self that comes from active membership in a community of peers. Spanish anarchists insisted that individuality and community were mutually reinforcing. Mujeres Libres built on that insight. The experience of both personal and collective empowerment, rooted in networks of support and shared commitment, was a crucial aspect of revolutionary transformation. The empowerment they experienced required, in turn, a community that respected and valued differences *among* its members.

## Difference, Diversity, and Community

Although Mujeres Libres understood empowerment as a communal process, it also recognized that not all communities empower. For example, societies structured hierarchically along lines of class, race, and gender, empower some while disempowering others. A second legacy of Mujeres Libres, then, is its effort, through a focus on gender, to create a community that fully incorporates *all* its members—in this case, respecting both women's similarities to, and differences from men.

Mujeres Libres demanded that the call for recognition and respect for diversity include women as well as men. It insisted that the anarchist movement and the new society it was attempting to create *treat women equally with men while, at the same time, respecting women's differences from men*. The women of Mujeres Libres did not always agree about what those differences or their sources were. But all insisted that women had to be accepted in their particularity: to be addressed in ways that acknowledged their different life situation—without necessarily assuming its permanence—and that women must be allowed, in fact encouraged, to contribute their unique perspective to the movement and the new society.

Their experiences parallel those of contemporary feminists in important ways, and offer suggestions for dealing with some of the more pressing questions on the contemporary feminist agenda: (1) How do we acknowledge differences among people (whether differences between men and women or differences of class, ethnicity, and culture among women) without precluding the possibilty of change? (2) Once those differences are acknowledged and named, what "difference" should they make? How ought they be incorporated organizationally? What could it mean for us to create a society that recognizes diverse groups of people with diverse needs without treating the perspectives and characteristics of some as the norm for all?

## Women's Difference, Different Politics?

Prevailing definitions and expectations of what constitute legitimate political issues and forms of political behavior have important implications for our understandings of politics, for what we recognize as political activism or protest, and for the creation of policies and programs. In the political realm, the claim that women are fundamentally different from men has been used both to justify women's relative marginality from political and social power and to blame women for it.[13] Unions and political parties have set their agendas according to male-defined criteria, ignored issues of primary concern to women (such as maternity leave, equal pay for equal work, child care), and devoted little attention to mobilizing women into their ranks. In addition, they have tended to ignore, ridicule, or deny the political significance of protest actions women did undertake, whether on their own or others' behalf. As a result, women have rarely seen themselves, or been seen by others, as "political animals" capable of engaging in joint action to address issues of common concern.[14]

The experience of women within the Spanish anarchist and anarcho-syndicalist movements has illustrated some of the ways in which these understandings of difference constrained women's activism within the movement. A burgeoning literature on women in social protest movements, particularly in socialist organizations, makes clear that the frustrations Spanish anarchist women experienced were hardly unique.

In western Europe and the United States, political parties and workplace-based unions have been the dominant normative structures of social and political participation. But with a few notable exceptions, each of these types of organization has appealed overwhelmingly to men. Denied the right to vote through the nineteenth century and well into the twentieth on the grounds that it would "defeminize" them, women were largely ignored by political party organizations, except when these organizations were pressured on the question of suffrage.[15] Although women were joining the paid industrial work force in increasing numbers during the early years of the twentieth century, only rarely did unions actively mobilize women as members or make women's issues their priority demands in negotiations with management. Prevailing gender ideology constructed work as a male responsibility and treated any women who did engage in paid work as, somehow, anomalies. With the exception of unions inspired by traditions of direct action (for example, the Wobblies in the United States, in addition to the CNT in Spain), women seemed largely to disappear from the consciousness of both party and union.[16] In Spain, for example, during the early years of this century, only the Catholic church and related organizations took the plight of women workers seriously enough to mount substantial organizing drives.

Socialism and feminism arose in western Europe more or less simultaneously, sparked by related economic and cultural phenomena—the promises of freedom and universal citizenship offered by the French Revolution and the promises of abundance and economic growth offered by the Industrial Revolution. Both socialism and feminism highlighted the contradictions of these revolutions and of the democratic political regimes that struggled into being during the course of the nineteenth century. Socialists challenged the protection of private property built into democratic constitutions and the mockery it made of any process of universal suffrage. Feminists, too, focused on the contradiction between theory and practice: "The Declaration of Rights of Man and Citizen did not exclude women from social and political spheres; it did what was far worse: it established their absence."[17] In such a context, feminists and socialists might have turned to one another as allies, both struggling against limited notions of citizenship that, in not recognizing differences (whether of class or of sex), masked and perpetuated relations of domination and subordination.

In fact, European socialists and feminists did make common cause on many occasions. But as Barbara Taylor noted in *Eve and the New Jerusalem*, the "sex equality radicalism" that characterized British utopian socialism in the early nineteenth century was lost with the development of Marxist, scientific socialism, which forefronted class as the central category of analysis. "Organized feminism was increasingly viewed not as an essential component of the socialist struggle, but as a disunifying diversionary force with no inherent connection to the socialist tradition."[18] Socialism lost its feminist component; mainstream feminism lost its concern with class and "collectivity," providing the backdrop to the equal rights, liberal individualist feminism that is the dominant contemporary variety, at least in the United States.[19] The British experience was far from unique. In France, Italy, the United States, and even in the USSR, as well as in Spain, left-wing opposition groups were no less affected than were mainstream parties by the bifurcation of sex- and class-based critiques and by polarized understandings of women's differences from men. Women in European socialist movements were repeatedly forced to choose between socialism (posed as loyalty to the working class) and feminism (cross-class loyalty to women).

Socialist women throughout Europe challenged this polarization and attempted to create a socialist feminism that recognized women's specificity *within* the working class. They called on socialist movements to recognize women *with* their gender differences. But they were largely unsuccessful.[20] Forced to choose between loyalties, most of these women, whose political identities were rooted in socialist organizations and who certainly had little sympathy for bourgeois feminists, felt they had no option but to "choose socialism," effectively abandoning their efforts to appeal to women workers in their particularity. Constructions of women's difference and gendered understandings of politics and protest combined to assure that both parties and union movements, even those committed to radical social transformation, accepted gendered definitions of what was an appropriate issue and of how people ought to be mobilized around it. Dominant understandings of "women's difference" either denied the significance of any differences between men and women—and therefore of the need to make a special appeal to working women—or else defined women so completely in terms of their difference from men that there seemed to be no place for them within party or union organizations. The pattern of "forced choice," in fact, continues to our own day. Yasmine Ergas has noted in her discussion of women in the Italian Left in the post–World War II decades, for example, that women confronted a "bipolar process of validation [between the mutually exclusive categories of 'woman as mother' or 'woman as worker'], based on the alternative between specificity and marginality on one side, and integration and assimilation on the other."[21]

While the approaches may have differed, the consequences were similar. Women were thoroughly underrepresented in organized socialist movements in western Europe in the early years of this century, and those women who were present fought a losing battle for attention to their needs as women. Although socialist parties and organizations recognized that prevailing understandings of politics were biased against the working class, they were unable to recognize the social construction of their own views about women. Women's "otherness" was as encoded into the programs of socialist oppositional groups as it was into the policies of the capitalist regimes they opposed.

As I noted earlier, a parallel set of blinders affected many feminist movements. With the exception of working-class suffragists in England, for example, virtually all feminist organizing effectively ignored the class dimension to their critique of "male hierarchy."[22] It was, of course, for this reason that Mujeres Libres refused to identify itself as "feminist."

If women are marginalized in mainstream politics, there is also a further sense in which gender differences are inscribed in prevailing definitions of "the political." Both revolutionary activists and scholars of social movements often fail to recognize women's activism when it does not follow conventional lines. And women's activism often does not. Women are much less likely than men to take on leadership roles in union movements, for example, especially when the work force is a mixed (male-female) one. Women's activism tends to focus, more than does men's, on quality of life issues, which may be centered in communities rather than in workplaces or which cross the boundaries between home, workplace, and community. Most dramatically, women's activism often takes forms that, by conventional standards, appear as "spontaneous," "unplanned," or "disorganized."[23]

In effect, the social construction of gender differences creates different contexts for women's organization and protest activities. As Frances Fox Piven and Richard Cloward noted, people protest those institutions in those contexts and with those means to which they have access.[24] To the extent that the sexual division of labor and other institutional forms of oppression structure women's lives differently from men's, the contexts in which they experience and resist oppression must necessarily be different. Even unionized women may not have the full support of unions for the specificity of their situations as women. The expectation that they bear prime responsibility for household maintenance and for child care, for example, may render it impossible for them to participate fully in union meetings.

It should not be at all surprising, then, to find that the contexts and forms of women's resistance often differ quite markedly from those of most men. They often depend less on work-related or formally structured organizations and more on local networks of friends, family, associates, or co-workers. Much more so than men's, women's protests tend to be of the direct action sort, functioning as much to mobilize and raise the consciousness of participants as to influence those in power. The experience of participating in protest actions in those arenas of life formerly marked out as "private" or "personal" can have a major radicalizing effect. While according to Marxist theory, men are most likely to come to a consciousness of class in workplace-based organizations such as unions, the sources of changing consciousness for women may be quite different. As Myrna Brietbart and I have argued, "neighborhoods, like workplaces, are neither all-encompassing footholds of domination nor the loci of revolution . . . but they may contain the possibility for emancipatory struggle."[25]

Formally structured organizations, particularly those constructed along hierarchical lines such as union organizations and political parties, are defined as political. More loosely structured and non-hierarchically organized "spontaneous" forms of protest such as food riots, rent strikes, peace demonstrations, and public shaming—the predominant forms that much female activism has taken—are often dismissed as nonpolitical. Paradoxically, as Jacquelyn Dowd Hall and Nancy Hewitt have reported of women workers' resistance activities in the early part of this century in North Carolina and in Florida, the more effective the women's protests became, the more they were labeled "disorderly" and their characters and actions devalued. This labeling seems to have been the consequence of a number of factors. First, it suggests a denial of the legitimacy of organizations structured differently from the norm: the truly political is the formally structured; temporary organization is not deserving of that title. Second, it may also reflect an attempt to undermine and devalue those activities by women that challenge male dominance.[26]

One way this latter process is effected is through the use of sexuality to label and undercut the activities of women protesters. On the one hand, those women who claim the same prerogatives to sexual freedom that men enjoy are often made the butt of ridicule designed to negate the seriousness of their activism. But even those who do not make sexual freedom a focus of their protest often find themselves defined by their sexuality. Thus, both Nancy Hewitt and Jacquelyn Hall have noted that radical women labor union activists and organizers in the southern United States met frequently with sexual innuendos and slurs, not only from representatives of management, but even from male unionists who apparently resented their independence and autonomy. Such labeling recalls the ways in which members of Mujeres Libres were taunted with the epithet "Mujeres Liebres."

In such cases, gender again becomes a constitutive element of what is defined as political. Women, as women, cannot be political beings. But this splitting of sexuality from activism or, more properly, from personhood is not required of men. In fact, to the contrary, male political activists tend to be described, and to describe themselves, in language that emphasizes their maleness as a component of their "politicalness." Of course, not all men are allowed the free expression of their sexuality, either. A focus on sexuality has been used in the United States to control black men as well as all women.

These patterns of gender differentiation may help to explain some of what has happened to women in traditional mixed-sex organizations. The Spanish case illustrates this point. The forms of activism most common to women—through which many of them came to consciousness and became active in more traditional unions or protest organizations—were devalued by the male members of those organizations. For example, although "quality of life" strikes mobilized many thousands of women in the first two decades of this century and many anarchist men recognized that women's protests had accomplished much that traditional union activity had not been able to achieve, the CNT did not change its sense of the *form* that organization ought to take or of how to mobilize women. The vast majority of the women who participated in those strikes were never fully incorporated into the anarchist movement because the movement was unable to acknowledge *difference*, either in forms of participation or in its definitions of activism.

On the other hand, even when women did join unions and other movement organizations (such as the FIJL, ateneos, and the FAI), many were drawn in by the more nontraditional structures, especially ateneos and youth groups. But once they were in the mainstream organizations such as unions, the agendas of those organizations rarely changed to accommodate them. If Teresina Torrelles Graells was able to report that her textile workers' union advocated equal pay for equal work and maternity leave for women workers as early as 1931, her case was exceptional—an exception she attributed to the strength of the women's group in the union. Very few unions adopted the call for equal pay or concerned themselves with maternity leave or child care—concerns which were, of necessity, primary to many women workers.

Although the movement's commitment to a politics of direct action provided for the *possibility* that its practices would address the specificity of women's lives, movement organizations rarely took that step. Instead, their agendas relegated issues of concern to women to a secondary (or tertiary) status, treating them as special interests, rather than as issues that affected all workers. In such a context, it is hardly surprising that women did not join these movements in equal proportion to men or that they were only minimally active when they did join. The pattern in Spain up until the time of the Civil War was barely different from that found in most working-class organizations in western Europe or the United States.

## Mujeres Libres and the Politics of Women's Difference

Mujeres Libres attempted to address this marginalization of women and of women's concerns through its insistence on a separate and autonomous status. Independence allowed the women of Mujeres Libres to define their own agenda for organizing and capacitación and to retain their focus despite the demands of the war situation. Having created an independent base for themselves, they could reject the bipolar analysis that destroyed the visions of so many socialist women, who were forced to choose between class and gender. Instead, they were able to forge an analysis and a program that spoke to the needs and aspirations of working-class women in their particularity. That is not to say that the realities of war and of interorganizational competition with AMA and other Communist-affiliated organizations did not affect Mujeres Libres' programs. We have already seen that they did. But organizational autonomy, so precious to Mujeres Libres' members and so threatening to the mainstream organizations, partially shielded Mujeres Libres from the control that male-dominated movement organizations attempted to exercise over it.

Still, Mujeres Libres paid a price for its autonomy. It never had the funds or the organizational support that its leaders desired. Further, although most of the leadership of Mujeres Libres continued to be active in other organizations of the libertarian movement, their influence was relatively limited. As long as Mujeres Libres was denied *organizational* access to ongoing discussions and policy debates (a limitation it attempted to overcome through its claim for autonomous incorporation into the movement in October 1938), the libertarian movement never fully incorporated women or issues of concern to women into its agenda. In fact, the FIJL's decision to create a Women's Bureau illustrates the widespread perception that women were not adequately engaged in the movement as a whole. As it was, independent women's voices were marginalized. Autonomy allowed Mujeres Libres to continue its work *with women* virtually unconstrained except financially, but it did not necessarily help the organization to make its case effectively with men.

Mujeres Libres' claim to organizational autonomy was based both on its understanding of the gender dynamics of intraorganizational relations and on its views of women's "difference" from men. In its argument that women were triply oppressed by ignorance, by capitalism, and as women, we can find an attempt to articulate a perspective on the workings of institutional oppression. Mujeres Libres drew from its analysis the lesson that these forms of institutional oppression were problems not just for women, but for all workers. Consequently, overcoming the subordination of women—whether in the home, at the workplace, or in the larger culture—was essential to the well-being of *all* workers, men as well as women. Therefore, Mujeres Libres argued, the appropriate response of working-class organizations (e.g., the CNT and FAI) to differences between men and women based in institutional oppression was to struggle to eliminate them.

Nevertheless, many of Mujeres Libres' writings and programs seemed to assume that at least *some* of the differences between men and women were not based solely in oppression. These differences also represented values that ought to be retained in the new society. A number of articles in *Mujeres Libres,* for example, seem almost to foreshadow Carol Gilligan's call for listening to that "different voice" often associated with women. We read in an editorial celebrating the founding of the National Federation of Mujeres Libres in August 1937:

> In identifying its goals with the CNT and the FAI, [Mujeres Libres] has gathered the most genuinely Spanish and the most authentically revolutionary and enriched it with the best of its own specifically feminine characteristics. Mujeres Libres desires that the new social structure not be afflicted by that same unilateral quality that has been the undoing of the world to date. Mujeres Libres desires that in the new Society, the two angles of vision—masculine and feminine—will converge—that they will provide the equilibrium necessary on which to pour the foundations of

the new justice. There cannot be a just society unless masculine and feminine are present in equal proportions.[27]

Here, the writer seemed to be discussing the incorporation of a special perspective that women bring to political/social life. Another article in the same issue, which addressed problems of food distribution in the republican zone, made the case even more explicitly:

> The bars and restaurants of the rich and propertied must be controlled by workingmen [*obreros*] or, better, by workingwomen [*obreras*] because it is women and mothers who know what it is not to have milk for a weak or sick child, meat for a husband tired out from hard work in war industries. . . . Control of food must be in the hands of community women.[28]

Such arguments can easily slide into, or reinforce, assumptions about some "eternal female" characteristics. *Mujeres Libres* was not completely immune to such constructions, despite the anarchist insistence on the social construction of personality and of sexuality. Many articles in the journal seemed to presume the existence of some timeless notion of "femininity," omitting any reference to its social construction. Others focused on the particular hardships women faced as mothers, and took it for granted that women would be the ones most affected by what happened to their children.

As an organization, Mujeres Libres did not articulate a definitive position about the differences between men and women, what their sources were, or which of them ought to be retained and revalued in the revolutionary society. At times, Mujeres Libres seemed to agree with Emma Goldman and Federica Montseny, who had ridiculed feminist claims that women were morally superior to men. Given the opportunity to exercise power over others, Goldman and Montseny had insisted, women would be just as likely as men to abuse it. Their writings, and those of Lucía Sánchez Saornil and Amparo Poch, implied that any existing differences in attitude or perspective between men and women were rooted in societal oppression and would disappear in a more egalitarian society.

More commonly, however, Mujeres Libres seemed to assume that women were somehow different from men, that those differences had not found full articulation in the existing oppressive society, and that a fully egalitarian anarchist society would incorporate the female along with the male. Although Mujeres Libres did not develop an analysis of these differences comparable to that which has since been articulated by contemporary feminist "difference theorists,"[29] the group attempted both to revalue those differences and to develop a strategy for incorporating them into a newly organized society. Whatever the source of women's higher levels of concern for children and for morality in the social-political arena, they argued, that perspective was valuable. The anarcho-syndicalist movement could only be enriched by incorporating it.

Mujeres Libres demanded of its members that they see themselves as fully capable social beings and act accordingly. Its programs of education, consciousness-raising, and apprenticeship provided opportunities for women to educate themselves and to develop skills in organizing, public speaking, and building self-esteem—skills they would need to act effectively in mixed-sex organizations. Female solidarity as a context for changing consciousness was essential to the capacitación for which they aimed. The separation Mujeres Libres insisted on was strategic and temporary—necessary only until sufficient numbers of women had developed the requisite skills and self-confidence that they could then rely on their numbers and the force of their arguments and personalities to influence the mainstream organizations from within. Until then, Mujeres Libres would stand as a kind of direct-action reminder of the significance of gender to the movement.

## From "Difference" to "Diversity"

This review of Mujeres Libres' analysis and experience returns us to an earlier question: What difference should differences make? Neither Mujeres Libres nor contemporary feminist theorists have articulated a methodology for distinguishing between those differences which are temporary, socially constructed manifestations of women's social and political subordination and those particularities which, although they might now be rooted in relations of domination, are worth valuing and retaining in a future society, either as special characteristics of women or as characteristics of both men and women. The early feminist tendency to deny the significance of differences has, in fact, been replaced more recently by a countertendency to emphasize them, although feminists have never agreed on what those differences might be.

A number of significant common themes emerge from contemporary feminist efforts to deal with differences. Feminists inspired by the work of Michel Foucault and literary deconstructionists have focused on patterns of cultural dominance and subordination, as well as the resistance expressed in "submerged discourses." They suggest that we need to attend not only to differences between women and men, but also to different orientations to life and politics that are captured under the rubric of gender and then ascribed differentially to women and men.[30] Others focus on the particular life and social circumstances of women (or members of the working class) that generate different orientations to politics and social life.[31] Still others have adopted methodologies focusing on the development (or blocks to development) of subnational collective or communal identities, which may generate cultural and political perspectives different from the dominant norm.[32]

While the variations among these groups are significant, we can see them contributing to the development of an emerging perspective on difference. Such a perspective rejects the notion of woman (or person of color, or worker) as "other," insisting that we must de-center the dominant definitions, understandings, and institutions and make room to claim and validate a variety of perspectives. It insists on locating women within collectivities, while recognizing that many, if not most, women are located within a variety of collectivities, not just one. It therefore refuses the choice so many political women have had to confront between solidarity with other women and solidarity with their class or racial-ethnic group. At the same time it affirms the multilayered character of women's (and of all people's) identities. It would replace a politics of difference, in which all are defined relative to one norm, with a politics of diversity, which recognizes and validates distinct ways of being without ranking them according to some hierarchically defined norm.[33] Those in Mujeres Libres who affirmed the importance of a "women's perspective" in the anarchist movement, and those of our own day who insist on hearing women's "different voices," all urge women to value their particular strengths. At the same time, they insist that society as a whole would be better off if many of those characteristics were more widely shared.

We must challenge the hierarchical ranking of the dominant value system and begin to conceptualize a society (or movement) in terms of diversity, rather than of differences from one particular norm (however it may present itself as "universal"). Such a perspective underlies the calls by Audre Lorde, Adrienne Rich, Marilyn Frye, and others for feminists to confront racism, heterosexism, and class oppression within the women's movement and within the society at large.[34] It is also one way to understand what Mujeres Libres was attempting in its insistence on a separate status. One approach to de-centering the male-defined norms of the anarchist and anarcho-syndicalist movements, they seemed to be arguing, was to incorporate into that movement another organization with a different set of valued characteristics.

Mujeres Libres' very existence, then, was a form of direct action. The incorporation of Mujeres Libres into the libertarian movement as a fully equal organizational partner would have challenged the normativeness of male-defined visions, not only of women and their capabilities, but also of the range of human nature and, more generally, of the possibilities of a truly egalitarian society.

### Toward a New Conception of Politics

What lessons can we draw from Mujeres Libres that might contribute to contemporary feminist and participatory democratic politics in the

United States? Although Mujeres Libres' explicit focus vis-à-vis other leftist movements was gender, its experience offers us the model of an independent, but nonseparatist, strategy for dealing with diversity.

Specifically, beyond a focus on empowerment and on the incorporation of differences, the history of Mujeres Libres points to the importance of a community of orientation in the process of consciousness-change. Feminists and socialists, as well as anarchists, have argued that truly meaningful political participation can take place only within a more or less egalitarian, mutually respectful political community. But the question remains, What kind of community meets those criteria? Mujeres Libres identified itself not with other women's organizations, but with the libertarian movement.

Feminists, workers, and people of color have argued repeatedly in the contemporary context that we need subcommunities of people like ourselves in order to feel validated and valuable in our specificity.[35] Mujeres Libres insisted that however important and necessary these subcommunities might be, they are, in the end, insufficient and partial. No one group by itself can provide the sole basis for a movement to transform society. A movement must incorporate many such collectivities under a larger umbrella that respects the differences among them, values the particular contributions each group has to offer to the whole, and can take advantage of the power that comes from united action. Concepts of difference and diversity can provide us with new ways of thinking about the constitution of empowering communities. I will end by focusing on two related aspects of Mujeres Libres' legacy: the challenge to the gendered and class-biased construction of "the political" and the beginnings of a conceptualization of a politics of diversity.

Critics of liberal democratic polities point to the class bias built into the structure and very conceptualization of politics. As E. E. Schatt-schneider once put it, "The flaw in the pluralist heaven is that the heavenly chorus sings with a strong upper-class accent."[36] Poor and working-class people are disproportionately underrepresented among those who participate in politics, and they are fundamentally disadvantaged in the outcomes. As generations of critics have noted, the "rules of the game" of liberal democracy—the emphasis on isolated individuals with independently constructed interest profiles—benefit those already in power and prevent others from recognizing their differing needs, let alone articulating and struggling for them in the political arena.[37] Politics, as both Marxists and anarchists insist, is not simply about the distribution of positions in a "political opportunity structure." It is about the structuring of power in the society as a whole. Thus Marxists and, more especially, anarchists have insisted on the practice of widespread popular participation in a variety of forums. Marxists focused primarily on unions and workers' parties; Spanish anarchists added

cultural struggle and community-based organizing. Much current protest politics in the United States, beginning with the civil rights and
antiwar movements of the 1950s and 1960s and including education,
tenant organizing, ecological, and antinuclear protests, has been based
on nonunion organizational forms: neighborhood or community
groups, racial-ethnic cultural communities, and coalitions formed
around shared political/social concerns.

Feminists have added another dimension to this critique of liberal
democratic politics, pointing out that our conceptions (and practices) of
politics have gender as well as class encoded into them. When "the
political" is defined as those matters which take place in some public
sphere, allegedly separate from (and superior to) the private or domestic sphere, the concerns of many women and men are defined as outside
of politics; the political nature of their activities is denied or made
invisible. Carole Pateman has noted in *The Sexual Contract*, for example,
that the subordination of women was not problematized in liberal
political theory. Since, she argues, the assumption of these theories is
that women are related to society through men, women's exclusion
from the social contract has barely been noticed. Her claim, I believe, is
related to my earlier one that when women are seen totally in terms of
their "specificity," the actual concerns of real women are often neglected. Entire dimensions of human concern and collective action are
thus devalued, and the community as a whole is diminished.[38]

In highlighting the collective nature of the oppression that both men
and women experienced as members of the working class, Mujeres
Libres insisted that liberation from oppression required collective action and could only be evaluated according to collective norms: success
could not be defined as individual women making it in the political or
corporate world. Hierarchical structures had to be abolished, and
women had to be involved both in that process and in the creation of the
new society. Issues of class and gender must be addressed simultaneously.

Many feminists (both in Spain and elsewhere in Europe and in the
United States) share an aspect of that insight, arguing that women are
oppressed as a group and can redress their grievances only through
collective action. The class component of the analysis, however, has all
too often been neglected. This neglect resulted in feminism becoming
identified with the efforts of women to achieve favored positions in
existing hierarchical institutions and organizations. There have been
exceptions, of course—working-class women's suffrage organizations in
Great Britain, efforts to organize socialist feminist groups in France,
"material feminists" in the United States who attempted to assert
control over the so-called domestic sphere. But many of these were
ultimately unable to sustain the joint focus on gender and class issues.
As Dolores Hayden argues with respect to material feminists in the

United States, for example, many of the collective strategies the women proposed to address the isolation and discrimination they experienced as women were open only to other middle-class women like themselves. They ignored the extent to which their programs relied on the continued exploitation of working-class women.[39] Over time, feminism came to be identified with the goal of access to, rather than fundamental restructuring of, existing hierarchies of privilege.

In the contemporary United States, protest groups have argued that prevailing conceptions of politics are biased not only along class and gender lines but also along lines of racial-ethnic identity, sexual orientation, physical ability, etc. The "universal citizen" of liberal democratic theory is not only an upper-class male, but also a white, able-bodied, heterosexual family head.[40] In treating all people as mere bearers of interests, liberal democratic individualism masks structures of power and, in particular, relations of domination and subordination that affect people (and structure their "interests") as members of subnational collectivities.

At the same time, the individualist paradigm provides little or no place for the conscious articulation of interests and perspectives deriving from differing cultural, ethnic, religious, or gender backgrounds. That paradigm treats these either as generating different "interests" around which individuals may gather or, more commonly, as occasions for oppression or discrimination, on the basis of which members of particular groups are denied equal access to social goods. But being a part of a collectivity is not simply a matter of experiencing oppression as a member of that collectivity. To say that blacks, women, gays, Jews, Muslims, or the disabled are discriminated against (or disadvantaged) in a system that takes the normative citizen to be a white, Christian, heterosexual, able-bodied male should not deny that there are positive characteristics and values that members of those groups have developed—even if they have developed them partly in response to their oppression. Liberal individualism would "wash out" all those differences in the name of universal citizenship. Marxist socialism would wash out all but those based on class in the name of the workers' revolution. Similarly, some radical feminists would wash out all but those based on gender, in the name of "sisterhood." But those who are now finding strength in their identities as members of one or more of these collectivities are rightly unwilling to abandon them as the price of fully inclusive citizenship.

The challenge is to develop a conception of politics and political life that moves beyond both individualism and a narrow class or gender analysis. Such a reconceptualization must recognize people not as bearers of interests, but as participants in a variety of communities that contribute important components to their identity. When French socialist women were forced to choose between "women" and "the working class," their own identity as working-class women disappeared. Similarly, when black or Jewish women in the United States are forced (whether by members of their ethnic-cultural group or by other women) to choose between a loyalty to other women or a loyalty to their ethnic-cultural group, their own identities are denied. It is not surprising in this context that many working-class or ethnic minority women in the United States are wary of "the feminist movement," even though they may express support for many feminist goals. Individualist appeals deny or demean the bonds that working-class or ethnic minority people feel toward one another. It appears that the promise of individual achievement and fulfillment is to be won at the cost of abandoning group identity and solidarity.[41] At the same time, these appeals divide working-class women (whether white or of color) from middle-class white women by denying the separate reality of each situation.

No one should be forced to choose among aspects of her or his identity as the price for political or communal belonging. We are each whole beings, capable of multiple commitments to a variety of collectivities. Those commitments enrich our lives and empower us. Although, as in the case of Mujeres Libres, they are often labeled "divisive," they need not be so. In fact, multiple commitments are divisive only in the context of communities that make claims to exclusive loyalty. If we can move away from prevailing hierarchical patterns, in which one sort of commitment is conceived as primary or superior, and acknowledge that each of us has a variety of commitments of different intensities to different groups—the importance of which may change over time—then we can begin to create communities that recognize those commitments and do not make exclusive claims on our loyalties. Perhaps we can then claim for ourselves the legacy Mujeres Libres struggled so hard to create.

> We took the first steps . . . toward emancipation, first steps that have been taken up by women's liberation movements of today. They were first steps; we couldn't take the "giant steps," because of the war and the exile, which cut our struggle short. . . . Now, the world has changed. . . . Our children have to be the pacesetters for the future. But our memories, such beautiful memories, of that struggle so hard and so pure. . . . Is it possible that it has been of some use?[42]

# APPENDIX A

**Schematic Organization of the National
Confederation of Labor of Spain**

**Syndicate:** General assembly of members
Administrative committee

section of a syndicate: General assembly of the section
Administrative Committee

*Administrative committee of delegates from each syndicate*
**Local federation:** Meeting of administrative committees of the syndicates
of a community

**(Comarcal)** Committee composed of delegates from each syndicate
**Cantonal Federation:** in the canton

**Regional Committee:** Named by local federation of community in which
Regional committee sits (one delegate from each
syndicate in locality except in Catalonia)

**Regional Plenum:** Composed of delegates from each local and each cantonal
federation in the region

**Regional Congress:** Composed of delegates from each syndicate in the region

**National Committee:** Named by local federation of town in which (by
decision of a National Congress) the Committee sits
(one delegate/syndicate)

**Plenum of Regionals
(National Plenum):** Composed of delegates from each regional committee

**National Congress:** Composed of delegates from every syndicate in the
country

SOURCE: A. Schapiro (Association Internationale des Travailleurs), *Rapport sur
l'activité de la Confederation Nationale du Travail d'Espagne*, 16 de-
cembre 1932–26 fevrier 1933. Strictement confidentiel, 2.

183

# APPENDIX B

## Publications of Mujeres Libres

*Actividades F. N. Mujeres Libres,* (1938)
Comaposada Guillén, Mercedes. *Esquemas* (Barcelona: Mujeres Libres, 1937)
"Como organizar una agrupación Mujeres Libres," (Barcelona, 1937?), 16 pp.
Condé, Carmen. *Enseñanza nueva* (1936)
———. *Poemas en la Guerra* (1937)
———. *La composición literaria infantil* (1938).
Federn, Etta. *Mujeres de las Revoluciones* (Barcelona: Mujeres Libres, n.d.
    [1938]), 62 pp.
Poch y Gascón, Amparo. *Niño* (Barcelona: Mujeres Libres, n.d., [1937]), 20 pp.
———. *La ciencia y la enfermedad* (1938)
Sanchez Saornil, Lucía. *Horas de Revolución* (Barcelona: Mujeres Libres, n.d.
    [1937]), 62 pp.
———. *Romancero de Mujeres Libres* (Barcelona: Mujeres Libres, n.d. [1938])
Dr. Salud Alegre, *Sanatorio de optimismo* (Barcelona: Mujeres Libres, 1938)

(In addition to thirteen issues of the journal *Mujeres Libres* and numerous articles in newspapers and journals of the libertarian movement.)

# APPENDIX C

### Proposal for the Creation of Wedding Factory

Comrade Revolution has made us aware of his great affliction. People continue to marry. . . . Comrade Revolution thought that people's morals and spirit had improved somewhat, but he realizes that the spirit and morals of people are not susceptible to improvement. People are continuing to marry. . . . In the face of this inescapable reality, we attempt to alleviate some of its inevitable consequences. People continue loving the modes of their oppression. At the least, let us see if we can lighten the chains. . . .

### Proposal

#### Location
The wedding factory will be located far from every urban nucleus. It is not good that tragedies take place in the public eye, because they will demoralize the people. Besides, the difficulties of access to the factory will force the stupid ones to think [about what they're doing].

#### Materials for construction
Should be of such kind that dampen noise. What goes on inside is not anyone's business, and it's always better not to hear the statements of those who come to complain about how theirs have gone wrong.

#### Subdivisions
A waiting room, divided into two-person cubicles by partial partitions. Isolation is essential in case of epidemic. One room for ceremonies and an exit ramp.

Speed is important so that people shouldn't have time to change their minds. . . .

#### Material
Of two kinds: (a) necessary and (b) voluntary

(a) A cold shower; a committee convinced of the importance of its mission; a seal that says: "Enter, if you dare"; a stamp pad of red or red and black for the seal.

(b) A stake.

#### Library
One copy of the Laws of Common Sense.

#### Related institutions
A shop for rivets, collars, rings, and chains. An allegorical tricolor of Freedom.

#### Functioning of the factory
It is quick. Individuals wait, by pairs, in the two-person cubicles.

Later they will pass into the ceremonial room. They can do nothing, absolutely nothing, without the proper stamp. [An official] stamps a small piece of paper, their cheeks, and their underwear.

Then, with a very hollow voice, the Committee reads them the Laws of Common Sense, which can be reduced to three:

1. When there were priests, the priest deceived you; when there were judges,

the judge deceived you; now we are deceiving you ourselves, since you came here.

2. He who cannot go on without a guarantee of property and fidelity deserves the most vile oppressions upon his heart (danger of asphyxiation).

3. The act of passing through the factory gives evidence of idiocy, and predisposes to two or three afflictions per day. We know what we are doing!

The ceremony is free. Those who go have already suffered enough misfortune. Afterwards, rings and chains are put on them, they are made to kiss the tricolor picture of libertarian communism, and they are thrown down the ramp.

In order to avoid disturbances to the normal functioning of the factory, it is a good idea to place the following poster at the exit:

NO COMPLAINTS ACCEPTED.

SOURCE:  "Proyecto para la creación de una fábrica de bodas en serie (Churros auténticos)" *Mujeres Libres*, no. 7.

# NOTES

## Introduction

1. Confederación Nacional del Trabajo (National Confederation of Labor), the anarcho-syndicalist labor union confederation; and the Federación Ibérica de Juventudes Libertarias (Iberian Federation of Libertarian Youth), also known simply as the Juventudes, the movement-affiliated youth organization. Virtually all of the activists in Mujeres Libres were also activists in one or both of these movement organizations.

2. I use the term *libertarian movement* to refer to the complex of organizations and activities undertaken by anarchist and anarcho-syndicalist organizations in Spain. These included, most importantly, the CNT, the Federación Anarquista Ibérica (the Iberian Anarchist Federation), or FAI, and the FIJL, which joined together as the "libertarian movement" only during the war. Nevertheless, I use the term here as a shorthand to refer to anarchist, anarcho-syndicalist, and related organizations. The organizational details are explored in greater depth in chap. 2.

3. A perspective, of course, shared by many elements of the early feminist movement in the United States, dubbed "the tyranny of structurelessness" by "Joreen" in her article by that title, *The Second Wave* 2, no. 1 (1972): 20–25.

4. Suceso Portales, interview, Móstoles (Madrid), June 29, 1979.

5. Ana Cases, personal communication, August 10, 1981.

6. Lola Iturbe, interviews, Alella (Barcelona), August 3, 1981, and Barcelona, August 4, 1981.

7. Azucena Barba, interviews, Perpignan, France, August 14–15, 1981.

8. Enriqueta Rovira, interview, Castellnaudary, France, December 29, 1981.

9. Sara Berenguer Guillén, interview, Montady, December 28, 1981.

10. Sara Berenguer, *Entre el sol y la tormenta: Treinta y dos meses de guerra (1936–1939)* (Barcelona: sueBa, 1988).

11. At this time, during the dictatorship of Primo de Rivera, the CNT was outlawed and operated clandestinely. See chap. 2.

12. Pepita Carpena, interviews, Montpellier, France, December 30–31, 1981, and Barcelona, Spain, May 3–4, 1988.

13. Soledad Estorach, interview, Paris, January 6, 1982; personal communication, October 1989.

14. By communalist anarchism, I refer to the tradition represented in the works of Pierre-Joseph Proudhon, Michael Bakunin, Peter Kropotkin, Errico Malatesta, and Emma Goldman, among others. I first explored the evolution of these ideas in my doctoral dissertation, "The Possibility of Anarchism: The Theory and Practice of Non-Authoritarian Organization," Department of Politics, Princeton University, 1976.

15. See Nancy Cott, *The Grounding of Modern Feminism* (New Haven: Yale University Press, 1987); Zillah Eisenstein, *The Radical Future of Liberal Feminism* (New York: Longman, 1981); and Barbara Taylor, *Eve and the New Jerusalem* (New York: Pantheon, 1983). Benjamin Barber notes in *The Death of Communal Liberty* (Princeton: Princeton University Press, 1984), for example, that Swiss communes understood freedom as "collaborative self-reliance."

16. Among early articles are Temma Kaplan, "Female Consciousness and Collective Action: The Case of Barcelona, 1910–1918," *Signs* 7, no. 3 (Spring 1982): 545–66; Kaplan, "Class Consciousness and Community in Nineteenth-Century Andalusia," *Political Power and Social Theory* 2 (1981): 21–57; Paula Hyman, "Immigrant Women and Consumer Protest: The New York City Kosher Meat Boycott of 1902," *American Jewish History* 70 (Summer 1980): 91–105; and Laurel Thatcher Ulrich, "A Friendly Neighbor: Social Dimensions of Daily Work in Northern Colonial New England," *Feminist Studies*, 6, no. 2 (Summer 1980): 392–405. For more recent studies exploring the importance of community- and workplace-based networks to women's political activism, see Ruth Milkman, ed., *Women, Work and Protest: A Century of U.S. Women's Labor History* (Boston: Routledge and Kegan Paul, 1985) and Ann Bookman and Sandra Morgen, eds., *Women and the Politics of Empowerment* (Philadelphia: Temple University Press, 1988).

17. Floya Anthias and Nira Yuval-Davis, "Contextualizing Feminism: Gender, Ethnic and Class Divisions," *Feminist Review*, no. 15 (1983); Michelle Barrett and Maureen McKintosh, "Ethnocentrism and Socialist-Feminist Theory," *Feminist Review*, no. 20 (1985); Bell Hooks, *Ain't I a Woman: Black Women and Feminism* (Boston: South End Press, 1981).

18. I have reviewed much of this literature in "Sisters or Comrades? The Politics of Friends and Families," in *Families, Politics and Public Policies*, ed. Irene Diamond (New York: Longman, 1983), 339–56, and, with Irene Diamond, in "Gender and Political Life: New Directions in Political Science," in *Analyzing Gender: Social Science Perspectives*, ed. Beth B. Hess and Myra Marx Ferree (Beverly Hills: Sage, 1988). See also Ruth L. Smith and Deborah M. Valenze, "Mutuality and Marginality: Liberal Moral Theory and Working-Class Women in Nineteenth-Century England," *Signs* 13, no. 2 (Winter 1988): 277–98.

19. Taylor, *Eve and the New Jerusalem*, passim.

20. Starhawk, *Truth or Dare: Encounters with Power, Authority, and Mystery* (San Francisco: Harper and Row, 1988), especially 8–10.

21. Audre Lorde, *Sister Outsider* (Trumansburg, N.Y.: Crossing Press, 1984); Diane K. Lewis, "A Response to Inequality: Black Women, Racism, and Sexism," *Signs* 3, no. 2 (Winter 1977): 339–61; Margaret A. Simons, "Racism and Feminism: A Schism in the Sisterhood," *Feminist Studies* 5, no. 2 (Summer 1979): 389–410; Bonnie Thornton Dill, "Race, Class and Gender: Prospects for an All-Inclusive Sisterhood," *Feminist Studies* 9, no. 1 (Spring 1983): 131–50.

22. One early exploration of the connections between racism and sexism is Lillian Smith, *Killers of the Dream* (New York: Norton, 1961). See also Elizabeth V. Spelman, *Inessential Woman* (Boston: Beacon Press, 1988); Adrienne Rich, "Disloyal to Civilization: Feminism, Racism, and Gynephobia," in *On Lies, Secrets, and Silence: Selected Prose 1966–1978* (New York: Norton, 1979), 275–310; Phyllis Marynick Palmer, "White Women/Black Women: The Dualism of Female Identity and Experience in the United States," *Feminist Studies* 9, no. 1 (Spring 1983): 151–70; Elly Bulkin, Minnie Bruce Pratt, and Barbara Smith, *Yours in Struggle* (New York: Long Haul Press, 1984).

23. María C. Lugones and Elizabeth V. Spelman, "Have We Got a Theory for You! Feminist Theory, Cultural Imperialism, and the Demand for 'The Woman's Voice,'" *Women's Studies International Forum* 6, no. 6 (1983): 573–81; Martha Ackelsberg, "Personal Identities and Collective Visions: Reflections on Being a Jew and a Feminist," lecture, Smith College, March 8, 1983.

## 1. Anarchist Revolution and the Liberation of Women

1. Anarcho-syndicalism was the particular creation of Spanish theorists and activists, a unique blend of anarchist vision with a revolutionary syndicalist strategy. See chap. 2.

2. Peter Kropotkin, *Fields, Factories, and Workshops Tomorrow*, ed. Colin Ward (New York: Harper and Row, 1974). See also Myrna M. Breitbart, "Peter Kropotkin: Anarchist Geographer," in *Geography, Ideology and Social Concern*, ed. David Stoddart (New York: Oxford University Press, 1982), 134–53. For parallels with contemporary ecofeminist analysis see Susan Griffin, *Women and Nature: The Roaring Inside Her* (New York: Harper and Row, 1978); Carol Christ, "Finitude, Death, and Reverence for Life," in *Laughter of Aphrodite: Reflections on a Journey to the Goddess* (San Francisco: Harper and Row, 1987), 213–28; Ynestra King, "Feminism and the Revolt of Nature," *Heresies* 4, no. 1 (1981): 12–16.

3. Ralf Dahrendorf, "On the Origin of Social Inequality," in *Philosophy, Politics, and Society*, 2d series, ed. Peter Laslett and W. G. Runciman (Oxford: Basil Blackwell, 1962), 105.

4. Max Weber, "Politics as a Vocation," *From Max Weber: Essays in Sociology*, ed. Hans H. Gerth and C. Wright Mills (New York: Oxford University Press, 1958); Robert Michels, *Political Parties*, ed. and trans. Eden and Cedar Paul (New York: Free Press, 1962), especially 326, 344–66; and V. I. Lenin, *What Is to Be Done? Burning Questions of Our Movement* (New York: International, 1929), especially parts II–IV.

5. Isaac Puente, "Independencia económica, libertad y soberanía individual," *Estudios*, no. 121 (September 1933): 22–23.

6. Fernando Tarrida del Mármol, *Problemas trascendentales* (Barcelona: Biblioteca de "La Revista Blanca", 1930), 118–21; Ricardo Mella, "Breves apuntes sobre las pasiones humanas," prize essay originally written in 1889, reedited in 1890 and 1903, and reprinted in *Breves apuntes sobre las pasiones humanas* (Barcelona: Tusquets, 1976), 20–21; and Federico Urales (Juan Montseny), "Consideraciones morales sobre el funcionamiento de una sociedad sin gobierno," *La Revista Blanca* 1, no. 4 (July 15, 1923), 5 (August 1, 1923), 6 (August 15, 1923), and 7 (September 1, 1923). For a contemporary view, see Richard Sennett, *The Uses of Disorder* (New York: Pantheon, 1970).

7. *A las mujeres,* Conferencia leída en el 'Centro Obrero' de Sabadell y en el 'Centro Fraternal de Cultura' de Barcelona, October 18 and 24, 1903 (Barcelona: Biblioteca Editorial Salud, 1923), 14–15.

8. Mariano Gallardo, "Tendencias del instinto sexual humano," *Estudios*, no. 136 (December 1934). See also "Influencia de las instituciones sociales sobre el carácter humano," ibid., no. 137 (January 1935): 63; and Gregorio Marañón, "Sexo, Trabajo y Deporte," and "Maternidad y Feminismo," in *Tres ensayos sobre la vida sexual*, 5th ed. (Madrid: Biblioteca Nueva, 1929), especially 43, 80, 87ff, and 129ff.

9. Isaac Puente, *El comunismo libertario: Sus posibilidades de realización en España* (Valencia: Biblioteca de Estudios, 1933), 9; Michael Bakunin, "The International and Karl Marx," in *Bakunin on Anarchism*, ed. Sam Dolgoff (Montreal: Black Rose Books, 1980), 318; and Errico Malatesta, *Anarchy* (London: Freedom Press, 1949 [pamphlet originally published 1891]), 12–15.

10. A substantial part of this analysis was developed in collaboration with Kathryn Pyne Parsons Addelson and Shawn Pyne, in a paper delivered to the Philosophy Club at North Carolina State University at Raleigh, March 22, 1978; see Martha Ackelsberg and Kathryn Addelson, "Anarchism and Feminism" in

*Impure Thoughts: Essays on Philosophy, Feminism and Ethics,*· ed. Addelson (Philadelphia: Temple University Press, 1991).

11. William Chafe, *Women and Equality* (New York: Oxford University Press, 1977); Kathy E. Ferguson, *The Feminist Case against Bureaucracy* (Philadelphia: Temple University Press, 1984), especially chaps. 1, 2, and 5.

12. Carol P. Christ, *Diving Deep and Surfacing: Women Writers on Spiritual Quest* (Boston: Beacon Press, 1980); Judith Plaskow, *Sex, Sin, and Grace: Women's Experience and the Theologies of Reinhold Niebuhr and Paul Tillich* (Washington, D.C.: University Press of America, 1980), especially chap. 1. See also W. E. B. DuBois, *The Souls of Black Folk* (Chicago: A. C. McClurg, 1903), especially chap. 2.

13. José Prat, *Necesidad de la asociación* (Madrid: Ediciones el Libertario, n.d.), 10; Ricardo Mella, *Organización, agitación y revolución*, Cuadernos de Educación Social (Barcelona: Ediciones Tierra y Libertad, 1936), 5; Isaac Puente, "Mi concepto del apoliticismo," *Solidaridad Obrera*, January 8, 1936, 8; and Federico Urales,·"Consideraciones morales sobre el funcionamiento de una sociedad sin gobierno."

14. Mella, "Breves apuntes sobre las pasiones humanas," 34.

15. Federico Urales, "Comunistas y comunismos," *La Revista Blanca* 1, no. 2 (June 15, 1923): 2, 4; Federica Montseny, "El espíritu gregario y el individuo," ibid., 2 (1924): 9–11 and "Influencias marxistas en el anarquismo," ibid., 10 (1932): 265–67; and Ricardo Mella, "El socialismo anarquista," *Natura*, nos. 17 and 18 (June 1904), reprinted in *Breves apuntes sobre las pasiones humanas*, 53–54. Among non-Spanish anarchist writers see, for example, P. J. Proudhon, "Philosophie Populaire: Programme," in *De la justice dans la révolution et dans l'église*, in *Oeuvres complètes de P. J. Proudhon*, 14 vols., new ed., ed. Roger Picard (Paris: Marcel Rivière, 1930), vol. 9: 206; and Emma Goldman, "Anarchism: What It Really Stands For," in *Anarchism and Other Essays*, ed. Richard Drinnon (New York: Dover, 1969), 47–67, especially 55, 59, 62.

16. Pilar Grangel, "Trabajo intelectual y manual de la mujer," *Mujeres Libres*, no. 12.

17. José Prat, *Necesidad de la asociación*, 1, 2, and 4; Tarrida del Mármol, "Los siete enigmas del universo," *Problemas trascendentales*, 25–26.

18. Mella, "El socialismo anarquista," 55–56; Errico Malatesta on solidarity in *Anarchy*, 19–20; Malatesta, "El individualismo en el anarquismo," "La anarquía," and "Nuestro programa," all in *Socialismo y anarquía* (Madrid: Editorial Ayuso, 1977), 55–62, 189–238; and "Organisation," in *Malatesta: Life and Ideas*, ed. Vernon Richards (London: Freedom Press, 1977), especially 86–87. See also Nathan Rotenstreich, "Community as a Norm," in *Communal Life: An International Perspective*, ed. Yosef Gorni, Yaacov Oved, and Idit Paz (Efal, Israel: Yad Tabenkin; New Brunswick, N.J.: Transaction Books, 1987), 21–27.

19. See, for example, Carole Pateman, *The Sexual Contract* (Stanford: Stanford University Press, 1988), and Teresa Brennan and Carole Pateman, " 'Mere Auxiliaries to the Commonwealth': Women and the Origins of Liberalism," *Political Studies* 27, no. 2 (1978): 183–200.

20. P. J. Proudhon, *What Is Property?* trans. Benj. R. Tucker (London: William Reeves, n.d.), 57; José Prat, *Necesidad de la asociación*, 6–7; Fernando Tarrida del Mármol, "Interpretación matemática del interés," *Problemas trascendentales*, 106–107; and Puente, *El comunismo libertario*, 20–21. All drew on Peter Kropotkin. See his "Anarchist Communism: Its Basis and Principles," in *Kropotkin's Revolutionary Pamphlets*, ed. Roger N. Baldwin (New York: Vanguard Press, 1927); and *The Conquest of Bread* (London: Chapman and Hall, 1913), 34.

21. P. J. Proudhon, *Du principe fédératif et de la nécessité de reconstituer la Parti de la Révolution* (Paris: E. Dentu, 1863), 73–74; Puente, *El comunismo libertario*,

especially 16–19; Mella, "Breves apuntes sobre las pasiones humanas," 35; and George Woodcock, *Railways and Society: For Workers' Control* (London: Freedom Press, 1943).

22. Christian Cornelissen, *El comunismo libertario y el régimen de transición,* Spanish version by Eloy Muñiz (Valencia: Biblioteca Orto, 1936), 29–30; Puente, *El comunismo libertario,* 116–20.

23. Soledad Gustavo, "El sindicalismo y la anarquía," *La Revista Blanca* 1, no. 3 (July 1, 1923): 2.

24. Federica Montseny, "Sindicalismo revolucionario y Comunismo anarquista: Alrededor de un artículo de Pierre Besnard," *La Revista Blanca* 10, no. 2 (1932): 330, 332.

25. Puente, *El comunismo libertario,* 29–30. See also "Ensayo programático del Comunismo libertario," *Estudios,* no. 117 (May 1933), 23–29.

26. I compare Spanish anarcho-syndicalism and other European working-class movements in the conclusion of this book.

27. Mella, *Organización, agitación y revolución,* 19; "Breves apuntes," 15.

28. Marañón, "Maternidad y feminismo," *Tres ensayos sobre la vida sexual,* especially 123–25, 129, 140, 149.

29. Nash, "Estudio Preliminar," *"Mujeres Libres" España, 1936–1939* (Barcelona: Tusquets, 1976), 10–11.

30. See the statement of the Zaragoza Congress of the Spanish movement of 1870, cited in Anselmo Lorenzo, *El proletariado militante* (2 vols.; Toulouse: Editorial del Movimiento Libertario Español, CNT en Francia, 1947) II, 17–18.

31. Javierre, "Reflejos de la vida rusa en el régimen familiar," *Solidaridad Obrera,* October 13, 1935, 8; also Federica Montseny, "La tragedia de la emancipación femenina," *La Revista Blanca* 2 (1924): 19.

32. Kyralina [Lola Iturbe], "Temas femeninos: El comunismo anárquico libertará a la mujer," *Tierra y libertad* (supplement) 2, no. 11 (June 1933): 197–99.

33. On British groups, see Barbara Taylor, *Eve and the New Jerusalem,* and Ruth L. Smith and Deborah M. Valenze, "Mutuality and Marginality." On Fourier and his French followers see *The Utopian Vision of Charles Fourier: Selected Texts on Work, Love and Passionate Attraction,* trans. and ed. Jonathan Beecher and Richard Bienvenu (Columbia: University of Missouri Press, 1983); and Jonathan Beecher, *Charles Fourier: The Visionary and His World* (Berkeley: University of California Press, 1986).

34. *La Revista Blanca* was published by the Montseny family (Juan Montseny [Federico Urales] and Soledad Gustavo) in Madrid from 1898 until 1906, and then from 1923 through 1936 in Barcelona. *Estudios* was published in Valencia during the 1920s and 1930s.

35. A. G. Llauradó, "Por el sensualismo," *Estudios,* no. 134 (October 1934); Antonio de Hoyos y Vinent, "De, en, por, sin, sobre la moral sexual," *Estudios,* no. 138 (February 1935); Mariano Gallardo, "Experimentación sexual," *Estudios,* no. 146 (October 1935); Llauradó, "La marcha triunfal del sexo," *Estudios,* no. 119 (July 1933): 19–20.

36. Martí-Ibáñez wrote regularly for *Estudios* on a variety of topics related to sex and sexuality. During 1936–1937, he published a regular column of questions and answers, "Consultorio Psíquico-Sexual," reprinted in a book of the same title, ed. Ignacio Vidal (Barcelona: Tusquets, 1976).

37. Martí-Ibáñez, "Nueva moral sexual," *Estudios,* no. 134 (October 1934): 13–15; Martí-Ibáñez, "Erótica, matrimonio y sexualidad," ibid., no. 136 (December 1934): 21–23.

38. Martí-Ibáñez, "Carta a Buenos Aires, a don Rafael Hasan," *Estudios,* no. 144 (August 1935): 13. Compare Audre Lorde, "Uses of the Erotic: The Erotic as Power," in *Sister Outsider* (Trumansburg, N.Y.: Crossing Press, 1984), 55–57.

39. Martí-Ibáñez, "Carta a una muchacha española sobre el problema sexual," *Estudios*, no. 138 (February 1935): 5–6.

40. Martí-Ibáñez, "Consideraciones sobre el homosexualismo," *Estudios*, no. 145 (September 1935): 3–5. Similar assumptions about the "naturalness" of heterosexuality are to be found in Marañón's *Tres ensayos* and throughout the discussions of sexuality in *Estudios*.

41. María Lacerda, "El trabajo femenino," *Estudios*, no. 111 (November 1932), cited in Mary Nash, "El estudio del control de natalidad en España: ejemplos de metodologías diferentes," in *La mujer en la historia de España (Siglos XVI–XX)*, Proceedings of the II Interdisciplinary Research Conference (Madrid: Seminario de Estudios de la Mujer, Universidad Autónoma de Madrid [1984]), 252.

42. Juan Lazarte, "Significación cultural y ética de la limitación de nacimientos," *Estudios*, no. 120 (August 1933) through no. 128 (April 1934).

43. Lazarte, "Significación cultural y ética," *Estudios*, no. 126 (February 1934); Diógenes Ilurtensis, "Neomaltusianismo, maternidad consciente y esterilización," *Estudios*, no. 125 (special issue; January 1934): 12–14. For a discussion of anarchist neomalthusianism more generally see Mary Nash, "El neomaltusianismo anarquista y los conocimientos populares sobre el control de natalidad en España," in *Presencia y protagonismo: aspectos de la historia de la mujer*, ed. Mary Nash (Barcelona: Ediciones del Serbal, 1984), 307–40; and "El estudio del control de natalidad en España," especially 248–53.

44. Federica Montseny, "En defensa de Clara, II," *La Revista Blanca* 2, no. 47 (May 1, 1925): 26–28; Leonardo, "Matrimonio y adulterio," *Estudios*, no. 113 (January 1933); Hugo Treni, "El amor y la nueva ética sexual en la vida y en la literatura," *Estudios*, no. 118 (June 1933); and Marañón, "Maternidad y feminismo."

45. Mariano Gallardo, "Tendencias del instinto sexual humano"; and Brand, "El problema del amor," *La Revista Blanca* 2 (1924): 23.

46. Amparo Poch y Gascón, "Nuevo concepto de pureza," *Estudios*, no. 128 (April 1934): 32.

47. Lacerda de Moura, "Cuando el amor muere," *Estudios*, no. 127 (March 1934): 20–21; "Qué es el amor plural?" ibid., no. 128 (April 1934): 24–25; "El amor plural frente a la camaradería amorosa," ibid., no. 129 (May 1934): 22–24; and "Amor y libertad," ibid., no. 132 (August 1934): 18–19.

48. Soledad Gustavo, "Hablemos de la mujer," *La Revista Blanca* 1, no. 9 (October 1, 1923): 7–8.

49. Federica Montseny, "En defensa de Clara, III," *La Revista Blanca* 2, no. 48 (May 15, 1925): 23–25; also "En defensa de Clara II," 29; and Brand, "El problema del amor," 23.

50. Montseny, "La tragedia de la emancipación femenina," 20–21. See Goldman, "The Tragedy of Woman's Emancipation," in *Anarchism and Other Essays*, especially 223–25. Two recent biographies of Emma Goldman highlight her confusion and frustrations. See Alice Wexler, *Emma Goldman: An Intimate Life* (New York: Pantheon, 1984) and Candace Falk, *Love, Anarchy and Emma Goldman* (New York: Holt, Rinehart and Winston, 1984).

51. V. R., "Por caminos autoritarios no se consigue la libertad," *Acracia* 2, no. 250 (May 13, 1937). According to Federico Arcos (personal communication, July 25, 1989), V. R. was probably Vicente Rodriguez García (Viroga), a member of a group of young anarchists, Los Quijotes. See "Los Quijotes: Anarchist Youth Group, Spain 1937," *The Fifth Estate* 24, no. 2 (Summer 1989): 10.

52. Peter Kropotkin, quoted in Diego Abad de Santillán, *En torno a nuestros objetivos libertarios* (Madrid: Edición de la sección de propaganda del Comité de Defensa confederal del centro, n.d.), 18.

53. Enriqueta Rovira, interview, Castellnaudary, France, December 28, 1981.

54. Martha Ackelsberg and Kathryn Pyne Addelson, "Anarchist Alternatives to Competition," in *Competition: A Feminist Taboo?* ed. Valerie Miner and Helen E. Longino (New York: Feminist Press, 1987), especially 227–31.

55. For contemporary articulations see Chafe, *Women and Equality;* Frances Fox Piven and Richard A. Cloward, *Poor People's Movements* (New York: Pantheon, 1977); and Sara M. Evans and Harry C. Boyte, *Free Spaces: The Sources of Democratic Change in America* (New York: Harper and Row, 1986).

56. Isaac Puente, *El comunismo libertario,* 15.

57. Mella, *Organización, agitación y revolución,* 23, 31–32.

58. Soledad Estorach, interviews, January 4 and 6, 1982; personal communication, October 1989.

59. Mella, "Breves apuntes sobre las pasiones humanas," especially 35–36; Proudhon, *Système des contradictions economiques ou Philosophie de la misère,* in *Oeuvres complètes de P. J. Proudhon.*

60. Federica Montseny, interview, Toulouse, France, February 1, 1979.

61. Max Nettlau, "La actividad libertaria tras la revolución," *La Revista Blanca* 10 (May 15, 1932); and Ricardo Mella, *Organización, agitación y revolución,* 10–11.

62. Higinio Noja Ruíz, *La revolución española: Hacia una sociedad de trabajadores libres* (Valencia: Ediciones Estudios, n.d.), 62.

63. P. A. Kropotkin, "Must We Occupy Ourselves with an Examination of the Ideal of a Future System?" in *Selected Writings on Anarchism and Revolution,* ed. Martin A. Miller (Cambridge: MIT Press, 1970), 94–95; Bakunin, "The Policy of the International," in *Bakunin on Anarchism,* ed. Dolgoff, 167.

64. Eliseo Reclus, *A mi hermano el campesino* (Valencia: Ediciones Estudios, n.d. [originally published in 1873]); Higinio Noja Ruiz, *Labor constructiva en el campo* (Valencia: Ediciones librestudio, n.d.); and Camilo Berneri, "Los anarquistas y la pequeña propiedad agraria," *La Revista Blanca* 10 (November 1932) through 11 (May 1933).

65. Emma Goldman, "Anarchism: What It Really Stands For," in *Anarchism and Other Essays,* 50.

66. Enriqueta Rovira, interview, Castellnaudary, France, December 29, 1981.

67. Michael Taylor, *Community, Anarchy and Liberty* (Cambridge: Cambridge University Press, 1982), especially 123–29. See also John Rawls, *A Theory of Justice* (Cambridge: Harvard University Press, 1970).

68. "Breves apuntes," 24–26; and "La coacción moral," 62, 64. Also Proudhon, *De la justice,* in *Oeuvres Complètes* 12: 363–64.

69. Proudhon, *What Is Property?,* 221, 223; Proudhon, *De la Justice,* in *Oeuvres Complètes* 11: 334–43.

70. Mella, "La coacción moral," 66, 67. Compare Brian Barry, *The Liberal Theory of Justice: A Critical Examination of the Principal Doctrines in "A Theory of Justice" by John Rawls* (Oxford: Clarendon Press, 1973), 137–38.

71. Pat Mainardi, "The Politics of Housework," in *Sisterhood Is Powerful: An Anthology of Writings from the Women's Liberation Movement,* ed. Robin Morgan (New York: Vintage Books, 1970), 447–54.

72. Prat, *A las mujeres,* 28–29; Montseny, "El ocaso del donjuanismo," *La Revista Blanca* 2, no. 46 (April 15, 1925): 9–11; Gustavo, "Hablemos de la mujer," 9.

## 2. Community Mobilization and Union Organization

1. Xavier Cuadrat, *Socialismo y anarquismo en Cataluña: los orígenes de la CNT* (Madrid: Ediciones de la Revista de Trabajo, 1976); Murray Bookchin, *The*

*Spanish Anarchists: The Heroic Years, 1868–1936* (New York: Free Life, 1977); Juan Gómez Casas, *Historia del anarcosindicalismo español* (Madrid: ZYX, 1969). Joaquín Romero Maura, *"La Rosa de Fuego": republicanos i anarquistas. La política de los obreros barceloneses entre el desastre colonial y la semana trágica, 1899–1909* (Barcelona: Grijalbo, 1974) focuses on the earlier decade but discusses the background to the creation of anarcho-syndicalism.

2. Temma Kaplan, *Anarchists of Andalusia* (Princeton: Princeton University Press, 1977), 164–65, 161–62.

3. George Esenwein, *Anarchist Ideology and the Working-Class Movement in Spain, 1868–1898* (Berkeley: University of California Press, 1989), 107–108, 128–33, and chap. 8.

4. See Edward Malefakis, *Agrarian Reform and Peasant Revolution in Spain* (New Haven: Yale University Press, 1970), especially 3–15; Juan Martínez-Alier, *Labourers and Landowners in Southern Spain* (London: Allen and Unwin, 1971); Gerald Brenan, *The Spanish Labyrinth: The Social and Political Background to the Spanish Civil War* (Cambridge: Cambridge University Press, 1943), 87–131.

5. Joseph Harrison, *An Economic History of Modern Spain* (New York: Holmes and Meier, 1978), 5. But see also Juan Pablo Fusi, "El movimiento obrero en España, 1876–1914," *Revista de Occidente*, no. 131 (February 1974): 207.

6. Josep Fontana, "Formación del mercado nacional y toma de conciencia de la burguesía," *Cambio económico y actitudes políticas en la España del siglo XIX* (Esplugues de Llobregat: Ariel, 1973), 33.

7. Antonio-Miguel Bernal, *La lucha por la tierra en la crisis del antiguo régimen* (Madrid: Taurus, 1979), 302–306, 312–13 (map 18); Fontana, "Formación del mercado nacional," especially 24–37, 41–53.

8. Josep Fontana, *La revolución liberal: Política y hacienda en 1833–1845* (Madrid: Instituto de Estudios Fiscales, Ministerio de Hacienda, n.d.), 336.

9. Bernal, "Persistencia de la problemática agraria andaluza durante la Segunda República," *La propiedad de la tierra y las luchas agrarias andaluzas* (Barcelona: Ariel, 1974), 142.

10. Susan Friend Harding, *Remaking Ibieca: Rural Life in Aragon under Franco* (Chapel Hill: University of North Carolina Press, 1984), 53–55.

11. Susan Tax Freeman, *Neighbors: The Social Contract in a Castilian Hamlet* (Chicago: University of Chicago Press, 1970), 17.

12. Juan Pablo Fusi, "El movimiento obrero," 206; Harrison, *An Economic History of Modern Spain*, 69.

13. Fusi, "El movimiento obrero," 213. See also Alvaro Soto Carmona, "Cuantificación de la mano de obra femenina (1860–1930)," in *La mujer en la historia de España (Siglos XVI-XX)* (Madrid: Seminario de Estudios de la Mujer, Universidad Autónoma de Madrid [1984]), 279–98.

14. Bernal, *La lucha por la tierra*, 390–93, 414–15.

15. Fernando de los Ríos, "The Agrarian Problem in Spain," *International Labour Review* 11, no. 6 (June 1925): 840, 844–45; Jerome M. Mintz, *The Anarchists of Casas Viejas* (Chicago: University of Chicago Press, 1984), especially 33–63; and Bernal, "Burguesía agraria y proletariado campesino en Andalucía durante la crisis de 1868," in *La propiedad de la tierra*, 107–36.

16. Ildefonso Cerdá, "Monografía estadística de la clase obrera a Barcelona en 1856," *Teoría general de la urbanización* (Madrid: Instituto de Estudios Fiscales, 1968), vol. II, 657, cited in Fontana, "Nacimiento del proletariado industrial y primeras etapas del movimiento obrero," *Cambio económico y actitudes políticas*, 85.

17. See, for example, Ignasi Terradas Saborit, *Les colonies industrials: un estudi entorn del cas de l'Ametlla de Merola* (Barcelona: Laia, 1979).

18. Rosa María Capel Martínez, *El trabajo y la educación de la mujer en España (1900–1930)* (Madrid: Ministerio de Cultura, Dirección General de Juventud y Promoción Socio-cultural, n.d.), especially 61–75, 224–34; also Mary Nash, *Mujer, familia y trabajo en España, 1875–1936* (Barcelona: Anthropos, Editorial del Hombre, 1983), 315–62; Albert Balcells, "La mujer obrera en la industria catalana durante el primer cuarto del siglo XX," *Trabajo industrial y organización obrera en la Cataluña contemporánea, 1900–1936* (Barcelona: Laia, 1974), 7–121.

19. Bernal, *La lucha por la tierra*, 394–95.

20. For 1878, see María Laffitte, Condesa de Campo Alange, *La mujer en España: Cien años de su historia 1860–1960* (Madrid: Aguilar, 1964), 26. For the later years, Rosa María Capel Martínez, "La mujer en el reinado de Alfonso XIII: Fuentes, metodología y conclusiones de un estudio histórico," *Nuevas perspectivas sobre la mujer* (Madrid: Seminario de Estudios de la Mujer, Universidad Autónoma de Madrid, 1982), 182.

21. Juan Bosch Marín, *El niño español en el siglo XX* (Madrid: Gráficas Gonzalez, 1947), 43–50; Margarita Nelken, *La condición social de la mujer en España: Su estado actual, su posible desarrollo* (Barcelona: Minerva, n.d.), 119.

22. Joaquín Costa, "Colectivismo agrario," in *Oligarquía y caciquismo, colectivismo agrario, y otros escritos*, ed. Rafael Pérez de la Dehesa (Madrid: Alianza, 1969 [originally published, 1898]), 50. Juan Díaz del Moral, *Historia de las agitaciones campesinas andaluzas—Córdoba* (Madrid: Revista de Derecho Privado, 1929; reissued Madrid: Alianza Editorial, 1967), 39–40.

23. Fontana, "Nacimiento del proletariado industrial," 60–62; Constancio Bernaldo de Quirós y Pérez, *El espartaquismo agrario andaluz* (Madrid: Reus, 1919) and "La expansión libertaria," *Archivos de psiquiatría y criminología* 5 (1906): 432–38; and Constancio Bernaldo de Quirós y Pérez and Luís Ardila, "El bandolerismo en Andalucía," pt. 1 of *El bandolerismo en España y en México* (Mexico: Jurídica Mexicana, 1959).

24. Most notably E. J. Hobsbawm, *Primitive Rebels* (New York: Norton, 1959).

25. Bernal, *La lucha por la tierra*, 442–44. See Kaplan's similar evaluation of Andalusian anarchist organizing in *Anarchists of Andalusia*, especially chap. 8.

26. Anselmo Lorenzo, *El proletariado militante* 1: 22–27; Josep Termes, "La Primera Internacional en España (1864–1881)," in *Federalismo, anarcosindicalismo y catalanismo* (Barcelona: Anagrama, 1976), 13; and Max Nettlau, *Miguel Bakunin, La Internacional y la Alianza en España (1868–1873)*, ed. Clara E. Lida (New York: Iberama, 1971), especially chaps. 1 and 2.

27. See Termes, *Federalismo*, 12–13; Fusi, "El movimiento obrero en España"; and Esenwein, *Anarchist Ideology*.

28. Termes, *Federalismo, anarcosindicalismo y catalanismo*, 7–9; C. A. M. Hennessey, *The Federal Republic in Spain* (Oxford: Clarendon Press, 1962); Esenwein, *Anarchist Ideology*.

29. Cited in Clara E. Lida, *Anarquismo y revolución en la España del XIX* (Madrid: Siglo XXI, 1972), 150.

30. Termes, *Federalismo*, 17–23; Joaquín Romero Maura, "The Spanish Case," *Government and Opposition* 5, no. 4 (Autumn 1970): 462–64; Romero Maura, "Les origines de l'anarcho-syndicalisme en Catalogne: 1900–1909," in *Anarchici e Anarchia nel mondo contemporaneo* (Torino: Fondazione Luigi Einaudi, 1971), 110–12; Renée Lamberet, "Les travailleurs espagnols et leur conception de l'anarchie de 1868 au debut de XXe siècle," ibid., 78–94.

31. Kaplan, *Anarchists of Andalusia*, 140.

32. Ibid., 135–36; see also Clara Lida, "Agrarian Anarchism in Andalusia," *International Review of Social History* 14 (1969): part 3, especially 334–37. George Esenwein argues that these differences are overstated in *Anarchist*

*Ideology*, 107–108.

33. Kaplan, *Anarchists of Andalusia*, 166–67; see also her "Class Consciousness and Community in Nineteenth-Century Andalusia," *Political Power and Social Theory* 2 (1981), 21–57.

34. George Esenwein, *Anarchist Ideology*, 110–16.

35. Azucena Barba, interviews, August 14, 1981; January 1, 1982.

36. Kaplan, *Anarchists of Andalusia*, 202–205. See also Díaz del Moral, *Historia de las agitaciones*; and Victor Pérez Díaz, "Teoría y conflictos sociales," *Revista de occidente*, no. 131 (February 1974), especially 252–56.

37. Fusi, "El movimiento obrero en España"; Romero Maura, *La rosa de fuego*, especially chaps. 1 and 2.

38. Laffitte, *La mujer en España*, 144–45. Ellen Gates Starr, who, together with Jane Addams, was to found Hull House in Chicago, was struck by the militancy of female tobacco workers in Seville during her travels in Spain in 1888. See EGS to her parents, May 2, 1888, Ellen Gates Starr papers, Sophia Smith Collection, Smith College, box 7, file 2.

39. Balcells, "La mujer obrera," 6–22.

40. Fusi, "El movimiento obrero," 204; Capel Martínez, *El trabajo y la educación*, 42–43, 211–30; Soto Carmona, "Cuantificación de la mano de obra femenina," 280–81; and Balcells, "La mujer obrera," 45.

41. Summarized in José González Castro, *El trabajo de la mujer en la industria: Condiciones en que se efectúa y sus consecuencias en el porvenir de la raza. Medidas de protección necesaria*. Instituto de Reformas Sociales, Sección segunda (Madrid: Imprenta de la sucesora de m. Minuesa de los Ríos, 1914), 8.

42. González Castro, 11, 12, 27; see also José-Ignacio García Ninet, "Elementos para el estudio de la evolución histórica del derecho español del trabajo: regulación de la jornada de trabajo desde 1855 a 1931, II parte," *Revista de trabajo*, no. 52 (4th trimester 1975): 30–32; and Juan Paulís, *Las obreras de la aguja* (Barcelona: Ibérica, 1913), especially 19–25.

43. Marta Bizcarrondo, "Los orígenes del feminismo socialista en España," in *La mujer en la historia de España (siglos XVI-XX)*, 136–38; Antonio Elorza, "Feminismo y socialismo en España (1840–1868)," *Tiempo de historia* (February 1875): 46–63.

44. Bizcarrondo, "Los orígenes," 139, 144, 146; Geraldine Scanlon, *La polémica feminista en la España contemporánea (1868–1974)*, trans. Rafael Mazarrosa (Madrid: Siglo XXI, 1976), 234.

45. Aurora de Albornoz, "Virginia González, Mujer de acción," *Tiempo de historia*, no. 32 (July 1977): 26–29; Mary Nash, *Mujer y movimiento obrero en España, 1931–1939* (Barcelona: Fontamara, 1981), chap. 4.

46. Nelken, *La condición social de la mujer en España*, 61–62 (quotation), 99, 119.

47. Robert Kern, "Margarita Nelken: Women and the Crisis of Spanish Politics," in *European Women on the Left: Socialism, Feminism, and the Problems Faced by Political Women, 1880 to the Present*, ed. Jane Slaughter and Robert Kern (Westport, Conn.: Greenwood Press, 1981), 159. George A. Collier discusses the failure of Huelva's socialists fully to incorporate women, and the consequences for women during the postwar repression in "Socialists of Rural Andalusia, 1930–1950: The Unacknowledged Revolutionaries," unpublished manuscript, Stanford University, 1984, especially 51–52. This theme is addressed indirectly in Collier's book, *Socialists of Rural Andalusia: Unacknowledged Revolutionaries of the Second Republic* (Stanford: Stanford University Press, 1987), chap. 9.

48. Cited in Capel Martínez, *El trabajo y la educación*, 228.

49. *El liberal* (Madrid), April 30, 1891, cited in Bizcarrondo, "Los orígenes," 143.

50. On the 1901 strikes see Romero Maura, *"La rosa de fuego,"* 206–11; for the 1902 Barcelona strike see Balcells, "La mujer obrera," 48; also Lola Iturbe, *La mujer en la lucha social y en la Guerra Civil de España* (Mexico, D.F.: Editores Mexicanos Unidos, 1974), 52–56; Romero Maura, *"La rosa de fuego,"* 215; and Temma Kaplan, "Female Consciousness and Collective Action: The Case of Barcelona, 1910–1918," *Signs* 7, no. 3 (1982): 545–67.

51. Romero Maura, "Les origines," 115; *"La Rosa de Fuego,"* 498ff; Cesar Lorenzo, *Les anarchistes espagnols et le pouvoir, 1868–1969* (Paris: Les editions du seuil, 1969), 45–52.

52. Cristina Piera, interview, Santa Coloma, August 6, 1981.

53. Lola Iturbe, interview, Barcelona, August 4, 1981.

54. Joan Connelly Ullman, *The Tragic Week* (Cambridge: Harvard University Press, 1968), especially 215, 227, 232, 236, 241–44, 281, 292–93.

55. *Congreso de constitución de la Confederación Nacional del Trabajo (CNT)*, ed. José Peirats (Barcelona: Cuadernos Anagrama, 1976); see also *Congresos anarcosindicalistas en España 1870–1936* (Toulouse: CNT, n.d.), 35–40.

56. *Congreso de constitución*, 65, 90.

57. Capel Martínez, *El trabajo y la educación*, 208–209.

58. Balcells, "La mujer obrera," 46; Capel Martínez, *El trabajo y la educación*, 234–35, 245.

59. Cited in Balcells, "La mujer obrera," 47.

60. Kaplan, "Female Consciousness and Collective Action," especially 557–59; Bizcarrondo, "Los orígenes," 142–53.

61. Lola Iturbe, interview, Barcelona, August 4, 1981; Balcells, "La mujer obrera," 49; and Capel Martínez, *El trabajo y la educación*, 234–42.

62. González Castro, *El trabajo de la mujer en la industria*, 20–21.

63. María de Echarri, *Conferencia a las señoras de Pamplona, 1912*, cited in Capel Martínez, *El trabajo y la educación*, 223; see also 217–22, 258–62. On Catholic unionizing efforts see Mercedes Basauri, "El feminismo cristiano en España (1900–1930)," *Tiempo de Historia*, no. 57 (August 1979): 22–33; and Basauri, "La mujer social: Beneficiencia y caridad en la crisis de la Restauración," ibid., no. 59 (October 1979): 28–43.

64. Kaplan, "Female Consciousness and Collective Action," especially 560–64; Lester Golden, "Les dones com avantguarda: El rebombori del pa del gener 1918," *L'avenç*, no. 44 (December 1981): 45–52; and Martha Ackelsberg and Myrna B. Breitbart, "Terrains of Protest: Striking City Women," *Our Generation* 19, no. 1 (Fall 1987): 151–75.

65. Syndicalist from Badalona, cited in Golden, "Les Dones com avantguarda," 50.

66. Balcells, "La mujer obrera," 49.

67. Comicios Históricos de la CNT, *Memoria del Congreso celebrado en Barcelona los días 28, 29 y 30 de junio y 1 de julio de 1918* (Toulouse: CNT, 1957), 83–84.

68. Dolores Prat, interview, Toulouse, France, April 28, 1988.

69. Eduardo Pons Prades, *Un soldado de la República: Memorias de la Guerra Civil española, 1936–1939* (Madrid: G. del Toro, 1974), 23.

70. Capel Martínez, *El trabajo y la educación*, 370, 374–75. See also "La mujer en el reinado de Alfonso XIII," 182.

71. Azucena Barba, interview, Perpignan, France, August 15, 1981.

72. Clara Lida, "Educación anarquista en la España del ochocientos," *Revista de occidente*, no. 197 (April 1971): 33–47, especially 40–42; Paul Avrich, *The*

*Modern School Movement: Anarchism and Education in the United States* (Princeton: Princeton University Press, 1980), 7.

73. From a letter from Francisco Ferrer i Guardia to José Prat, cited in Avrich, *The Modern School Movement*, 6.

74. Ferrer i Guardia, *La escuela moderna: Póstuma explicación y alcance de la enseñanza racionalista* (Barcelona: Tusquets, 1976); Pedro Costa Musté, "La escuela y la educación en los medios anarquistas de Cataluña, 1909–1939," *Convivium*, nos. 44–45 (1975), reproduced as the prologue to the Tusquets edition of *La escuela moderna;* Père Solà, *Las escuelas racionalistas en Cataluña (1909–1936)* (Barcelona: Tusquets, 1978), 22–25; and Felix Carrasquer, *Una experiencia de educación autogestionada: Escuela 'Eliseo Reclús,' calle Vallespir, 184. Barcelona. Años 1935–36* (Barcelona: Felix Carrasquer, 1981), especially chaps. 1 and 2.

75. Cristina Piera, interview, Santa Coloma, August 6, 1981.

76. Solà, *Escuelas racionalistas*, 203–14; Tina Tomasi, *Ideología libertaria y educación* (Madrid: Campo Abierto, 1978), especially 179–86; and Alejandro Tiano Ferrer, *Educación libertaria y revolución social. España 1936–39* (Madrid: Universidad nacional de educación a distancia, 1987), chap. 2.

77. Igualdad Ocaña, interview, Barcelona, February 14, 1979.

78. Ana Cases, personal communication, August 1981.

79. Valero Chiné, interview, Fraga (Aragon), May 11, 1979.

80. Arturo Parera, interview, Barcelona, July 5, 1979.

81. Juan Padreny, *Necesidad del excursionismo y su influencia libertaria en los individuos y los pueblos* (Barcelona: Ateneo libertario del Clot, "Sol y Vida," Sección excursionismo, 1934), 32.

82. Enriqueta Rovira, interview, Castellnaudary, December 28, 1981.

83. Soledad Estorach, interview, Paris, January 6, 1982.

84. Azucena Barba, interview, Perpignan, January 1, 1982.

85. Enriqueta Rovira, interview, December 29, 1981.

86. Mercedes Comaposada, interview, Paris, January 5, 1982.

87. Interview, Paris, January 3, 1982.

### 3. Civil War and Social Revolution

1. Gabriel Jackson, *The Spanish Republic and the Civil War, 1931–1939* (Princeton: Princeton University Press, 1965); Shlomo Ben-Ami, *The Origins of the Second Republic in Spain* (Oxford: Oxford University Press, 1978); Richard A. H. Robinson, *The Origins of Franco's Spain: The Right, the Republic and Revolution, 1931–1936* (Pittsburgh: The University of Pittsburgh Press, 1970); Paul Preston, *The Coming of the Spanish Civil War: Reform, Reaction and Revolution in the Second Republic 1931–1936* (New York: Barnes and Noble Books, 1978), chaps. 3–7; Josep Fontana, "La Segunda República: una esperanza frustrada," in *La II República: Una esperanza frustrada*, Proceedings of the April 1986 Conference on the Spanish Republic, held in Valencia (Valencia: Alfons el Magnanim, Institució Valenciana d'Estudis i Investigació, 1987), 9–22; and Manuel Tuñón de Lara, "Crisis de la Segunda República?" ibid., 23–36.

2. Pierre Broué and Emile Témime, *The Revolution and the Civil War in Spain*, trans. Tony White (Cambridge: MIT Press, 1970), 75–78. See also Gabriel Jackson, "The Spanish Popular Front, 1934–37," *Journal of Contemporary History* 5 (1970): 21, 28; and Stanley Payne, *The Spanish Revolution* (New York, 1970).

3. For further details on these struggles, see Adrian Shubert, *The Road to Revolution in Spain: The Coal Miners of Asturias, 1860–1934* (Urbana: University of Illinois Press, 1987); Gerald Brenan, *The Spanish Labyrinth*, 284–95; and José

Peirats, *La CNT en la revolución española* (3 vols.; Paris: Ruedo Ibérico, 1971), I: 93–104.

4. Ronald Fraser, *Blood of Spain: An Oral History of the Spanish Civil War* (New York: Pantheon, 1979), 83–104 and 513–74; Bookchin, *The Spanish Anarchists*, chaps. 9 and 10. On agrarian reform see Edward Malefakis, *Agrarian Reform and Peasant Revolution in Spain;* Malefakis, "El problema agrario y la República," in *La II República*, 37–48.

5. Pepita Carpena, interview, Montpellier France, December 30, 1981.

6. Cristina Piera, interview, Badalona, August 6, 1981.

7. Soledad Estorach, interview, Paris, January 4, 1982.

8. Enriqueta Rovira, interview, Castellnaudary, France, December 29, 1981.

9. George Orwell, *Homage to Catalonia* (Boston: Beacon Press, 1955), especially 3–6. The most comprehensive recent study of collectivization is Walther L. Bernecker, *Colectividades y revolución social: el anarquismo en la Guerra Civil Española, 1936–1939* (Barcelona: Crítica, 1982); see also Aurora Bosch, *Colectivistas (1936–1939)* (Valencia: Almudín, 1980); and Bosch, "Las colectivizaciones: estado de la cuestión y aspectos regionales," in *La II República*, 147–68.

10. José Peirats, interview, Montady, France, January 22, 1979. Compare Kropotkin, *The Conquest of Bread.*

11. Estorach, interview, Paris, January 4, 1982.

12. Orwell, *Homage to Catalonia*, 5.

13. Estorach, interview, Paris, January 6, 1982.

14. "Decret: Creació del Consell de l'Escola Nova Unificada," July 27, 1936, cited in Albert Manent, "L'Obra Cultural de la Generalitat," *Documents*, no. 8 (Barcelona: Edicions 62, 1977).

15. Emma Goldman to a friend, September 9, 1936, NYPL-EG.

16. EG to Rudolf and Milly, October 1, 1936; see also EG to Stella [Ballantine], September 19, 1936, NYPL-EG.

17. Rovira, interview, Castellnaudary, December 29, 1981.

18. Eduardo Pons Prades directed me to Tapiolas 10, Barcelona and told me about the remains of the workplace and recreational center. Reports from the unified building and construction trades union can be found in AHN/SGC-S, P.S. Barcelona: 1411, 1419, 628, 174, 855, 889, and 1323; also *Memoria del primer Congreso regional de sindicatos de la Industria de la Edificación, Madera y Decoración de Cataluña, celebrado en Barcelona, los días 26, 27, y 28 de junio de 1937* (CNT-AIT, n.p., n.d.), AMB A.M. Entid. 259-4.8; *Memoria del primer Congreso de sindicatos de la Industria de la Edificación, Madera y Decoración* (Valencia: CNT, 1937); *Memoria del primer Pleno de Comarcales de la Industria de la Edificación Madera y Decoración de Cataluña, celebrado los días 5, 6 y 7 de marzo de 1938 en Barcelona* (AHN/SGC-S, Sección propaganda, no. 242). I am grateful to Rafael Pujol for providing me with copies of minutes from local committees, Carpeta 108, documentos 882 and 883.

19. Minutes of these meetings can be found in AHN/SGC-S, P.S. Barcelona: 182: September 29, 1936 (salary unification); October 20, 1936 (worker discipline); October 23–30, 1936 (efforts to purchase coal from Germany).

20. A book of minutes of the Sindicato Unico de la Metalurgía, Barcelona, CNT, Sección Caldareros en Cobre, for example, begins with the report of a meeting that took place on September 26, 1931, and continues through December 1936. AHN/SGC-S, P.S. Barcelona: 1428.

21. Dolores Prat, interview, Toulouse, France, April 28, 1988.

22. "Copia del texto que como manifiesto lanzó a los trabajadores la junta central del sindicato de industria fabril y textil de Badalona y su radio el día 22 de julio de 1936, aplastado el movimiento de las fuerzas armadas producido el

día 19 en Barcelona," and "Comunicado," La Junta Central del Sindicato de Industria Fabril y Textil de Badalona y su Radio, Badalona, July 29, 1936, both documents from the collection of Josep Costa.

23. Costa, interviews, February 12 and 19, 1979.

24. Pérez-Baró, interview, Barcelona, July 14, 1979. On worker control of trams, see Walter Trauber, "Les tramways de Barcelone collectivisés pendant la révolution espagnole (1936–1939)," *Bulletin d'Information F.I.E.H.S.*, no. 2 (March 1977): 8–54.

25. Prat, interview, Toulouse, France, April 28, 1988.

26. There were frequent features, for example, in *Sídero-metalurgía*, the journal of the CNT union of the Barcelona steel industry, and in *Espectáculo*, a review published by Barcelona entertainment workers (CNT).

27. Minutes of the Central Committee of Worker Control for the Electricity and Gas Industry in Catalonia, for example, reflect frequent discussions about the equalization of salary scales across the industry. "Reunión del Pleno del Comité Central de Control Obrero, celebrada a las 11.15 horas, del día 29 de Septiembre de 1936. . . ." AHN/SGC-S, P.S. Barcelona: 182. See also AHN/SGC-S, P.S. Barcelona: 626 (on textiles); and Trauber, "Les tramways de Barcelone," 29. Also interviews with Federica Montseny, Toulouse, February 1, 1979; José Peirats, Montady, France, January 22 and 23, 1979; Josep Costa Font, Barcelona, February 12, 1979; and Magi Mirabent, Barcelona, February 8, 1979.

28. Pepita Carnicer, interview, Paris, January 7, 1982.

29. Teresina Graells, interview, Montady, April 29–30, 1988.

30. On this point, the work of Mercedes Vilanova on a collectivized steel plant in Barcelona is instructive; her findings were echoed, at least in part, by anarchist activists, including Pons Prades (interview, Barcelona, August 1981), Andrés Capdevila (interview, Perpignan, France, July 1979); Igualdad Ocaña (interview, Barcelona, February 1979); Pepita Carpena (interview, Montpellier, December 1981).

31. Both Albert Pérez Baró and Andrés Capdevila reported in interviews that there had been many problems "disciplining" these women: they were reluctant to work under the new system. But neither suggested that the women's resistance might have a source other than laziness or stubbornness.

32. See, for example, the letter from a woman worker to the textile workers' union in Reus (Catalonia), in which she said she would have to resign from her union post and her role as factory committee delegate as a result of her forthcoming marriage. AHN/SGC-S, P.S. Barcelona: 857.

33. Estorach, interviews, Paris, January 4 and 6, 1982.

34. Material on the Lérida collective is based on documents located in AHN/SGC-S, most particularly, Sindicato Unico de Campesinos, Colectividad AIT, CNT, *Libro de Actas*, October 15, 1936, to November 2, 1937, P.S. Lérida: 3; and other documents of the same collective, P.S. Lérida: 3, 5, 14, and 57. Information on the distribution of landholdings is derived both from interviews and from *Reparto Rústica, Lérida*, AMHL, 35, no. 2,433.

35. Interviews, Lérida, May 1979. See also Juan Domenech to Juan García Oliver, May 1938, IISG/CNT: 35.

36. AHN/SGC-S, P.S. Aragón: 113.

37. For example, Arturo and Luzdivina Parera, interviews with author, Sitges, July 22 and 23, 1979; see also Fraser, *Blood of Spain*, especially 347–72. For contrary perspectives see Félix Carrasquer, *Las colectividades de Aragón: Un vivir autogestionado promesa de futuro* (Barcelona: Laia, 1986), especially 27–28; and Gaston Leval, *Espagne libertaire 36–39 (L'oeuvre constructive de la Révolution espagnole)* (Paris: Editions du Cercle, Editions de la Tête de Feuilles, 1971).

38. Susan Friend Harding, *Remaking Ibieca*, 72. For her discussion of the

constitution of the collective in Ibieca see 61–64.

39. Bosch, "Las colectivizaciones: estado de la cuestión y aspectos regionales," in *La II República*, 147–68.

40. See, for example, *Actas*, Sindicato Agrícola Colectivo de Alcañiz, December 4, 1936, September 4, 1937, AHN/SGC-S, P.S. Aragón: 136.

41. Myrna Margulies Breitbart, "The Theory and Practice of Anarchist Decentralism in Spain, 1936–39" (Ph.D. diss., Department of Geography, Clark University, 1977); and *Problèmes de la construction et du logement dans la révolution espagnole, 1936–39*, ed. and trans. Bernard Catlla (Saillagouse, France: n.p., 1976). Gonzalo Mata and Antonio Alcázar showed me some of the canals built by CNT collectives in Vilanova i la Geltru during the course of an interview, August 16, 1981.

42. Felix Carrasquer, interview, Barcelona, February 16, 1979. See also Rudolf de Jong, "El anarquismo en España," in *El movimiento libertario español: Pasado, presente, futuro, Cuadernos de Ruedo Ibérico* (special issue, 1974), 14–15; and Bosch, *Colectivistas*, xlvii.

43. See, for example, "En Motril, en vez de dinero existen bonos de relación," *Solidaridad Obrera*, September 27, 1936, 3; "Los pequeño burgueses no deben alarmarse," ibid., August 29, 1936, 1.

44. On Monzón and Miramel, interviews with Matilde Escuder and Félix Carrasquer, Barcelona, February 16, 1979. For an overview of wages in collectives in Catalonia see "L'Enquesta de la Consellería sobre la collectivització de la terra," *Butlletí del Departament d'Agricultura* 1, no. 3 (December 1936): 21–30; and 2, no. 4 (January 1937): 75–78.

45. Information on wages in Lérida comes from "Certificats de Treball," AHN/SGC-S, P.S. Lérida: 5. On Tabernes de Valldigna in Valencia, see "Colectividad productora 'El Porvenir,' de Tabernes de Valldigna." (UGT-CNT), *CLUEA*, no. 4 (July 1937): 11–13, reprinted in Bosch, *Colectivistas*, 29.

46. On Fraga, interview with Valero Chiné, Fraga, May 11, 1979. A similar plan seems to have been implemented in Alcañíz. See *Actas*, Sindicato Agrícola Colectivo, Alcañíz, November 21, 1937, AHN/SGC-S, P.S. Aragón: 136.

47. *Libro de Actas*, entries for December 20, 1936, and July 18, 1937.

48. See the rules of a collective in Binéfar, *Realizaciones revolucionarias y estructuras colectivistas de la Comarcal de Monzón (Huesca)* (Confederación Nacional del Trabajo de España, Regional de Aragón, Rioja, y Navarra: Cultura y Acción, 1977), 85. Susan C. Bourque and Kay B. Warren report similar patterns of defining "work" along sex lines in *Women of the Andes* (Ann Arbor: University of Michigan Press, 1981), 114–26.

49. See Eduardo Pons Prades, *Un soldado de la República: Memorias de la guerra civil española* (Madrid: G. del Toro, 1974), 93ff; and AHN/SGC-S, P.S. Barcelona: 1392 and 626.

50. Juan García Oliver, *El eco de los pasos* (Barcelona: Ruedo Ibérico, 1978), 171; Diego Abad de Santillán, *Por qué perdimos la guerra?* El Arca de Papel (Barcelona: Plaza y Janes, 1977), 88, 124–25; and Cesar Lorenzo, *Les anarchistes espagnols et le pouvoir, 1868–1969*, 102–10.

51. Emma Goldman communicated her fears about these arrangements to many friends and comrades. See EG to My dear Mark [Mrachny], October 3, 1936, NYPL-EG.

52. Burnett Bolloten, *The Spanish Revolution* (Chapel Hill: University of North Carolina Press, 1979); Pierre Broué and Emile Témime, *The Revolution and the Civil War in Spain;* and Douglas Little, *Malevolent Neutrality: The United States, Great Britain, and the Origins of the Spanish Civil War* (Ithaca: Cornell University Press, 1985).

53. For further details see Martha Ackelsberg, "Women and the Politics of the

Spanish Popular Front: Political Mobilization or Social Revolution?" *International Labor and Working-Class History*, no. 30 (Fall 1986): 1–12.

54. "Federica Montseny habla en Madrid ante el micrófono de Unión Radio," *Solidaridad Obrera*, September 2, 1936, 7.

55. "Es necesario que los trabajadores cooperan a la obra de los camaradas que ocupan los puestos de responsabilidad," *Solidaridad Obrera*, September 30, 1936, 1; related articles appeared on September 29 and October 2.

56. "Importantísimo manifiesto de la CNT," *Solidaridad Obrera*, October 1, 1936.

57. EG to Rudolf, Barcelona, November 3, 1936, NYPL-EG.

58. *Actas*, Comité Central de Control Obrer, Gas i Electricitat, November 18–19 and December 5, 1936, AHN/SGC-S, P.S. Barcelona: 182.

59. EG to Senia Flechine, London, February 23, 1937; EG to a comrade, Barcelona, December 7, 1936, NYPL-EG; EG to Rose Pesotta, February 1, 1938, NYPL-RP, Special Correspondence, Box 10.

60. For fuller details on these changes, see Franz Borkenau, *The Spanish Cockpit* (Ann Arbor: University of Michigan Press, 1963), especially chap. 2; George Orwell, *Homage to Catalonia*, chaps. 5, 7–12; Noam Chomsky, "Objectivity and Liberal Scholarship," in *American Power and the New Mandarins* (New York: Random House, 1969), especially 72–158; and Bolloten, *The Spanish Revolution*.

61. EG to Ethel Mannin, November 18, 1937, NYPL-EG.

62. Fraser, *Blood of Spain*, 321–47; Vernon Richards, *Lessons of the Spanish Revolution* (London: Freedom Press, 1953); García Oliver, *El eco de los pasos*, chap. 3; and "Actas del pleno nacional de regionales, CNT, septiembre 1937," 21ff, IISG/CNT, Paquete 48A.

63. EG to the Dutch Pacifist, Wim Jong, February 10, 1937, NYPL-EG, EG to Mollitchka [Mollie Stiemer], January 19, 1937, IISG/EG, no. 20094; her address to the Extraordinary Congress in Paris of the IWBA [*sic*], December 1937. NYPL-RP, Special Correspondence, Box 10; and EG to Max Nettlau, May 9, 1937, Labadie Collection, University of Michigan (Federico Arcos supplied me with a copy).

64. Mariano M. Vázquez, for the National Committee of the CNT, and Pedro Herrera, for the Peninsular Committee of the FAI, to EG, January 11, 1938, IISG/EG, #19187. I am grateful to Alice Wexler for calling these letters to my attention. See Wexler's *Emma Goldman in Exile* (Boston: Beacon Press, 1989), especially chap. 9.

65. Hugh Thomas, *The Spanish Civil War* (New York: Harper and Row, 1961). Gabriel Jackson, *The Spanish Republic and the Civil War, 1931–39;* Edward Malefakis, panel presentation, "Revolution and Counterrevolution," at the conference "1936–1986: From the Civil War to Contemporary Spain, Perspective on History and Society," Center for European Studies, Harvard University, November 14–16, 1986.

66. Vázquez to EG, Paris, February 21, 1939; March 5, 1939, IISG, Rocker Archives, file 107.

67. On the Franco years, see Louis Stein, *Beyond Death and Exile: Spanish Republicans in France* (Cambridge: Harvard University Press, 1979); Lidia Falcón, *Los hijos de los vencidos, 1939–1949* (Barcelona: Pomaire, 1979); Carlota O'Neill, *Trapped in Spain*, trans. Leandro Garza (Toronto: Solidarity Books, 1978); and Javier Tusell, *Los hijos de la sangre: La España de 1936 desde 1986* (Madrid: Espasa Calpe, 1986).

## 4. The Founding of Mujeres Libres

1. Kiraline [Lola Iturbe], "La educación social de la mujer," *Tierra y Libertad* 1, no. 9 (October 15, 1935): 4.

2. Enriqueta Rovira, interview, Castellnaudary, December 28, 1981. For contemporary parallels, see Sara Evans, *Personal Politics: The Roots of Women's Liberation in the Civil Rights Movement and the New Left* (New York: Knopf, 1979); and Ellen Kay Trimberger, "Women in the Old and New Left: The Evolution of a Politics of Personal Life," *Feminist Studies* 5 (Fall 1979): 432–50.

3. Azucena Barba, interview, Perpignan, December 27, 1981.

4. Pepita Carpena, interview, Montpellier, France, December 30, 1981.

5. Pura Pérez Arcos, interview, Windsor, Ontario, December 19, 1984.

6. Matilde Piller, "Adónde va la mujer?" *Estudios*, no. 133 (September 1934): 18–19. Mary Berta made a similar argument in "La verdadera madre," *Estudios*, no. 121 (September 1933): 40–41.

7. Montuenga, "Consideraciones sobre la mujer," *Solidaridad Obrera*, September 4, 1935, 4.

8. CNT, *El congreso confederal de Zaragoza. 1936*. Biblioteca "Promoción del Pueblo" (Madrid: Zero, 1978), 237.

9. Federica Montseny, "La mujer: problema del hombre," in *La Revista Blanca* (February–June 1927); see also Mary Nash, "Dos intelectuales anarquistas frente al problema de la mujer: Federica Montseny y Lucía Sánchez Saornil," *Convivium* (Barcelona: Universidad de Barcelona, 1975), 74–86.

10. Federica Montseny, "Feminismo y humanismo," *La Revista Blanca* 2, no. 33 (October 1, 1924); see also "Las mujeres y las elecciones inglesas," *La Revista Blanca* 1, no. 18 (February 15, 1924). For a different interpretation of Montseny's views, see Shirley Fredericks, "Feminism: The Essential Ingredient in Federica Montseny's Anarchist Thought," in *European Women on the Left*, ed. Slaughter and Kern, 125–45, especially 127–35.

11. See Geraldine Scanlon, *La polémica feminista en la España contemporánea (1868–1974)*, 195–209; and María Teresa González Calbet, "El surgimiento del movimiento feminista, 1900–1930," in *El feminismo en España: Dos siglos de historia*, ed. Pilar Folguera (Madrid: Pablo Iglesias, 1988), 51–56.

12. Federica Montseny, "La falta de idealidad en el feminismo," *La Revista Blanca* 1, no. 13 (December 1, 1923): 3; "Feminismo y humanismo."

13. Montseny, "La falta de idealidad en el feminismo," 4; see also Emma Goldman, "Woman Suffrage," especially 198–201, 208–11, and "The Tragedy of Woman's Emancipation," especially 215–17 in *Anarchism and Other Essays*.

14. Igualdad Ocaña, interview with author, Hospitalet (Barcelona), February 14, 1979.

15. Teresina Torrelles, interview, Montady, April 29, 1988.

16. The CNT and UGT had attempted a coordinated rising in October 1934 in protest against the reactionary policies of the government. In most areas, the revolt failed, largely through lack of communication and cooperation. In the mining communities of Asturias, however, UGT and CNT miners coordinated their activities and actually took over a number of towns and cities before they were crushed by Moorish troops sent by the government. The "revolution of October" became a model for proletarian unity and a rallying cry for working-class organizing in the ensuing years. See Adrian Shubert, *The Road to Revolution in Spain*.

17. Interviews with Pura Perez Arcos, Windsor, Ontario, December 16, 1984, and Mercedes Comaposada, Paris, January 1982, April 1988.

18. See chap. 2.

19. Mercedes Comaposada, interviews, Paris, January 3 and 5, 1982; April 22, 1988.

20. John Brademas, *Anarcosindicalismo y revolución* (Barcelona: Ariel, 1974), especially chaps. 5–7; Juan Gómez Casas, *Historia de la FAI* (Madrid: Zero, 1977); Gómez Casas, *Historia del anarcosindicalismo español* (Madrid: ZYX, 1968), especially 167–91; and Murray Bookchin, *The Spanish Anarchists: The Heroic Years*, especially 241–51.

21. Soledad Estorach, conversation, Paris, April 27, 1988.

22. Estorach, interview, Paris, January 6, 1982.

23. Soledad Estorach, interview with author, Paris, January 4, 1982. For more information about Federica Montseny and Libertad Ródenas see Lola Iturbe, *La mujer en la lucha social y en la Guerra Civil de España* (Mexico, D.F.: Mexicanos Unidos, 1974), 64–71.

24. Mercedes Comaposada, interview, Paris, April 22, 1988.

25. Soledad Estorach, interview, Paris, January 4, 1982.

26. Mariano Vázquez, "Mujer: factor revolucionario," appeared in *Solidaridad Obrera*, on September 18, 1935; "Avance: Por la elevación de la mujer," appeared in *Solidaridad Obrera* on October 10, 1935, in response to Sánchez Saornil's first three. "La cuestión femenina en nuestros medios" appeared in five parts on September 26 and October 2, 9, 15, and 30, 1935; "Resúmen al márgen," appeared on November 8. Sánchez Saornil's pieces are reprinted in Mary Nash's important collection, *"Mujeres Libres" España, 1936–1939*, 43–66.

27. See Miguel Benjumea García, "La mujer ante la revolución," *Solidaridad Obrera*, October 6, 1935, or Peter, "Una proposición a la mujer," ibid., October 10, 1935.

28. Strikingly, *Solidaridad Obrera* published an article a few days later illustrating her point, "Crónica del día: El trabajo de la mujer," *Solidaridad Obrera*, October 25, 1935, 6.

29. Sánchez Saornil's article drew on María Luísa Cobos, "A la mujer, no; a vosotros, proletarios," *Solidaridad Obrera*, October 8, 1935, 3.

30. See also José Alvarez Junco, *La ideología política del anarquismo español, 1868–1910* (Madrid: Siglo XXI, 1976), 302n; and Kahos, "Mujeres, Emancipaos!" *Acracia*, November 26, 1937, 4.

31. Similar claims appeared periodically in various anarcho-syndicalist journals. See, for example, "Femeninas," *Obrero Balear*, Organo de la Federación Socialista Balear, October 30, 1931, and a series of articles in *Cultura Obrera*, Órgano de la Confederación Regional del Trabajo de Baleares y Portavoz de la CNT, January 7, 1935, and February 14, 1935. I am grateful to Neus for providing me with copies of these documents.

32. Letters, both from the editorial collective of *Mujeres Libres* to would-be distributors and from supporters back to the editorial board, can be found in AHN/SGC-S, P.S. Madrid: 432. I am grateful to Mary Nash for alerting me to the location of these documents.

33. The first issue appeared toward the end of May 1936. According to a list prepared by Mercedes Comaposada, there were four issues of the journal edited before the war (of which two were of the brief newsletter sort). A second issue appeared in June. Issue no. 4 was apparently being prepared when the war broke out on July 19, but was never published. The second extant issue (officially no. 5) dated Día 65 de la Revolución, appeared in October 1936. I am grateful to Pura Pérez Arcos for providing me with a list, "Revista Mujeres Libres," prepared by Mercedes Comaposada.

34. Letter to Emma Goldman from the editors of *Mujeres Libres*, Madrid, April 17, 1936, AHN/SGC-S, P.S. Madrid: 432. Goldman commented on her

receipt of the letter in a note to a comrade, April 24. This letter is reproduced in David Porter, ed., *Vision on Fire: Emma Goldman on the Spanish Revolution* (New Paltz, N.Y.: Commonground Press, 1983), 254.

35. From a letter to María Luísa Cobos, April 20, 1936. AHN/SGC-S, P.S. Madrid: 432.

36. Lucía Sánchez Saornil to Federica Montseny, Madrid, May 24, 1936; also Mujeres Libres to Compañero Hernandez Domenech (La Unión), Madrid, May 27, 1936.

37. Mujeres Libres to Compañero Celedonio Arribas (Soria), Madrid, May 14, 1936; and Editorial Committee to Camarada Morales Guzmán (Granada), May 7, 1936.

38. Lucía Sánchez Saornil to Camarada Abad de Santillán (Barcelona), Madrid, May 6, 1936.

39. Lucía Sánchez Saornil, for the Editorial Committee to Compañero Director of *Solidaridad Obrera* (Barcelona), Madrid, May 28, 1936.

40. From the Editorial Committee to Compañera Josefa de Tena (Mérida), Madrid, May 25, 1936; and de Tena's response, June 3, 1936.

41. Lucía Sánchez Saornil to Compañera María Luísa Cobos, April 20, 1936.

42. Lucía Sánchez Saornil, for the editors, to Camarada Morales Gumán [*sic*] (Granada), Madrid, June 14, 1936.

43. See, for example, Carol Gilligan, *In a Different Voice* (Cambridge: Harvard University Press, 1982); and Sara Ruddick, *Maternal Thinking: Toward a Politics of Peace* (Boston: Beacon Press, 1989). For a critical review of this literature see Martha Ackelsberg and Irene Diamond, "Gender and Political Life: New Directions in Political Science," in *Analyzing Gender: A Handbook of Social Science Research*, ed. Myra Marx Ferree and Beth B. Hess (Beverly Hills: Sage, 1987), 515–18.

44. This article became part of her booklet *Niño* (Barcelona: Mujeres Libres [1937]).

45. One example of such a journal in an earlier period is *La mujer: Periódico Científico, Artístico y Literario*, published in Barcelona in 1882.

46. For example, AHN/SGC-S, P.S. Madrid: 432.

47. Mercedes Comaposada, "Orígen y actividades de la Agrupación 'Mujeres Libres'" *Tierra y Libertad*, no. 11 (March 27, 1937): 8.

48. "Henos aquí otra vez. . . ." *Mujeres Libres*, no. 5 (October 1936).

49. "Mujeres de Madrid: Preparáos a vencer," *Mujeres*, no. 12 (October 29, 1936): 3; see also Aurora Morcillo Gómez, "Feminismo y lucha política durante la II República y la Guerra civil," in *El feminismo en España*, ed. Pilar Folguera, 75–76.

50. *Companya* 1, no. 1 (March 11, 1937). See also my "Women and the Politics of the Spanish Popular Front."

## 5. Education for Empowerment

1. "Estatutos de la Agrupación de Mujeres Libres," 4 pp., Alfáfar (Valencia), n.d., AHN/SGC-S, P.S. Madrid: 432, Legajo 3270; also Federación Nacional "Mujeres Libres," Comité Nacional, "A todos los Comités Regionales y Provinciales de la Federación Nacional Mujeres Libres" (Barcelona, July 12, 1938), 1, IISG/FAI: 48.c.1.a.

2. "Mujeres Libres tiene una personalidad," *Mujeres Libres*, no. 8; and Etta Federn, *Mujeres de las revoluciones* (Barcelona: Mujeres Libres [1938]), 58.

3. "Anexo al informe que la federación Mujeres Libres eleva a los comités superiores del movimiento libertario y al pleno del mismo," 2. Federación

Nacional 'Mujeres Libres,' Comité Nacional, Barcelona, October 1938, IISG/ CNT: 40.c.4.

4. "Resumen al márgen de la cuestión femenina," *Solidaridad Obrera*, November 8, 1935. See also Emma Goldman, "La situación social de la mujer," *Mujeres Libres*, no. 6.

5. "El problema sexual y la revolución," *Mujeres Libres*, no. 9, and "Liberatorios de prostitución," *Mujeres Libres*, no. 5. Compare José Luís Aranguren, "La mujer, de 1923 a 1963," *Revista de Occidente* (Segunda época), nos. 8–9 (November-December 1963): 231–43.

6. "Un acontecimiento histórico," *Mujeres Libres*. no. 11.

7. See, for example, Carol Gilligan, *In a Different Voice;* Sara Ruddick, *Maternal Thinking;* Mary Field Belenky et al., eds., *Women's Ways of Knowing: The Development of Self, Voice, and Mind* (New York: Basic Books, 1986); and, for critical perspectives, Mary G. Dietz, "Citizenship with a Feminist Face," *Political Theory* 13, no. 1 (1985): 19–37; and Martha Ackelsberg and Irene Diamond, "Gender and Political Life."

8. Instituto Mujeres Libres, *Actividades de la F. N. Mujeres Libres* (Barcelona: Mujeres Libres, [1938]). See also "Realizaciones de Mujeres Libres: Organización, Cultura, Trabajo, Maternidad," *Tierra y Libertad*, July 30, 1938; and Soledad Estorach, "Caracteres de nuestra lucha," *Tierra y Libertad*, December 3, 1938.

9. See the advertisement "Mujeres Libres," *Tierra y Libertad*, no. 47 (December 10, 1938): 3. On the literacy campaign more generally see "Salvemos a las mujeres de la dictadura de la mediocridad: Labor cultural y constructiva para ganar la guerra y hacer la Revolución," *Ruta*, 2, no. 29 (April 30, 1937): 8; also "Realizaciones de 'Mujeres Libres,': La Mujer ante el presente y futuro social," in *Síderometalurgía* (Revista del sindicato de la Industria síderometalúrgica de Barcelona) 5 (November 1937): 9.

10. As announced in *Mujeres Libres*, no. 11 (1937).

11. Pepita Carpena, interviews, Montpellier, December 30, 1981 and Barcelona, May 3, 1988; Conchita Guillén and Amada de Nó, interviews, Montady, April 29 and 30, 1988.

12. Anna Delso de Miguel, "Demarche évocatrice," *Trois cents hommes et moi* (Montréal: Editions de la pleine lune, 1989): 48–55; interviews.

13. "Reglament per a l'Applicació del Decret del 10 de Juliol del 1937 que Crea l'Institut d'Adaptació Profesional de la Dona," IISG/CNT: 001.A.3.

14. "Informes: Instituto de Adaptación Profesional de la Mujer," IISG/CNT: 001.A.3.; Federación Local de Sindicatos Unicos, "Acerca del Instituto de Adaptación Professional," *Boletín de Información*, CNT-FAI, no. 393, September 24, 1937; Generalitat de Catalunya, *Escola professional per a la dona—Reglament* (Barcelona: Casa d'A.F. Maciá, 1937); and Generalitat de Catalunya, Departament de Cultura, *Les noves institucions jurídiques i culturals per a la dona* (Setmana d'Activitats Femenines, February 1937) (Barcelona: Gráficas Olivade Vilanova, 1937).

15. "Realizaciones de 'Mujeres Libres,'" *Tierra y Libertad*, July 30, 1938.

16. Interview, Paris, January 4, 1982. See also Soledad Estorach, "Escucha, compañera," *Acracia*, February 6, 1937.

17. Lucía Sánchez Saornil, for the National Committee of Mujeres Libres, to the national or peninsular committees of the CNT, FAI, and FIJL (December 13, 1938) and to Juan Negrín, president of the Council of Ministers (December 21, 1938), IISG/FAI: 48.C.1.a.

18. For many months, Amada de Nó was responsible for this kiosk. Interview, Montady, April 30, 1988.

19. "Acta de la Segunda Sesión de la Conferencia Nacional de 'Mujeres

Libres' Celebrada en Valencia el Día 21 de agosto 1937," and "Acta de la Tercera Sesión de la Conferencia Nacional de Mujeres Libres Celebrada en Valencia en 21 de agosto a las Cuatro de la Tarde," 6–8, AHN/SGC-S, P.S. Madrid: 432.

20. Those named included Sara Berenguer (now Guillén) (Barcelona), Propaganda; Angela Colomé (Badalona), Pepita Margallo (Mataró), Angelina Cortez (Guixols), and Pepita Carpena (Barcelona), Cultura; and María Luísa Cobos (Barcelona) and Águeda Abad (Barcelona), Propagandistas y Organizadoras. "Presupuesto de los gastos mensuales del Comité Regional 'Mujeres Libres' de Cataluña," Barcelona, November 3, 1938, IISG/CNT: 40.C.4.

21. Pepita Carpena, interview, December 30, 1981.

22. Soledad Estorach, interview, January 4, 1982.

23. "Realizaciones de 'Mujeres Libres,'" *Tierra y Libertad*, July 30, 1938, 4.

24. Mercedes Comaposada, interview, Paris, January 5, 1982.

25. "El trabajo" and "El accidente espiritual," *Mujeres Libres*, no. 6.

26. "La mujer como productora," *Mujeres Libres*, no. 11.

27. Pilar Grangel, "El trabajo intelectual y manual de la mujer," *Mujeres Libres*, no. 12; see also "Mujeres con carga," *Mujeres Libres*, no. 10, and "Campesinas," *Mujeres Libres*, no. 8.

28. "Trabajo: Redoblemos el esfuerzo," *Mujeres Libres*, no. 6 (December 1936).

29. "El trabajo," *Mujeres Libres*, no. 13.

30. Mercedes Comaposada, "Nivelación de salarios," *Tierra y Libertad*, February 27, 1937, cited in Nash, *"Mujeres Libres,"* 150–52.

31. "Actas del Pleno Nacional de Regionales del Movimento Libertario," Barcelona, October 1938, 160, IISG/CNT: 92.A.3. See also "Hasta cuando?" *Mujeres Libres*, no. 10.

32. "Hay sitio para todas," *Mujeres Libres*, no. 7.

33. "Mujeres de España," *Mujeres Libres*, no. 12. See also Pilar Grangel, "El trabajo intelectual y manual de la mujer," and "La mujer y la técnica" (in the same issue).

34. "El trabajo," *Mujeres Libres*, no. 13.

35. "La mujer como productora," *Mujeres Libres*, no. 11.

36. "La incorporación de las mujeres al trabajo," *Mujeres Libres*, no. 12.

37. "Las mujeres en los primeros días de lucha," *Mujeres Libres*, no. 10.

38. Pura Pérez Arcos, interview, Windsor, Ontario, December 16, 1984; and personal communication, June 5, 1989.

39. As reported by María Gimenez, "Una colectividad: Amposta," *Mujeres Libres*, no. 11; see also, in that same issue, María Pérez, "Utiel revolucionario"; also María Gimenez, "Aragon revolucionario," in no. 10, and "Campesina," in no. 13.

40. Soledad Estorach, interview, January 4, 1982.

41. Comité Nacional de Mujeres Libres, "Circular a los Comités regionales," May 10, 1938, fragment in IISG/FAI; 59; also cited in "Informe que esta federación eleva a los comités nacionales del movimiento libertario y a los delegados al pleno del mismo," 6, IISG/CNT: 40.C.4. For a direct appeal to women see "La mujer en el Sindicato," *Acracia*, November 19, 1937, 2.

42. "Actas," August 21, 1937, 6; and Aurea Cuadrado, "Adaptación Profesional de la Mujer," *Mujeres Libres*, no. 11.

43. Those by Etta Federn were later published as *Mujeres de las revoluciones;* those by Kiralina [Lola Iturbe] appeared in *La mujer en la lucha social*.

44. Amada de Nó, interview, Montady, April 30, 1988. *Mujeres Libres* ran a brief article on the 70th Brigade, accompanied by a picture of Mika Etchebéhère, Captain of its 14th Division, in issue no. 10. See also Etchebéhère, *Ma guerre d'Espagne à moi*, Dossiers des lettres nouvelles (Paris: Denoël, 1976).

45. On women at the battlefronts see "La capitana de Somosierra," *Mujeres Libres*, no. 13. The shooting range for women in Madrid was noted in *Actividades de la F.N. Mujeres Libres*, 2; and the section on "war sports" in Catalonia in "Actividades de Mujeres Libres," *Mujeres Libres*, no. 12.

46. Federn, *Mujeres de las Revoluciones*, 5; also Lucía Sánchez Saornil, "El día de la mujer, conmemorado por el Comité de Mujeres contra la Guerra y el Fascio," *Horas de Revolución* (Barcelona: Mujeres Libres [1937]), 52.

47. Federica Montseny, "Acción de la mujer en la paz y en la guerra: El progreso es la obra de todos," *Mujeres Libres*, no. 13.

48. Aurea Cuadrado, "Superación," *Mujeres Libres*, no. 13; Mercedes Comaposada, *Esquemas* (Barcelona: Mujeres Libres, n.d.); and Comité Nacional, Mujeres Libres, *Cómo organizar una agrupación Mujeres Libres* (Barcelona: Mujeres Libres, n.d.). The latter two are reprinted in Mary Nash's anthology, *"Mujeres Libres" España, 1936–1939* (Barcelona: Tusquets, 1976), 115–18, 75–85.

49. Ilse, "La doble lucha de la mujer," *Mujeres Libres*, no. 7; see also "La mujer y el problema de la libertad," *Acracia*, June 15, 1937.

50. Mercedes Comaposada, interview, Paris, January 5, 1982. On conscientious motherhood in the U.S. context, see Linda Gordon, *Woman's Body Woman's Right: A Social History of Birth Control in America* (New York: Penguin, 1974).

51. Lucía Sánchez Saornil, "La cuestión femenina en nuestros medios, IV" *Solidaridad Obrera*, October 15, 1935, 2.

52. Pilar Grangel, "En vez de crítica: soluciones," *Mujeres Libres*, no. 13.

53. Etta Federn, "Maternidad y Maternalidad," *Mujeres Libres*, no. 12; and "Maternidad," *Mujeres Libres*, no. 13.

54. On Alexandra Kollantai, 45, and on Angelica Balabanoff, 37, in *Mujeres de las revoluciones*.

55. Amparo Poch y Gascón, *Niño* (Barcelona: Mujeres Libres, n.d. [1937]).

56. Teresina Torrelles, interview, Montady, France, April 29, 1988.

57. "Puericultura," *Mujeres Libres*, no. 13.

58. Aurea Cuadrado, "Nuestra labor en la casa de maternidad de Barcelona," *Mujeres Libres*, no. 7.

59. "Notas Informativas," Instituto de puericultura y maternología, Barcelona, April 3, 1938. See also "Manifiesto de los compañeros responsables técnicos, sindicales, y administrativos del Instituto de Puericultura y Maternología, Hospital del Pueblo, y Hospital de Sangre de Pueblo Nuevo, a Todos los Militantes y Affiliados que pertenecen a los sindicatos de la Confederación Nacional del Trabajo de Barcelona," May 3, 1938 (both in IISG/CNT: 40.C.).

60. For example, "Niños," in *Mujeres Libres*, no. 5; and "Niños," by Florentina in *Mujeres Libres*, nos. 9 and 11.

61. Etta Federn, "La crueldad y la ira del niño," *Mujeres Libres*, no. 11.

62. Florentina, "Niños," *Mujeres Libres* nos. 8, 9, 10, 11, and 12; "Educar es equilibrar," *Mujeres Libres*, no. 7; and Etta Federn, "Mi ideal de una escuela," *Tiempos nuevos* (July–August 1937), nos. 7–8.

63. On the importance of a "fit" between educational institutions and authority relations in society see Harry Eckstein, *Division and Cohesion in Democracy* (Princeton: Princeton University Press, 1966), chap. 7; Carole Pateman, *Participation and Democratic Theory* (Cambridge: Cambridge University Press, 1970), chap. 2; Dennis F. Thompson, *The Democratic Citizen* (Cambridge: Cambridge University Press, 1970); John Rawls, *A Theory of Justice*, chaps. 5 and 8; and Michael Walzer, *Spheres of Justice: A Defense of Pluralism and Equality* (New York: Basic Books, 1983), chap. 8.

64. Florentina, "Niños," *Mujeres Libres*, no. 8; also "Infancia sin escuela,"

*Mujeres Libres*, no. 12; Pilar Grangel, "Pedagogía," *Mujeres Libres*, no. 10; Etta Federn, "Eliminad el miedo," *Mujeres Libres*, no. 9; "De poco servirán todos los sacrificios," *Mujeres Libres*, no. 13.

65. Summarized from "Enseñanza nueva," *Mujeres Libres*, no. 6.

66. Poch y Gascón, *La vida sexual de la mujer* (Valencia: Cuadernos de Cultura, 1932), especially 22, 26, 31; "La autoridad en el amor y en la sociedad," *Solidaridad Obrera*, September 27, 1935, 1; and "La convivencia, antídoto del amor," *Solidaridad Obrera*, December 19, 1936, 8.

67. Federn, *Mujeres de las revoluciones*, 44.

68. See also "Ante que te cases, mira lo que haces," *Mujeres Libres*, no. 7.

69. Sara Guillén, interview, Montady, April 29, 1988; see also Antonina Rodrigo, "Nuestras mujeres en la Guerra civil," *Vindicación feminista*, no. 3 (September 1, 1976): 37.

70. "La ceremonía matrimonial o la cobardía del espíritu," *Horas de revolución*, 24–26, citation from 25; see also "Con la libertad sexual los hombres y las mujeres dejarían de ser esclavos incluso de la moral más roja," *Acracia*, August 19, 1936.

71. Michel Froidevaux, "Les avatars de l'anarchisme: la révolution et la guerre civile en Catalogne (1936–1939), vues au travers de la presse anarchiste," 2 vols., typescript, International Institute for Social History, Amsterdam, 212.

72. "Liberatorios de Prostitución," *Mujeres Libres*, no. 5.

73. For example, "Nota local," *Acracia*, July 14, 1937; "Saboteando la revolución," *Acracia*, January 1, 1937; and "Mujeres Libres," *Ruta*, January 21, 1937.

74. For example, Nita Nahuel, "Los que deshonran al anarquismo," *Mujeres Libres*, no. 7.

75. Pepita Carpena, interview, Barcelona, May 3, 1988.

76. "El problema sexual y la revolución," *Mujeres Libres*, no. 9. See also Amparo Poch, *La vida sexual de la mujer*, 25; and Lucía Sánchez Saornil, "La cuestión femenina en nuestros medios: V," *Solidaridad Obrera*, October 30, 1935, 2.

77. "Acciones contra la prostitución," *Mujeres Libres*, no. 11. Compare Emma Goldman, "The Traffic in Women," especially 178–79, 184–86, and "Marriage and Love," especially 228–31, both in *Anarchism and Other Essays*.

78. See "Nuestra labor en la casa de maternidad de Barcelona," *Mujeres Libres*, no. 7; "La enorme labor del Ministerio de Sanidad y Asistencia Social," *Mujeres Libres*, no. 8, "Nuevas conquistas para Asistencia Social," *Mujeres Libres*, no. 10.

79. Lola Iturbe, in particular, emphasized the importance of this reform, and the number of women who took advantage of it, in an interview August 4, 1981. A few articles in the column "La mujer en la lucha" of *Tierra y Libertad* made reference to the availability of abortion (see, for example, July 3, 1937); but there was no mention in *Mujeres Libres*. See also Mary Nash, "El neomaltusianismo anarquista y los conocimientos populares sobre el control de natalidad en España."

80. Julia Mirabé de Vallejo, interview, in Isabella Cuenca, "La mujer en el movimiento libertario de España durante la Segunda República (1931–1939)," thesis, Université de Toulouse Le Mirail, Institut d'Etudes Hispaniques et Hispano-Americaines, 1986. I am grateful to Sara Berenguer Guillén for lending me her copy of this thesis.

81. The puritan streak was also evident in articles in *Mujeres Libres*. See, for example, Etta Federn, "Maternidad y Maternalidad," *Mujeres Libres*, no. 12; "Fiestecitas que no deben propagarse," *Mujeres Libres*, no. 13; and "Valencia: Carteleras permanentes," *Mujeres Libres*, no. 8.

82. Enriqueta Rovira, for example, was effectively ostracized by many of her

movement comrades for ending a relationship with her compañero after the war. Sara Guillén, Pepita Carpena, and Azucena Barba all reported observing similar attitudes.

83. Suceso Portales, interview, Móstoles (Madrid), June 29, 1979; Pepita Carpena, interview, Barcelona, May 3, 1988. Others I interviewed, though they did not use the word "lesbian," made frequent reference to Lucía's compañera, Mary.

84. See, for example, letter from Felisa de Castro, secretary of Mujeres Libres in Barcelona, to SIA, June 9, 1938, IISG/CNT: 64.C.4.

85. Anna Delso de Miguel, *Trois cents hommes et moi*, especially 42–56.

86. Conchita Guillén, interview, Montady, April 30, 1988.

87. Amada Victoria de Nó Galindo, interview, Montady, April 30, 1988.

88. Sara Berenguer Guillén, interview, Capestang, France, April 30, 1988; personal communication, August 1989.

89. Federación Nacional Mujeres Libres, Comite Nacional, "A todos los Comités Regionales y Provinciales de la Federacion Nacional Mujeres Libres."

## 6. Separate and Equal?

1. "La personnalité de 'Femmes Libres,'" *Mujeres Libres: Bulletin d'Information* IISG/FAI: 48.c.1.a; also "Anexo al informe que la Federación Mujeres Libres eleva a los comités superiores del movimiento libertario."

2. "Anexo al informe," 1. See also "Algunas consideraciones del Comité Nacional de Mujeres Libres al de la CNT sobre la importancia política de aquella organización," undated, contained in memorandum from CNT National Committee to organizational delegates, Barcelona, January 20, 1938, p. 1, IISG/CNT: 45.B.17.

3. Nash, *Mujer y movimiento obrero*, 176.

4. See *La mujer ante la revolución*, Publicaciones del secretariado femenino del POUM (Barcelona, 1937); Nash, *Mujer y movimiento obrero;* Ackelsberg, "Women and the Politics of the Spanish Popular Front: Political Mobilization or Social Revolution?", 5; and Antonina Rodrigo, "Nuestras mujeres en la Guerra Civil," 39–40.

5. Emilia Elias, *Por qué luchamos?* cited in Nash, *Mujer y movimiento obrero*, 244.

6. Mujeres Libres, "Algunas consideraciones del Comité Nacional"; "Informe que esta federación eleva a los comités nacionales del movimiento libertario y a los delegados al pleno del mismo," Barcelona, September 1938, pp. 1, 8, IISG/CNT: 40.C.4; Federación Nacional Mujeres Libres, Comité Nacional, Circular n., Barcelona, July 12, 1938, IISG/FAI: 48.C.1.a; and Emma Goldman to Mariano Vásquez, October 7, 1938, IISG/CNT: 63.C.2.

7. "Informe que esta Federación eleva," 6.

8. The text is reproduced in ibid., 2–3.

9. Ibid., 7. Nevertheless, letters and articles in *Acracia*, the anarchist daily in Lérida, appealed to anarchist women to participate in the AMA. Anna Cunsigne, "Lletres de dona," *Acracia*, December 2, 1937, 1; and Una de ellas, "Las mujeres de retaguardia por los luchadores del frente," ibid., December 3, 1937, 4.

10. Comité Regional Mujeres Libres "Circular no. 1 de Información," March 7, 1938, IISG/CNT: 40.C.4.

11. Lucía Sánchez Saornil, "Actitud clara y consecuente de Mujeres Libres. En respuesta a Dolores Ibarruri," *Solidaridad Obrera*, August 11, 1938, reprinted in Nash, *"Mujeres Libres,"* 109–12.

12. Mercedes Comaposada, interview, Paris, January 5, 1982.

13. Federación Nacional Mujeres Libres, "Actas de la conferencia nacional celebrada en Valencia," August 21–23, 1937," AHN/SGC-S, P.S. Madrid: 432.

14. Mercedes Comaposada, interviews, Paris, January 1 and 3, 1982.

15. "ACTAS de la conferencia nacional," 9.

16. Ibid., August 21, 1937.

17. "Anexo al informe," 3.

18. Mujeres Libres, Valencia, to Peninsular Committee of the FAI, August 17, 1937, IISG/FAI: 48.C.1.a.

19. Letter from J. Domenech, Secretary, Catalan Regional Committee of the CNT, November 11, 1937, transmitting Circular no. 11 from CNT National Committee, Valencia, November 6, 1937, IISG/CNT: 48.B.1.

20. Amada de Nó, interviews, Montady, April 30, 1988.

21. "Una publicación interesante Mujeres Libres," *Acracia*, July 27, 1937, p. 1; "Día tras día: Transformación social sin decretos," ibid., September 4, 1937, p. 1; "Mujeres Libres," ibid., November 23, 1937, p. 4.

22. Mercedes Comaposada, interview, Paris, January 7, 1982. Letters can also be found in AHN/SGC-S, P.S. Madrid: 432.

23. See the minutes of the organization of ateneos libertarios of Madrid, July 29, 1937, August 19, 1937, September 16, 1937, February 19, 1938, April 14, 1938. Circular no. 7 of the Commission on Anarchist and Confederal Propaganda, Madrid, January 29, 1938, similarly included Mujeres Libres in its scope. Both documents in AHN/SGC-S, P.S. Madrid: 1712.

24. "Informe que esta Federación eleva," 8–9.

25. Propaganda Section, Levantine Regional Committee, Mujeres Libres, to Peninsular Committee, FAI, 3-1-1938, and response, IISG/FAI: 48.C.1.c.; Catalan Regional Committee, Mujeres Libres, to Catalan Regional Committee, CNT, February 2 and 26 and October 6, 1938, and responses, IISG/CNT: 40.C.4.; National Propaganda Section, Mujeres Libres, to Peninsular Committee, FAI, March 1938, IISG/FAI: 48.C.1.a.; and the exchange of letters between Lucía Sánchez Saornil, for the National Committee of Mujeres Libres, to Germinal de Sousa, Peninsular Committee, FAI, November 22, 1938, IISG/FAI: 48.C.1.a. Copies of correspondence between the Catalan Regional Committee of Mujeres Libres and the Catalan Regional Committee of the CNT can also be found in AHN/SGC-S, P.S. Barcelona: 1049.

26. See Nancy Hewitt and Jacqueline Hall, presentations in "Disorderly Women: Gender, Politics and Theory," Berkshire Conference, Wellesley College, June 1987; and Marie Marmo Mullaney, *Revolutionary Women: Gender and the Socialist Revolutionary Role* (New York: Praeger, 1983), 53–96.

27. For example, Lucía Sánchez Saornil, for the National Committee, Mujeres Libres, to the Peninsular Committee, FAI, Valencia, October 6, 1937, IISG/FAI: 48.C.1.a. and Regional Committee, Mujeres Libres to Regional Committee, CNT, August 2, 1938, IISG/CNT: 40.C.4.

28. Federación Nacional Mujeres Libres, "Algunas consideraciones del Comité Nacional de Mujeres Libres al de la CNT," especially 3.

29. U.G.T., Federación Local Barcelona, Secretario de Organización de la Federacion Local U.G.T., "Al Sindicato . . ." Barcelona, March 16, 1938, AHN/SGC-S, P.S. Barcelona: 628.

30. Mujeres Libres' letter, March 12, 1937; response, March 20, IISG/FAI: 48.C.1.a.

31. Mercedes Comaposada, Barcelona, June 1937, IISG/FAI: 48.C.1.a.

32. Propaganda Section, Levantine Regional Committee, Mujeres Libres, to Peninsular Committee, 31-1-1938; and response from the Peninsular Committee, February 1, 1938; IISG/FAI: 48.C.1.c.; also Lucía Sánchez Saornil to Penin-

sular Committee, FAI, March 10, 1938.

33. Goldman to Vázquez, October 7, 1938, IISG/CNT: 63.C.2.

34. Vázquez to Goldman, October 11, 1938, IISG/CNT: 63.C.2.

35. Pepita Carpena, interview, Barcelona, May 3, 1988. For a slightly different version of the story see Pepita Carpena, "Spain 1936: Free Women. A Feminist, Proletarian and Anarchist Movement," 51, in *Women of the Mediterranean*, ed. Monique Gadant, trans. A. M. Berrett (London: Zed Books, 1986).

36. FIJL, National Committee, Women's Bureau, Circular no. 1, Valencia, November 4, 1937; FIJL, Women's Bureau, Circular no. 1, April 19, 1938, both in IISG/FAI: 48.C.1.d. See also "La juventud actual y la emancipación juvenil femenina," *Acracia*, January 11, 1937.

37. FIJL, National Committee, Women's Bureau, Circular no. 3, Valencia, November 25, 1937, 2 pp. typescript. IISG/FAI: 48.C.1.d. See also "Dictamen Que Presenta la Ponencia a la Consideración del Congreso, Sobre el 4º Punto del Orden del Día Apartado Tercero" (from the second National Congress of FIJL, February 1938), 1 p. typescript, AHN/SGC-S, P.S. Barcelona: 903; and Carmen Gomez, for the FIJL Women's Bureau to the FAI Peninsular Committee, March 22, 1938, IISG/FAI 48.C.1.a.

38. "Del Movimiento de Mujeres Libres" AHN/SGC-S, P.S. Barcelona: 903.

39. Carmen Gómez, from the Peninsular Committee, Women's Bureau, FIJL, to Regional Committee, Barcelona, July 23, 1938. AHN/SGC-S, P.S. Barcelona: 903. See also "Conversación con la compañera Suceso Portals [*sic*], Secretaria del Subcomité Nacional de Mujeres Libres en el día 16 de diciembre de 1938," 2 pp. typescript, IISG/FAI: 48.C.1.d.

40. "Formas y Actividades a Desarrollar por la Secretaría Femenina, Poniendo en Práctica Diversos Procedimientos a Nuestro Alcance," 3 pp. typescript, p. 2, AHN/SGC-S, P.S. Barcelona: 903.

41. FIJL, Comité Penínsular, Secretaría Femenina, "Informe que presenta la Secretaría Femenina del Comité Peninsular sobre el sexto punto del orden del día del próximo pleno nacional de regionales de la FIJL que ha de celebrarse en Barcelona," Barcelona, October 1, 1938; see also "Exposición del problema de las relaciones de las secretarías femeninas de la FIJL con Mujeres Libres, que presenta a estudio de las regionales la Secretaría Femenina Penínsular," Barcelona, September 8–9, 1938. AHN/SGC-S, P.S. Barcelona: 140.

42. "Informe que presenta," 6. See also "Dictamen Que Presenta la Ponencia a la Consideración y Aprobación del Congreso" and "Formas y Actividades a Desarrollar."

43. Pura Pérez Arcos, interviews, Windsor, Ontario, Canada, December 16, 1984; and New York City, September 10, 1989; and Pura Pérez Arcos, "Evocación de un viaje," unpublished manuscript, 1985.

44. "Actas del Pleno Nacional de Regionales del Movimiento Libertario, CNT-FAI-FIJL (celebrado en Barcelona durante los días 16 y sucesivos del mes de octubre de 1938)," Barcelona, 1938, 226 pp. typescript. IISG/CNT: 92.A.3.; see also José Peirats, *La CNT en la revolución española*, 3 vols. (Paris: Ruedo Ibérico, 1971), III: 253.

45. "Anexo al informe."

46. "Actas del Pleno Nacional de Regionales," 162, 163.

47. "Dictamen que la Federación Nacional Mujeres Libres elabora a petición del Pleno de Conjunto Libertario, para su discusión por la base de las tres organizaciones, FAI, CNT, FIJL," 2 pp., undated, IISG/CNT: 40.C.4.

48. Nash, *'Mujeres Libres' España, 1936–1939*, 19.

49. "Actas del Pleno Nacional de Regionales," 158; also Juan García Oliver, *El eco de los pasos*, 128.

50. "Actas," 210–13; "Dictamen que emite la ponencia nombrada para el

estudio del cuarto punto del orden del día: 'Forma de ayudar a las JJ.LL.,'" 2 pp. typescript, Barcelona, October 27, 1938; and CNT, AIT, Comité Nacional, "Circular Nº 35: A los Comités Locales y Comarcales," 3 pp. typescript, Barcelona, November 11, 1938, both in IISG/CNT: 92.A.3.

51. "Dictamen que la Federación Nacional 'Mujeres Libres' elabora," 1.

52. National Federation, Mujeres Libres, to Peninsular Committee, FAI, November 12, 1938 (and response), IISG/FAI: 48.C.1.a.; Catalan Regional Committee, Mujeres Libres to Regional Committee, CNT, November 3, 1938, and response (November 7, 1938), IISG/CNT: 40.C.4.; and Peninsular Committee, FAI, "Circular Nº 51: A los Comités Regionales de la F.A.I.," 3 pp. typescript, Barcelona, November 25, 1938, IISG/FAI: 29.E.1.

53. Germinal de Sousa, for the Peninsular Committee, FAI, to National Committee, Mujeres Libres, December 20, 1938. IISG/FAI 48.C.1.a.; and Mujeres Libres, "Informe sobre los incidentes surgidos con motivo de la imposición del Ministero de Hacienda para que cedieramos el edificio del 'Casal de la Dona Treballadora' al Banco de España," Barcelona, December 20, 1938, AHN/SGC-S, P.S. Barcelona: 1049.

54. Lucía Sánchez Saornil, to Peninsular Committee of the FAI, December 21, 1938, and to National Committee of the CNT, Barcelona, December 20, 1938, 3 pp. typescript, IISG/FAI: 48.C.1.a.

55. Conchita Guillén, interview, Montady, April 29, 1988.

### Conclusion

1. Martha A. Ackelsberg, "Revolution and Community: Politicization, Depoliticization, and Perceptions of Change in Civil War Spain," in *Women Living Change*, ed. Susan C. Bourque and Donna R. Divine (Philadelphia: Temple University Press, 1985), 85–115.

2. Comité Nacional, Mujeres Libres, "Como organizar una agrupación Mujeres Libres" (Barcelona: Mujeres Libres, [1938?]).

3. Marge Piercy, "For Strong Women," in *The Moon Is Always Female* (New York: Knopf, 1980), 57.

4. Martha A. Ackelsberg, "Mujeres Libres, 1936–1986: Meaning, Memory, and the Politics of Repression," working paper, Center for European Studies, Harvard University, 1988.

5. See, for example, essays in Ann Bookman and Sandra Morgen, eds., *Women and the Politics of Empowerment*.

6. Carol Gilligan, *In a Different Voice;* Sarah Ruddick, "Maternal Thinking," *Feminist Studies* 6, no. 2 (1980): 342–67; and *Maternal Thinking: Toward a Politics of Peace* (Boston: Beacon Press, 1989); Sue J. M. Freeman, "Women's Moral Dilemmas: In Pursuit of Integrity," in *Women Living Change*, ed. Bourque and Divine, 217–54; M. Brinton Lykes, "Gender and Individualistic vs. Collectivist Bases for Notions about the Self," *Journal of Personality* 53, no. 2 (June 1985): 358–83.

7. Shirley Ardener, "Introduction," to *Perceiving Women* (New York: Wiley, 1975); Susan C. Bourque and Donna R. Divine, "Introduction: Women and Social Change" in *Women Living Change*, 1–21; Irene Diamond and Lee Quinby, "American Feminism and the Language of Control," in *Feminism and Foucault: Reflections on Resistance*, ed. Irene Diamond and Lee Quinby (Boston: Northeastern University Press, 1988), 193–206; Nancy Hartsock, *Money, Sex, and Power* (New York: Longman, 1983), especially chap. 10; T. Drorah Setel, "Feminist Insights and the Question of Method," in *Feminist Perspectives on Biblical Scholarship*, ed. Adela Yarbro Collins (Chico, Ca.: Scholars Press, 1985), 35–42;

Mary G. Dietz, "Context Is All: Feminism and Theories of Citizenship," *Daedalus* (Fall 1987): 1–24.

8. Martha Ackelsberg and Myrna Breitbart, "Terrains of Protest: Striking City Women," *Our Generation* 19, no. 1 (Fall/Winter 1988), especially 165–75; Ronald Lawson, Stephen E. Barton and Jenna Weissman Joselit, "From Kitchen to Storefront: Women in the Tenant Movement," in *New Space for Women*, ed. Gerda R. Wekerle, Rebecca Peterson, and David Morley (Boulder, Colo.: Westview Press, 1980), 255–71; Paula Hyman, "Immigrant Women and Consumer Protest: The New York City Kosher Meat Boycott of 1902," *American Jewish History* 70 (Summer 1980): 91–105; Wendy Luttrell, "The Edison School Struggle," in *Women and the Politics of Empowerment*, ed. Bookman and Morgen, 136–56, and Sandra Morgen, "It's the Whole Power of the City against Us," ibid., 97–115; Manuel Castells, *The City and the Grassroots: A Cross-Cultural Theory of Urban Social Movements* (Berkeley: University of California Press, 1983).

9. Ackelsberg and Breitbart, "Terrains of Protest," 172.

10. See, for example, Andrea Dworkin, *Right Wing Women* (New York: Coward, McCann and Geoghegan, 1982); Kathleen McCourt, *Working-Class Women and Grassroots Politics* (Bloomington: Indiana University Press, 1977); Faye Ginsburg, *Contested Lives: The Abortion Debate in an American Community* (Berkeley: University of California Press, 1989).

11. Temma Kaplan, "Class Consciousness and Community in Nineteenth-Century Andalusia," *Political Power and Social Theory* 2 (1981): 21–57; also Carol Stack, *All Our Kin: Strategies for Survival in a Black Community* (New York: Harper and Row, 1974); and Shulamit Reinharz, "Women as Competent Community Builders: The Other Side of the Coin," in *Social and Psychological Problems of Women: Prevention and Crisis Intervention*, ed. Annette U. Rickel, Meg Gerrard, and Ira Iscoe (Washington, D.C.: Hemisphere, 1984), 19–43.

12. Martin Buber, *Paths in Utopia*, trans. R. F. C. Hull (Boston: Beacon Press, 1958), 140.

13. Simone de Beauvoir, *The Second Sex*, trans. H. M. Parshley (New York: Bantam Books, 1961). On not viewing women as "political" beings, see Susan C. Bourque and Jean Grossholtz, "Politics as Unnatural Practice: Political Science Looks at Women's Participation," *Politics and Society* 4, no. 2 (1974): 225–66; Jean B. Elshtain, "Moral Woman and Immoral Man: A Consideration of the Public-Private Split and Its Ramifications," *Politics and Society* 4, no. 4 (1974): 453–73; and my "Communities, Resistance, and Women's Activism: Some Implications for a Democratic Polity," in *Women and the Politics of Empowerment*, ed. Bookman and Morgen, especially 301.

14. See, for example, Bookman and Morgen, eds., *Women and the Politics of Empowerment*, especially the essays by Sacks, Morgen, Costello, Zavella, and Susser; Mary Fainsod Katzenstein and Carol McClurg Mueller, eds., *The Women's Movements of the United States and Western Europe: Consciousness, Political Opportunity, and Public Policy* (Philadelphia: Temple University Press, 1987); Judith Friedlander, Blanche Wiesen Cook, Alice Kessler-Harris, and Carroll Smith-Rosenberg, eds., *Women in Culture and Politics* (Bloomington: Indiana University Press, 1986); Patricia Caplan and Janet M. Bujra, eds., *Women United, Women Divided: Cross-Cultural Perspectives on Female Solidarity* (London: Tavistock, 1978).

15. Suffrage was granted women in 1918 in England, 1920 in the United States, 1931 in Spain, and 1944 in France.

16. On the IWW see Ardis Cameron, "Bread and Roses Revisited: Women's Culture and Working-Class Activism in the Lawrence Strike of 1912," in *Women*,

*Work and Protest: A Century of U.S. Women's Labor History*, ed. Ruth Milkman (Boston: Routledge and Kegan Paul, 1985), 42–61.

17. Genevieve Fraisse, "Natural Law and the Origins of Nineteenth-Century Feminist Thought in France," in *Women in Culture and Politics*, ed. Friedlander et al., 322. See also Joan Landes, *Women and the Public Sphere in the Age of the French Revolution* (Ithaca: Cornell University Press, 1989); Francoise Picq, "'Bourgeois Feminism' in France: A Theory Developed by Socialist Women before World War I," in *Women in Culture and Politics*, ed. Friedlander et al., especially 332–35; and Charles Sowerwine, *Sisters or Citizens? Women and Socialism in France since 1876* (Cambridge: Cambridge University Press, 1982), 1–2.

18. Barbara Taylor, *Eve and the New Jerusalem*, xvi.

19. But see also Ruth Smith and Deborah Valenze, "Marginality and Mutuality: Liberal Moral Theory and Working-Class Women in Nineteenth Century England," *Signs* 13, no. 2 (Winter 1988): 277–98; and Ruth Smith, "Moral Transcendence and Moral Space in the Historical Experiences of Women," *Journal of Feminist Studies in Religion* 4, no. 2 (Fall 1988): 21–37.

20. Marilyn J. Boxer, "Socialism Faces Feminism: The Failure of Synthesis in France, 1879–1914," in *Socialist Women: European Socialist Feminism in the Nineteenth and Early Twentieth Centuries*, ed. Marilyn J. Boxer and Jean H. Quataert (New York: Elsevier, 1978), 75–111; and Boxer, "When Radical and Socialist Feminism Were Joined: The Extraordinary Failure of Madeleine Pelletier," in *European Women on the Left*, ed. Jane Slaughter and Robert Kern (Westport, Conn.: Greenwood, 1981), 51–73; Claire LaVigna, "The Marxist Ambivalence toward Women: Between Socialism and Feminism in the Italian Socialist Party," in *Socialist Women*, ed. Boxer and Quataert, 146–81; and Beverly Tanner Springer, "Anna Kuliscioff: Russian Revolutionist, Italian Feminist," in *European Women on the Left*, ed. Slaughter and Kern, 13–27.

21. Jasmine Ergas, "Convergencies and Tensions between Collective Identity and Social Citizenship Rights: Italian Women in the Seventies," in *Women in Culture and Politics*, ed. Friedlander et al., 303. See also Ergas, "1968–1979—Feminism and the Italian Party System: Women's Politics in a Decade of Turmoil," *Comparative Politics* 14 (April 1982): 253–80; and Ethel Klein, "The Diffusion of Consciousness in the United States and Western Europe," in *The Women's Movements*, ed. Katzenstein and Mueller, 41–42.

22. Jill Liddington and Jill Norris, *One Hand Tied Behind Us: The Rise of the Woman's Suffrage Movement* (London: Virago, 1978).

23. Temma Kaplan, "Female Consciousness and Collective Action"; Darlene Gay Levy, Harriet Branson Applewhite, and Mary Durham Johnson, *Women in Revolutionary Paris, 1789–1795* (Urbana: University of Illinois Press, 1979), especially 3–12.

24. Piven and Cloward, "The Social Structuring of Political Protest," in *Poor People's Movements* (New York: Pantheon, 1977); and Piven, "Hidden Protest: The Channeling of Female Innovation and Resistance," *Signs* 4, no. 4 (1979): 651ff. See also Herbert Gutman, *Work, Culture and Society in Industrializing America: Essays in American Working-Class and Social History* (New York: Knopf, 1976).

25. Ackelsberg and Breitbart, "Terrains of Protest" 174.

26. Jacquelyn Dowd Hall, "Disorderly Women: Gender and Labor Militancy in the Appalachian South," *Journal of American History* (September 1986): 354–82; roundtable discussion by Jacquelyn Hall, Nancy Hewitt, Ardis Cameron, and Martha Ackelsberg, "Disorderly Women: Gender, Politics and Theory," Berkshire Conference of Women Historians, Wellesley College, June, 1987; and

Amrita Basu, "When Indian Peasant Women Revolt," manuscript. The classic alternative view is E. J. Hobsbawm's, *Primitive Rebels.*

27. "Un acontecimiento histórico," *Mujeres Libres,* no. 11 (1937).

28. "Paralelismo," ibid.

29. Martha Ackelsberg and Irene Diamond, "Gender and Political Life: New Directions in Political Science," in *Analyzing Gender: A Handbook of Social Science Research,* ed. Hess and Ferree (Beverly Hills: Sage Publications, 1987), especially 515–18. See also Ava Baron, "Feminist Legal Strategies: The Powers of Difference," ibid., 474–503, and Cynthia H. Enloe, "Feminists Thinking about War, Militarism and Peace," ibid., 526–47.

30. See especially Ferguson, *The Feminist Case against Bureaucracy,* chap. 5; Joan Scott, "Gender: A Useful Category of Historical Analysis," *American Historical Review* 91, no. 5 (December 1986): 1053–75; and Scott, *Gender and the Politics of History* (New York: Columbia University Press, 1988).

31. In addition to Ruddick and Elshtain, see Isaac Balbus, *Marxism and Domination: A Neo-Hegelian, Feminist, Psychoanalytic Theory of Sexual, Political and Technological Liberation* (Princeton: Princeton University Press, 1982). For a critical perspective see Dietz, "Citizenship with a Feminist Face," 19–37.

32. Maria C. Lugones and Elizabeth V. Spelman, "Have We Got a Theory for You! Feminist Theory, Cultural Imperialism, and the Demand for 'The Woman's Voice' "; Audre Lorde, *Sister Outsider;* Floya Anthias and Nira Yuval-Davis, "Contextualizing Feminism—Gender, Ethnic and Class Divisions"; and Yuval-Davis and Anthias, eds., *Woman–Nation–State* (NY: St. Martin's, 1989).

33. I am much indebted to Iris Young's work, especially "The Ideal of Community and the Politics of Difference," *Social Theory and Practice* 12, no. 1 (Spring 1986): 1–26. See also Elizabeth V. Spelman, *Inessential Woman;* Marilyn Friedman, "Feminism and Modern Friendship: Dislocating the Community," *Ethics* 99 (January 1989): 275–90; and Joan Tronto, "Otherness in Moral Theory (or, If We're So Smart, Why Are We Racists, Sexists, Anti-Semites, Ethnocentrics, Homophobes, etc.?)," paper prepared for delivery at the annual meeting of the American Political Science Association, Chicago, September 1987.

34. Lorde, *Sister Outsider;* Adrienne Rich, "Disloyal to Civilization: Feminism, Racism, Gynephobia," in *On Lies, Secrets and Silence,* 275–310, and "Notes toward a Politics of Location," in *Blood, Bread and Poetry: Selected Prose 1979–1985* (New York: Norton, 1986), 210–31; Marilyn Frye, *The Politics of Reality* (Trumansburg, N.Y.: Crossing Press, 1983); and Myra Jehlen, "Against Human Wholeness," paper delivered at the Boston Area Feminist Theory Colloquium, spring 1984.

35. For example, Bernice Johnson Reagon, "Coalition Politics: Turning the Century," in *Home Girls: A Black Feminist Anthology,* ed. Barbara Smith (New York: Kitchen Table, Women of Color Press, 1983), 359.

36. E. E. Schattschneider, *The Semi-Sovereign People* (New York: Holt, Rinehart and Winston, 1960), 35.

37. Karl Marx, "On the Jewish Question" in Marx, *Early Writings,* ed. Lucio Coletti (New York: Vintage, 1975), 211–41; C. B. Macpherson, *The Political Theory of Possessive Individualism* (New York: Oxford University Press, 1962); Peter Bachrach and Morton Baratz, "Two Faces of Power," *American Political Science Review* 56 (1962): 947–52; Isaac Balbus, "The Concept of Interest in Pluralist and Marxian Analysis," *Politics and Society* 1, no. 2 (1971): 151–77; Lewis Lipsitz, "The Grievances of the Poor" in *Power and Community,* ed. Philip Green and Sanford Levinson (New York: Random House, 1970), 142–72.

38. Carole Pateman, *The Sexual Contract* (Stanford: Stanford University Press, 1988).

39. Dolores Hayden, *The Grand Domestic Revolution* (Cambridge: MIT Press, 1981):

40. John Rawls, *A Theory of Justice*, makes this point clearly, though un-self-consciously. See also Michael Walzer, *Spheres of Justice*. For criticism see Susan Moller Okin, "Justice and Gender," *Philosophy and Public Affairs* 16, no. 1 (Winter 1987): 42–72; and Carole Pateman, *The Disorder of Women: Democracy, Feminism and Political Theory* (Stanford: Stanford University Press, 1989), chaps. 6, 8, 9.

41. See, for example, Richard Sennett and Jonathan Cobb, *The Hidden Injuries of Class* (New York: Vintage, 1972); Lillian Rubin, *Worlds of Pain* (New York: Basic Books, 1976); and Carol Stack, *All Our Kin.*

42. Azucena Barba, interview, August 15, 1981.

# GLOSSARY

**agrupación**  Group, affinity group; the name given to local chapters of Mujeres Libres, and also to the affinity groups of the FAI
**ateneo**  Storefront school or cultural center
**barrio (barriada)**  Urban neighborhood
**bracero**  Rural day-laborer, also known as **jornalero**
**cacique**  Local political boss
**cambio de mentalidad**  Consciousness change
**campesino/a**  Peasant, rural landworker; one who lives in a rural area
**capacitación**  Empowerment; self-development; self-realization
**captación**  Mobilization into a particular party or group
**Casal de la Dona**  Mujeres Libres' women's institute in Barcelona
**casamientos a la libertaria**  Libertarian-style marriages; e.g., weddings formalized by union organizations
**compañero/a**  Comrade, member of the libertarian movement; also used to refer to lover or life-partner
**comité local**  Local committee; local group of a larger organization
**comunismo libertario**  Libertarian communism; communitarian anarchism
**Cortes**  Constituent Assembly; the Spanish parliament
**cortijo**  Large farm
**enseñanza integral**  Integral or holistic education; forerunner to rationalist education
**escuela libre**  Free school, rationalist school; school run neither by the state nor by the church
**Escuela Moderna**  Modern School; rationalist school founded by Francisco Ferrer in Barcelona in 1901
**formación social**  Political or social consciousness; education for social and political awareness
**Generalidad, Generalitat**  Autonomous government of Catalonia
**huerta**  Garden plot; usually refers to small area cultivated for home consumption
**jornalero**  Day-laborer
**jóven/es**  Young person/people (sometimes refers to contemporary young person, as distinct from those of the Civil War period)
**Juventudes**  Short for Juventudes Libertarias, the Libertarian youth organization
**latifundio**  Large landed estate
**liberatorios (de prostitución)**  Centers proposed by Mujeres Libres to retrain prostitutes for other work and new lives
**libertarias/os**  Libertarians; people identified with the anarchist or anarcho-syndicalist movement
**mayorazgo**  Primogeniture
**militante**  Activist in the movement
**municipio libre**  Free commune; basis for social organization in a communalist anarchist system
**obrero consciente**  Enlightened worker/self-taught teacher in the early days of the anarchist movement who carried the message to other workers

**pueblo**   Village or town; the common people

**sección (de trabajo)**   (Work) section, one of the task-oriented groups developed by Mujeres Libres

**secretaría**   Bureau, department

**Secretariado femenino**   Women's Bureau

**sindicato**   Union

**sueldo único**   Uniform salary; equalized salary scale

**viejas**   Older women (veterans); usually refers to those who were active in Mujeres Libres in the 1930s, as distinct from members of current groups

# INDEX

Jackson, Gabriel, 198n., 202n.
"Javierre," 25, 191n.
JJLL. *See* FIJL; Juventudes Libertarias
Johnson, Mary Durham, 215n.
Joreen, 187n.
Joselit, Jenna Weissman, 214n.
Juventudes Libertarias (JJLL), 8, 89, 91, 100–101, 154, 161, 187n. *See also* FIJL

Kahos, 204n.
Kaplan, Temma, 40, 46, 54, 188n., 194n., 196n., 197n., 214n.
Katzenstein, Mary Fainsod, 214n.
Kern, Robert, 196n., 215n.
Kessler-Harris, Alice, 214n.
King, Ynestra, 189n.
Kiralina. *See* Iturbe, Lola
Kiraline. *See* Iturbe, Lola
Klein, Ethel, 215n.
Kollontai, Alexandra, 65, 134, 208n.
Kropotkin, Peter, 21, 31, 187n., 189n., 190n., 192n., 193n.
Kyralina. *See* Iturbe, Lola

Lacerda de Moura, María, 28–30, 192n.
Laffitte, María (Condesa de Campo Alange), 195n.
Lamberet, Renée, 195n.
Landes, Joan, 215n.
Landholding, in Spain, 41–42, 44–45, 66, 67, 68, 70, 77–81
Largo Caballero, Francisco, 83
Laslett, Peter, 189n.
LaVigna, Claire, 215n.
Lawson, Ronald, 214n.
Lazarte, Juan, 28–29, 192nn.
Lenin, Vladimir Ilyich, 65, 189n.
Leonardo, 192n.
Leval, Gaston, 200n.
Levinson, Sanford, 216n.
Levy, Darlene Gay, 215n.
Lewis, Diane K., 188n.
Liaño, Conchita, 96, 141
*Liberatorios de prostitución*, 136, 139
Lida, Clara E., 58, 195nn., 197n.
Liddington, Jill, 215n.
Lipsitz, Lewis, 216n.
Lister, Enrique, 84
Little, Douglas, 201n.
Llauradó, A. G., 191n.
Longino, Helen E., 193n.
Lorde, Audre, 177, 188n., 191n.
Lorenzo, Anselmo, 191n.
Lorenzo, Cesar, 197n.
Lugones, María C., 188n.
Luttrell, Wendy, 214n.
Luxemburg, Rosa, 65
Lykes, M. Brinton, 213n.

Macpherson, C. B., 216n.

McCourt, Kathleen, 214n.
McKintosh, Maureen, 188n.
Mainardi, Pat, 193n.
Malatesta, Errico, 187n., 189n., 190n.
Malefakis, Edward, 194n., 202n.
Malthus, Thomas Herbert, 29
Manent, Albert, 199n.
Marañón, Gregorio, 20, 24, 28, 189n., 192n.
Margallo, Pepita, 207n.
Marriage, monogamous, 29–30, 35, 98, 117, 119, 133–35, 137–39, 185–86, 200n.32. *See also* Plural love; Sexuality
Martí-Ibáñez, Felix, 27–28, 191nn., 192nn.
Martínez-Alier, Juan, 194n.
Marx, Karl, 216n.
Marxism, 34, 45, 165, 171; distinguished from anarchism, 17; rejected by feminist critics, 13; on subordination of women, 144–45
Mata, Gonzalo, 201n.
"Material feminists," 179–80
Mella, Ricardo, 25, 35, 36, 189n., 190n.
Michel, Louise, 94
Michels, Robert, 189n.
Milkman, Ruth, 188n., 215n.
Miller, Martin A., 193n.
Mills, C. Wright, 189n.
Miner, Valerie, 193n.
Ministry of Health and Public Assistance, 137
Mintz, Jerome M., 194n.
Mirabé de Vallejo, Julia, 137, 209n.
Mirabent, Magi, 200n.
"Modern school movement," 58–60. *See also* Ateneos; Education; Escuela Moderna; Rationalist schools
Molina, Juan Manuel, 3
Montseny, Federica, 30, 38, 83, 137, 161, 190n., 191nn., 192nn., 193nn., 200n., 202n., 203nn., 204n., 208n.; criticism of feminism, 90–91; on gender differences, 175; on the *municipio libre*, 23–24; on necessity of preparation, 34; on women's activism, 127
Montseny, Juan. *See* Urales, Federico
Montuenga, 90, 203n.
Morales de Guzmán, Eduardo, 102
Morcillo Gómez, Aurora, 205n.
Morgan, Robin, 193n.
Morgen, Sandra, 188n., 214nn.
Morley, David, 214n.
Mueller, Carol McClurg, 214n.
*Mujeres* (PCE journal), 106–7, 128, 145
Mujeres Libres, 29, 35, 37, 38, 62, 76–77, 81, 86, 116; activists' experiences in ateneos, 61–65; ambiguity about women's nature, 118, 124–25; anarcho-syndicalism and subordination of women, 87–92; *captación* programs, 115–18, 125, 127, chap. 6 *passim*, Con-

MARTHA ACKELSBERG is Professor of Government and a member of the Women's Studies Program Committee at Smith College, where she teaches courses in political theory, urban politics, political activism, and feminist theory. She has published articles on Mujeres Libres and on women in the Spanish anarchist movement in *Feminist Studies, Radical America, Our Generation, International Labour and Working Class History,* and *Communal Societies.* She has also contributed to a variety of anthologies on women's political activism in the United States, on changing family structures, and on Jewish feminism.